Holy Souls Book

Reflections on Purgatory

A COMPLETE PRAYER-BOOK
Including
Special Prayers and Devotions in Behalf
of the Poor Souls in Purgatory

Edited by

Rev. F. X. Lasance
Author of "My Prayer-Book,"
etc.

Nihil Obstat

ARTHUR J. SCANLAN, S.T.D.,
Censor Librorum.

Imprimatur

PATRICK J. HAYES, D.D.,
Archbishop of New York.

New York, May 30, 1922.

Foreword

IN OFFERING the present volume to the faithful our object is to aid in cultivating among them, with the help of God's grace, a *special* devotion—a more fervent, a more persistent, a more practical, a more fruitful devotion—to the holy souls in Purgatory. This devotion, while it solaces the Holy Souls, in whose behalf it is directly exercised, is eminently pleasing to God, and beneficial to ourselves.

St. Francis de Sales says: "We do not sufficiently remember our dead."

The holy Curé d'Ars once said: "Oh, my friends, let us pray much, and let us obtain many prayers from others, for the poor dead; the good God will render us back the good we do to them a hundredfold. Ah! if every one knew how useful this devotion to the holy souls in Purgatory is to those who practise it, they would not be forgotten so often; the good God regards all that we do for them as if it were done to Himself."

We read in the Second Book of Machabees:

"It is a holy and wholesome thought to pray for the dead, that they may be loosed from sins."

It is hoped that the " Reflections " contained in the first part of this little book will stimulate the pious reader to make frequent use of the prayers and devotions which are found in the second part for the solace of the suffering souls in Purgatory. Let us heed the cry of these Holy Souls from the depths of torturing flame: " *Miseremini!* " " Have pity on us! " Day by day may the richly indulgenced versicles and responses for the dead fall, as it were, unceasingly from our lips:

V. Eternal rest give unto them, O Lord.
R. And let perpetual light shine upon them.
V. May they rest in peace.
R. Amen.

" ALL ye, who would honor
    The saints and their Head,
Remember, remember,
    To pray for the dead;

" And they, in return,
    From their misery freed,
To you will be friends
    In the hour of need."

Contents

PART TWO

Prayers and Devotions

PAGE

14 CONTENTS

PAGE

Table of Movable Feasts

Year of Our Lord	Septuagesima Sunday	Ash Wednesday	Easter Sunday	Ascension Day	Whit-Sunday	Corpus Christi	First Sunday of Advent	Sundays After Pentecost
1944	6 Feb.	23 Feb.	9 Apr.	18 May	28 May	8 June	3 Dec.	26
1945	28 Jan.	14 Feb.	1 Apr.	10 May	20 May	31 May	2 Dec.	27
1946	17 Feb.	6 Mar.	21 Apr.	30 May	9 June	20 June	1 Dec.	24
1947	2 Feb.	19 Feb.	6 Apr.	15 May	25 May	5 June	30 Nov.	26
1948	25 Jan.	11 Feb.	28 Mar.	6 May	16 May	27 May	28 Nov.	27
1949	13 Feb.	2 Mar.	17 Apr.	26 May	5 June	16 June	27 Nov.	24
1950	5 Feb.	22 Feb.	9 Apr.	18 May	28 May	8 June	3 Dec.	26
1951	21 Jan.	7 Feb.	25 Mar.	3 May	13 May	24 May	2 Dec.	28
1952	10 Feb.	27 Feb.	13 Apr.	22 May	1 June	12 June	30 Nov.	25
1953	1 Feb.	18 Feb.	5 Apr.	14 May	24 May	4 June	29 Nov.	26
1954	14 Feb.	3 Mar.	18 Apr.	27 May	6 June	17 June	28 Nov.	24
1955	6 Feb.	23 Feb.	10 Apr.	19 May	29 May	9 June	27 Nov.	25
1956	29 Jan.	15 Feb.	1 Apr.	10 May	20 May	31 May	2 Dec.	27
1957	17 Feb.	6 Mar.	21 Apr.	30 May	9 June	20 June	1 Dec.	24
1958	2 Feb.	19 Feb.	6 Apr.	15 May	25 May	5 June	30 Nov.	26
1959	25 Jan.	11 Feb.	29 Mar.	7 May	17 May	28 May	29 Nov.	27
1960	14 Feb.	2 Mar.	17 Apr.	26 May	5 June	16 June	27 Nov.	24
1961	29 Jan.	15 Feb.	2 Apr.	11 May	21 May	1 June	3 Dec.	27
1962	18 Feb.	7 Mar.	22 Apr.	31 May	10 June	21 June	2 Dec.	24
1963	10 Feb.	27 Feb.	14 Apr.	23 May	2 June	13 June	1 Dec.	25
1964	26 Jan.	12 Feb.	29 Mar.	7 May	17 May	28 May	29 Nov.	27
1965	14 Feb.	3 Mar.	18 Apr.	27 May	6 June	17 June	28 Nov.	24
1966	6 Feb.	23 Feb.	10 Apr.	19 May	29 May	9 June	27 Nov.	25
1967	22 Jan.	8 Feb.	26 Mar.	4 May	14 May	25 May	3 Dec.	28
1968	11 Feb.	28 Feb.	14 Apr.	23 May	2 June	13 June	1 Dec.	25
1969	2 Feb.	19 Feb.	6 Apr.	15 May	25 May	5 June	30 Nov	26
1970	25 Jan.	11 Feb.	29 Mar	7 May	17 May	28 May	29 Nov	27
1971	7 Feb.	24 Feb.	11 Apr.	20 May	30 May	10 June	28 Nov.	25

NOTE—*The first year in each division will be leap year.*

13

PART ONE
Reflections on Purgatory

Chapter 1

Purgatory

THE word *Purgatory* is sometimes taken to mean a place, sometimes as an intermediate state beween hell and heaven. It is, properly speaking, *the condition of souls* which, at the moment of death, are in the state of grace, but which have not completely expiated their faults, nor attained the degree of purity necessary to enjoy the vision of God.

Purgatory is, then, a transitory state which terminates in a life of everlasting happiness. It is not a trial by which merit may be gained or lost, but a state of atonement and expiation. The soul has arrived at the term of its earthly career; that life was a time of trial, a time of merit for the soul, a time of mercy on the part of God. This time once expired, nothing but justice is to be expected from God, whilst the soul can neither gain nor lose merit. She remains in the state in which death found her; and since it found her in the state of sanctifying grace, she is certain of never forfeiting that happy state, and of arriving at the eternal possession of God. Nevertheless, since she is burdened with certain debts of

temporal punishment, she must satisfy
Divine Justice by enduring this punishment
in all its rigor.

Such is the signification of the word
Purgatory, and the condition of the souls
which are there.

On this subject the Church proposes *two
truths* clearly defined as dogmas of faith:
first, *that there is a Purgatory;* second,
*that the souls which are in Purgatory may
be assisted by the suffrages of the faithful,
especially by the holy sacrifice of the Mass.*

*

Location of Purgatory

ALTHOUGH faith tells us nothing
definite regarding the location of
Purgatory, the most common opinion, that
which most accords with the language of
Scripture, and which is the most generally
received among theologians, places it in the
bowels of the earth, not far from the hell
of the reprobates. Theologians are almost
unanimous, says Bellarmine,[1] in teaching
that Purgatory, at least the *ordinary* place
of expiation, is situated in the interior of the
earth, that the souls in Purgatory and the
reprobate are in the same subterranean
space in the deep abyss which the Scripture
calls *Hell.*

" A very probable opinion," says St.
Thomas,[2] " and one which, moreover, corre-

---

[1] Catech. Rom., chap. vi. § 1.
[2] Supplem. part. iii. ques. ult.

sponds with the words of the saints in particular revelation, is that Purgatory has a double place for expiation. The first will be destined for the generality of souls, and is situated below, near to hell; the second will be for particular cases, and it is thence that so many apparitions occur."

The holy Doctor admits, then, like so many others who share his opinions, that sometimes Divine Justice assigns a special place of purification to certain souls, and even permits them to appear either to instruct the living or to procure for the departed the suffrages of which they stand in need; sometimes also for other motives worthy of the wisdom and mercy of God.

*

Purgatory in the Divine Plan

PURGATORY occupies an important place in our holy religion: it forms one of the principal parts of the work of Jesus Christ, and plays an essential rôle in the economy of the salvation of man.

Let us call to mind that the Holy Church of God, considered as a whole, is composed of three parts: The Church Militant, the Church Triumphant, and the Church Suffering, or *Purgatory*. This triple Church constitutes the mystical body of Jesus Christ, and the souls in Purgatory are no less His members than are the faithful upon earth and the elect in heaven. In the Gospel, the

Church is ordinarily called the *Kingdom of Heaven;* now Purgatory, just as the heavenly and terrestrial Church, is a province of this vast kingdom.

The three sister Churches have incessant relations with one another, a continual communication which we call the *Communion of Saints.* These relations have no other object than to conduct souls to eternal glory, the final term to which all the elect tend. The three Churches mutually assist in peopling heaven, which is the permanent city, the glorious Jerusalem.

What then is the work which we, members of the Church Militant, have to do for the souls in Purgatory? We have to alleviate their sufferings. God has placed in our hands the key of this mysterious prison: it is *prayer for the dead,* devotion to the souls in Purgatory. . . .

Prayer for the departed, sacrifices, and suffrages for the dead form a part of Christian worship, and devotion toward the souls in Purgatory is a devotion which the Holy Ghost infuses with charity into the hearts of the faithful. *It is a holy and wholesome thought,* says Holy Scripture, *to pray for the dead, that they may be loosed from sins.* (II Machab. xii, 46.) . . . .

In order to be perfect, devotion to the souls in Purgatory must be animated both by a spirit of fear and a spirit of confidence. On the one hand, the sanctity of God and

His justice inspires us with a salutary fear; on the other, His infinite mercy gives us boundless confidence. . . .

This fear of Purgatory is a salutary fear; its effect is, not only to animate us with a charitable compassion toward the poor Suffering Souls, but also with a vigilant zeal for our own spiritual welfare.

Think of the fire of Purgatory, and you will endeavor to avoid the least faults; think of the fire of Purgatory, and you will practise penance, that you may satisfy Divine Justice in this world rather than in the next.

Let us, however, guard against excessive fear, and not lose confidence. Let us not forget the mercy of God, which is not less infinite than His justice. *Thy mercy is great above the heavens,* says the Prophet;[1] and elsewhere, *The Lord is gracious and merciful: patient, and plenteous in mercy.*[2] This ineffable mercy should calm the most lively apprehensions, and fill us with a holy confidence, according to the words, *In te, Domine, speravi, non confundar in æternum* —" In Thee, O Lord, I have hoped; let me never be put to confusion."[3]

If we are animated with this double sentiment, if our confidence in God's mercy is equal to the fear with which His justice inspires us, we shall have the true spirit of devotion to the souls in Purgatory.

—Rev. F. X. Schouppe, S.J., *Purgatory.*

[1] Ps. cvii.   [2] Ps. cxliv.   [3] Ps. lxx.

Chapter 2

Proofs of the Existence of Purgatory

PURGATORY is a state of suffering where the souls of those who die in grace, but without having fully satisfied the justice of God, remain for a time, to pay the debt of temporal punishment due to their sins, and to be purified for heaven, into which, according to Holy Scripture, *nothing defiled can enter.*

Proofs of the existence of Purgatory are to be found:

1st. In Holy Scripture.

In the Old Testament we read of Judas Machabeus sending twelve thousand drachms of silver to Jerusalem, to be offered in sacrifice for the dead who died in battle; and we are told in the same chapter that *it is a holy and wholesome thought to pray for the dead that they may be loosed from sins.*

In the New Testament Our Lord plainly tells us there are sins which *shall not be forgiven in this world or in the world to come* (St. Matt. xii.); again in St. Matthew we read of a prison which the debtor shall not leave until he has paid the last farthing (St. Matt. v.); and St. Paul in his epistle to the Corinthians says: *Every man's work shall be manifest: for the day of the Lord shall declare it, because it shall be revealed in fire: and the fire shall try every man's work of what sort it is. If any man's work burn, he shall suffer loss: but he himself shall be saved: yet so as by fire.* (I Cor. iii. 13, 15.)

2d. In all tradition, which is thus incontestably confirmed by the following decree of the Council of Trent:

" If any one claim that a penitent sinner when he receives the grace of justification obtains the remission of the guilt and the eternal punishment, so that neither in this life nor in Purgatory has he any temporal punishment to undergo before he can enter heaven, let him be anathema! " (Sess. 6th.)

*

On the Sufferings of Purgatory

R EVELATION, which speaks very clearly of the existence of Purgatory, is not so clear on the state of the Suffering Souls, and we have no accurate knowledge of their place of suffering, or of the nature or the form of their sufferings. We know with certainty, however, that the pains of Purgatory are extremely great, and of two kinds. The first and most unendurable, says the Council of Florence, is the privation of God.

The soul released from the body comprehends God as the only object of its happiness, and the desire to see and possess Him is felt with extraordinary keenness in all its faculties. It is a burning thirst, a devouring hunger, a terrible void, a species of suffocation produced by the absence of God, the food and breath of the soul.

The second is suffering which subjects the soul to tortures more terrible than those inflicted on the martyrs. The Church has not defined the nature of this suffering; it is generally taught, however, with the permission of the Church, that Purgatory is a mysterious fire which, like that of hell, devours the soul without destroying it; and though this is not an article of faith, says *La Luzerne*, yet all authorities so strongly support the doctrine of an expiatory fire, that it is best not to depart from it.

*

On the Causes of Purgatory

THERE are two causes of Purgatory: 1st. The lack of sufficient satisfaction for remitted sin. It is of faith that God, in pardoning sins committed after Baptism, and remitting the eternal punishment due to mortal sin, usually leaves the absolved soul a debt of temporal punishment which it must pay in this life or the next.

2d. The venial sins which may mar the souls of the just when they depart this life.

*

On the State of the Souls in Purgatory

THOUGH in the midst of the most cruel sufferings, the Holy Souls never yield to impatience or despair; they are in a state of grace and charity, and their will is so at one with that of God that they cheerfully will all that He desires. They adore the hand that strikes them; and however ardently they yearn for their deliverance, they would only have it in the order of God's will. The certainty that they will never offend God more, and that they will one day possess Him in heaven, is a source of great consolation to them.

*

On the Duration of the Sufferings of Purgatory

THESE sufferings are of short duration compared to the eternity of the pains of hell, but considered in themselves they are long, very long. The Church authorizes anniversaries of prayers for years and even centuries after souls have departed this life; and eminent writers, Bellarmine among others, think that there are sinners who will remain in Purgatory until the end of the world.

There is a communication of the fruit of good works between the living faithful and the departed. The Catholic Church, enlightened by the Holy Spirit, and guided by the Scriptures and the traditions of the early Fathers, teaches in her Councils the existence of Purgatory, and that souls detained in this place of suffering are helped

by the suffrages of the faithful, and particularly by the precious Sacrifice of the Altar (Council of Trent, Sess. 25).
—*Little Month of the Souls in Purgatory.*

Chapter 3

"Have Pity on Us!"

ST. BRIDGET had once a vision of Purgatory, and there beheld the souls of the just being cleansed from every stain of sin, as iron is purified in a fiery furnace. She tells us that she heard an angel calling down the blessing of God upon the charitable Christians who hasten to the rescue of the Poor Souls, for unless they are released by the good works of the faithful, God in His ineffable justice is resolved to purify them by the flames of Purgatory. When the angel had spoken, there arose a most piteous moan from a great multitude of souls. They entreated the Eternal Judge to forget their many sins, to apply to them the merits of His sacred passion, and to admit them into His presence. They besought Him most earnestly to inspire the faithful, but particularly priests and nuns, to offer up prayers, Masses, alms, and indulgences in their behalf, because by doing this they would lessen and shorten their torments, and enable them to enjoy the sooner the beatific vision of Jesus, their Love. Suddenly a mysterious light, the brilliancy of which was tempered by a certain dull hue, broke forth and hovered over the dark prison. It was the symbol of approaching deliverance, and the poor souls greeted it with acclamations of joy. But they did not forget their benefactors; on the contrary, they asked our blessed Redeemer to reward a hundredfold the charity of those who had prayed for them.

*

WE HAVE it in our power to help these suffering friends of God. We can do so by prayer, almsdeeds, the Holy Mass, our indulgences, and to do so is certainly a work of mercy and charity. Understanding this full well, the saints, without exception, have been most earnest and constant in their efforts to help them. Some of them have made this devotion one of the strong characteristics of their sanctity, and we venture to say that no truly devout or sincere Catholic neglects this spiritual work of mercy.

In Ireland this devotion has obtained a strong hold on the faithful. Even the very poor make many sacrifices in order to secure for their departed relatives, and others also, the special benefits of the Holy Mass. May the same enlightened piety ever remain firmly rooted in the hearts of our people, and may the day never come when they will cease to follow beyond the grave with tender solicitude the souls of those they loved in life.

In praying for the dead and gaining indulgences for them, let us remember that every prayer we say, every sacrifice we make, every alms we give for the repose of the dear departed ones, will all return upon ourselves in hundredfold blessings. They are God's friends, dear to His Sacred Heart, living in His grace, and in constant communion with Him; and though they may not alleviate their own sufferings, their prayers in our behalf always avail. They can aid us most efficaciously. God will not turn a deaf ear to their intercession. Being Holy Souls, they are grateful souls. The friends that aid them, they in turn will also aid. We need not fear praying to them in all faith and confidence. They will obtain for us the special favors we desire. They will watch over us lovingly and tenderly; they will guard our steps; they will warn us against evil; they will shield us in moments of trial and danger; and when our hour of purgatorial suffering comes, they will use their influence in our behalf to assuage our pains and shorten the period of our separation from the Godhead.

*

ST. MALACHY having lost his sister by death, offered many fervent prayers and pious suffrages for her eternal repose.

Having after some time desisted from doing so, he heard one night an unknown voice say to him that his sister waited outside the church and asked him for assistance. The Saint well understood what the needs of his sister were, and having resumed the pious exercises which he had discontinued, he saw her some time after at the entrance of the church in robes of mourning, and having a sad and disconsolate aspect. This vision caused him to redouble his prayers in her behalf, nor did he allow any day to pass without performing many acts of piety for her relief. The soul on its next appearance had a less mournful garb and was inside the church, but durst not approach the altar. The Saint having his confidence in the efficacy of his suffrages thus sustained, multiplied them even more than before, and did his utmost to satisfy the Divine Justice in her behalf. On her third appearance, he was consoled with the assurance that his pious intention had been effected. He saw her clad in garments of dazzling brightness, and advancing to the altar, surrounded by a joyous band of blessed spirits, thus signifying to her holy brother that she had obtained admission into heaven.

The various states or stages in which this soul appeared, teach us the ordinary economy of God's providence—that He does not ordinarily liberate souls from Purgatory by an absolute act of His power and will, but exacts from them with the strictest justice the full payment of their debt, ever accepting the suffrages of the faithful in their behalf— which succors are the more advantageous to these poor souls the more frequently and fervently they are offered.

—*Forget-me-nots from Many Gardens.*

Chapter 4

Apparitions

ST. TERESA had great charity toward the souls in Purgatory, and assisted them as much as lay in her power by her prayers and good works. In recompense, God frequently showed her the souls she had delivered; she saw them at the moment of their release from suffering and of their entrance into heaven. Now, *they generally came forth from the bosom of the earth.* "I received tidings," she writes, "of the death of a Religious who had formerly been Provincial of that province, and afterward of another. I was acquainted with him, and he had rendered me great service. This intelligence caused me great uneasiness. Although this man was commendable for many virtues, I was apprehensive for the salvation of his soul, because he had been Superior for the space of twenty years, and I always fear much for those who are charged with the care of souls. Much grieved, I went to an oratory; there I conjured our divine Lord to apply to this Religious the little good I had done during my life, and to supply the rest by His infinite merits, in order that this soul might be freed from Purgatory.

"Whilst I besought this grace with all the fervor of which I was capable, I saw on my right side this soul come forth from the depths of the earth and ascend into heaven in transports of joy. Although this priest was advanced in years, he appeared to me with the features of a man who had not yet attained the age of thirty, and with a countenance resplendent with light.

"This vision, though very short, left me inundated with joy, and without a shadow of doubt as to the truth of what I had seen. As I was separated by a great distance from the place where this servant of God had ended his days, it was some time before I learned the particulars of his edifying death; all those who were witnesses of it could not behold without admiration how he preserved consciousness to the last moment, the tears he shed, and the sentiments of humility with which he surrendered his soul to God.

"A Religious of my Community, a great servant of God, had been dead not quite two days. We were saying the Office for the Dead for her in choir, a Sister was reading the lesson, and I was standing to say the versicle. When half of the lesson had been said, I saw the soul of this Religious come forth from the depths of the earth, like the one of which I have just spoken, and go to heaven.

"In this same monastery there died, at the age of eighteen or twenty years, another Religious, a true model of fervor, regularity, and virtue. Her life had been but a tissue of maladies and sufferings patiently endured. I had no doubt, after having seen her live thus, that she had more than sufficient merits to exempt her from Purgatory. Nevertheless, whilst I was at Office, before she was interred, and about a quarter of an hour after her death, I saw her soul likewise issue from the earth and rise to heaven." Behold what St. Teresa writes.

*

ACCORDING to St. Thomas and other Doctors, Divine Justice, in particular cases, assigns *a special place upon earth for certain souls.* This opinion we find confirmed by several facts, among which we quote the two mentioned by St. Gregory the Great in his "Dialogues."[1] "Whilst I was young and still a layman, I heard told to the seniors, who were well-informed men, how the Deacon Paschasius appeared to Germain, bishop of Capua. Paschasius, deacon of the Apostolic See, whose books on the Holy Ghost are still extant, was a man of eminent sanctity, devoted to works of char-

[1] Dialog., iv. 40.

ity, zealous for the relief of the poor, and most forgetful of self. A dispute having arisen concerning a pontifical election, Paschasius separated himself from the bishops, and joined the party disapproved by the Episcopacy. Soon after this, he died, with a reputation for sanctity which God confirmed by a miracle: an instantaneous cure was effected on the day of the funeral by the simple touch of his dalmatic. Long after this, Germain, bishop of Capua, was sent by the physicians to the baths of St. Angelo. What was his astonishment to find the same Deacon Paschasius employed in the most menial offices at the baths! 'I here expiate,' said the apparition, ' the wrong I did by adhering to the wrong party. I beseech of you, pray to the Lord for me: you will know that you have been heard when you shall no longer see me in these places.'

" Germain began to pray for the deceased, and after a few days, returning to the baths, sought in vain for Paschasius, who had disappeared. 'He had but to undergo a temporary punishment,' says St. Gregory, ' because he had sinned through ignorance, and not through malice.' "

The same Pope speaks of a priest of Centumcellæ, now Civita Vecchia, who also went to the warm baths. " A man presented himself to serve him in the most menial offices, and for several days waited upon him with the most extreme kindness, and even eagerness. The good priest, thinking that he ought to reward so much attention, came the next day with two loaves of blessed bread, and, after having received the usual assistance of his kind servant, offered him the loaves. The servant, with a sad countenance, replied, ' Why, Father, do you offer me this bread? I cannot eat it. I, whom you see, was formerly the master of this place, and, after my death, I was sent back to the condition in which you see me, for the expiation of my faults. If you wish to do me good, ah! offer up for me the Bread of the Eucharist.'

" At these words he suddenly disappeared, and he, whom the priest had thought to be a man, showed by vanishing that he was but a spirit.

" For a whole week the good priest devoted himself to works of penance, and each day offered up the Sacred Host in favor of the departed one: then, having returned to the same baths, he no longer found his faithful servant, and concluded that he had been delivered."

It seems that Divine Justice sometimes condemns souls to undergo their punishment in the same place where they have committed their sins. We read in the chronicles of the Friars Minor, that Blessed Stephen, Religious of that Order, had a singular devotion to the Blessed Sacrament, so that he passed a part of the night in adora-

tion before it. On one occasion, being alone
in the chapel, the darkness broken only by
the faint glimmer of the little lamp, he suddenly perceived a Religious in one of the
stalls. Stephen approached him, and asked
if he had permission to leave his cell at such
an hour. "I am a deceased Religious," he
replied. "Here, by a decree of God's justice, must I undergo my Purgatory, because
here I sinned by tepidity and negligence at
the Divine Office. The Lord permits me to
make known my state to you, that you may
assist me by your prayers."

Touched with these words, Blessed Stephen
immediately knelt down to recite the *De Pro-*
fundis and other prayers; and he noticed
that whilst he prayed, the features of the
deceased bore an expression of joy. Several
times, during the following nights, he saw
the apparition in the same manner, but more
happy each time as it approached the term of
its deliverance. Finally, after the last prayer
of Blessed Stephen, it arose all radiant from
the stall, expressed its gratitude to its liber-
ator, and disappeared in the brightness of
glory.

—Rev. F. X. Schouppe, S.J., *Purgatory.*

*

JOSEPH HAROLIUS tells us the following
touching story in his discourse of "The
Holy Souls."

Two Fathers of the same Order had con-

tracted a close and holy friendship, their
object in view being to exhort and encourage
each other in the service of God, and fervently to work out their eternal salvation.
Their mortifications were many, their penances austere, their prayers fervent, and
their example most edifying. They avoided
carefully infringing any rule of the Order,
being, above all, anxious always to arrive in
good time for the recitation of the Divine
Office. After some time, one of these Fathers fell ill, and all hopes for his recovery
were vain. Besides, an angel appeared to
him and warned him that his end was near,
telling him at the same time that on account
of his venial sins, he would have to go to
Purgatory until a Mass was offered up in his
behalf, and that then he should enter into
the joys of heaven, and receive the reward of
his zeal for the salvation of his fellow-men.
Full of joy, the Father told his friend of the
apparition, and entreated him, for the sake
of their long friendship, to say a Mass for
him as soon as possible after his death.
Deeply touched, his friend assured him he
would do as he wished, and he faithfully kept
his promise. Scarcely had the Father
closed his eyes in death on the morrow, than
his friend went into the sacristy, vested for
Mass and went to the altar. With great
fervor, he offered up the Holy Sacrifice and
besought God, in the name of the Victim on
the altar, to have pity on the soul of his

departed friend, and to admit him into the heavenly kingdom. After Mass, as he was making his thanksgiving, the soul of the dead Father appeared to him, beaming with happiness and holy joy. But with a sad voice, he reproached him, saying: "O brother, how badly you have kept your promise! you have left me in Purgatory a whole year, and during all this long time neither you nor any other of the Fathers have ever said a Mass for me. What cruel neglect, as you could so easily have delivered me from those awful flames." Awestruck by these words, the Father answered: "I have just finished saying the Mass, which I was able to begin directly after your death; you see your body still lying there, for it is not yet buried; I assure you, I have faithfully kept my promise." For a long time the apparition looked at him in speechless astonishment, but said at last, terror-struck: "Oh, how awful are the sufferings of Purgatory, that such a short time should appear to be a year. Blessed be God, who, in His mercy and goodness, has shortened them so much for me! Forgive me, dear brother, I thank you with all my heart for your love and faithful friendship. I hasten now to heaven, where I shall see my Beloved face to face. But I shall not forget to ask Him to bless you for all you have done for me and to beg Him to unite us again in His kingdom, where the friendship we have begun upon earth, will flourish through the ages of eternity. Farewell! In heaven we shall meet again."

*

ST. MARGARET of Cortona had been, at one time of her life, a great sinner, but by the grace of God, she became a great saint. Among the many virtues which adorned her soul after her conversion, was a great love and devotion to the poor souls in Purgatory. So great was her desire to assuage their sufferings, that she offered herself a living victim for them, and beautiful was the reward our blessed Lord bestowed upon her. When the hour of her death was approaching, a great number of souls, all of whom she had released from the flames of Purgatory, assembled round her bed and, ranging themselves like a guard of honor, escorted her to heaven. Our love is due, in the first place, to our parents; and for this reason, Margaret's first care was to pray for her dead father and mother. Many were the Masses, communions, and good works she offered up for them; and it was revealed to her that, owing to her, they were admitted into paradise much sooner than they would have been otherwise. But her charity embraced all, as we see from the number of souls who appeared to her at her death.

Two merchants were attacked and killed by robbers, as they were travelling across a desolate tract of country. Their souls appeared to St. Margaret and made known to her that, previous to their death, they had been truly sorry for their manifold transgressions, and had consequently found mercy in the eyes of God. Moreover, thanks to the intercession of the Blessed Virgin Mary, they had obtained the grace to receive the death-stroke in a true spirit of penance, and offered it in expiation for their sins. In their past lives they had, however, been unfair in their dealings, and for this sin they were suffering in the flames of Purgatory. They implored the servant of God to go and tell their relations to make satisfaction to all those they Had wronged in any way, to pay the debts they had contracted, and to give abundant alms in order to assuage their inconceivable sufferings, and eventually release them from Purgatory. St. Margaret herself they entreated to pray for them, which she promised to do with pleasure. And her prayer was heard; for a short time after, the souls of the two merchants took their flight to heaven. St. Margaret was not content to pray herself for the faithful departed, she also did all in her power to impart this useful and beautiful devotion to priests and nuns, as well as to people living in the world. Our divine Lord Himself commanded her once to recommend the poor souls in Purgatory to the charity of the Friars Minor of St. Francis in these words: "Recommend them, in My name, to think of the Poor Souls, whose number, at the present moment, is innumerable, because there are scarcely any people who pray for them."

This great zeal on the part of St. Margaret accounts for the multitude of souls, who, at the hour of her death, showed their gratitude by coming and escorting her to the gates of paradise.—*Voices from Purgatory.*

Chapter 5

We Owe It to God, to Our Neighbor, and to Ourselves, to Help the Poor Souls in Purgatory

LET us descend in spirit into the dark prison where the souls in Purgatory are detained until the entire and perfect expiation of their sins has been accomplished. Let us adore the infinite justice of God, who never passes over any fault, even the slightest; His ineffable purity, which cannot endure in His court anything which is not perfectly pure; His ineffable holiness, which cannot ally itself with the shadow of a stain; and at the sight of Purgatory, as well as at the sight of heaven, let us repeat the eternal canticle: "*Holy, holy, holy, is the Lord.*"

FIRST POINT

We Owe It to God, to Help the Souls in Purgatory

WHAT, in fact, in relation to God, are the souls in Purgatory? They are His elect, His beloved children, the heirs of His glory, called to bless Him eternally in heaven, His spouses whom He tenderly loves. His heart will delight to introduce them into His paradise, to inundate them with a torrent of delights; but His justice and His holiness require that all the satisfaction due from these souls should be paid down to the last farthing. If some Christian or other upon earth paid the debt of one of these souls, God would receive it with joy into His bosom, and a saint more would sing His praises in heaven. Now, things being thus, should we love God if, having at our disposition several means for reuniting to Him the souls He desires and loves, we should leave them separated from Him, without trying to put Him in possession of them? Should we love His honor and His glory if, being able to make new worshippers enter into heaven, and enable another mouth to sing His praises, another heart to love Him we took no trouble about it?

*

SECOND POINT

We Owe It through Charity toward Our Neighbor to Help the Souls in Purgatory

FOR, first, they are persons who are in great suffering; they suffer above all from the privation of God. Sighing with indescribable ardor for their reunion to the Supreme Good, they dart toward Him as the arrow shoots toward the target, and are always repelled. They endure in addition sufferings which are unknown to nature, the least of which, the saints tell us, incomparably surpass the greatest torments it is possible to suffer here below. Now, would there be charity in our hearts if, being able to obtain for these souls the great blessing for which they sigh, we were not to procure it for them; if, being able to withdraw them from the extreme sufferings they endure, we were not to withdraw them? Secondly, they are unfortunate beings who, sighing beneath the weight of misery, could not make their voices heard if they were to cry for help; and to whom could they cry?—to God? But justice, which is there, replies: The debt must be paid, the soul must be purified. If they were to cry to us, alas! we should not hear them; their only resource is to borrow the voice in which the Church speaks to-day, exclaiming: " Have pity on me, you at least.

my friends, because the hand of the Lord
hath touched me! "

*

THIRD POINT

We Owe It to Our Own Interests to help the Souls in Purgatory

FOR, first, these good souls which we
have withdrawn from their prison and
introduced into heaven, will be our protectors
in the presence of God, and will there pray
continually for us. Secondly, Jesus Christ
Himself will be our advocate, as being also
indebted to us, seeing that He was in prison
in the person of one of His members, and
we withdrew Him from it; He was thirsty,
and we made Him drink from the fountain of
life. Oh, if the works of mercy here below,
if the glass of cold water given to a poor man,
touch His heart and obtain for us an eternal
recompense, what will He not do in return
for the still more excellent mercy which is
exercised on behalf of the suffering souls in
Purgatory? Thirdly, if it be written that we
shall be treated as we treat others, God will
not permit us to be forgotten when we in our
turn shall be in the place of expiation, or He
Himself will apply to us the merits which
have no other destination, such as there are
when those for whom they are offered have
been damned or have already entered into
heaven; whilst He will allow those who have

not been helpful to their deceased brethren
to languish without any succor being given
them. Fourthly, at the same time that we
procure for ourselves such great advantages,
we shall lose nothing of the merits which we
offer for the solace of these souls; for there
will always remain to us the merit of charity
which abundantly compensates all that we
give up for their deliverance. Would it not
then be to understand our own interests very
badly if we had no zeal for the solace of the
souls in Purgatory?

—Hamon, *Meditations.*

Example

ST. PHILIP NERI was a great servant of
the Poor Souls, for whom he prayed
much and offered up the merit of all his good
works. Above all, he was zealous for the
deliverance of the souls whose spiritual
director he had been during their life,
believing he owed them more, because he
had once worked for the eternal salvation of
their souls. Many a time dead people appeared to him and asked for his prayers,
which he never refused. Our blessed
Redeemer always heard the supplications of
the Saint, and the released souls obtained by
their intercession innumerable graces for
him. After the death of this great servant
of God, a Franciscan Father was praying at
the bier on which St. Philip lay, when the
Saint appeared to him in the midst of a daz-

zling light and surrounded with heavenly spirits. Of these, he said, some were members of his Order, others were his benefactors, whilst a large part of them were souls he had freed from Purgatory and who had come to accompany him to heaven.

The spirit of devotion and sacrifice seemed to have gone over from the holy founder to the whole Order. A certain priest of the Order prayed nearly without ceasing for the dead; and splendid and encouraging were the results with which his zeal was crowned. He was the director of a child whose name was Elizabeth, and who lived at Aquila. Elizabeth was poor with regard to earthly possessions, but extremely rich in virtues. The only reason for which she regretted her poverty was that it proved an obstacle to her entering a convent, where she wished to consecrate her life to her heavenly Spouse. Her director comforted her, saying she need not be downcast, because, ere long, she would be for ever united to her Beloved. He bade her prepare herself for death, and added that she would not have to stay in Purgatory long. All happened as the priest had foretold. Elizabeth died, soon after, a happy death. Her family grieved for her most bitterly, but the good Father comforted them, and assured them that they had now a powerful advocate in heaven. Elizabeth appeared soon after to one of her brothers, and said to him: " Tell my father he need not pray for me any longer, because, through the prayers of my director, this friend of my soul, the hour of deliverance has arrived."

This priest used the numerous alms he received, partly for the poor and partly for Masses for the dead. To these he added his fasts, penances, and prayers. He even asked our blessed Lord to allow him to suffer part of their pain, so that the Poor Souls might experience some alleviation. This heroic wish was granted. He was at times seized with such intense suffering that he was totally unable to move.

For so many and such great things in their behalf, his children were not ungrateful. To them he owed innumerable graces and the preservation from the dangers of soul and body. Many appeared to him and, by words and action, showed their gratitude. Innumerable incidents are recorded of the gratitude of priests to those who have prayed for them after their death, and these ought to encourage us to pray much and fervently for these benefactors of our souls.

—*Voices from Purgatory.*

Chapter 6

Gratitude of the Holy Souls

By Their Prayers They Can Help Us

TO PROVE that the souls in Purgatory show their gratitude even by temporal favors, Father Rossignoli relates a fact that happened at Naples.

If it is not given to all to offer to God the abundant alms of Judas Machabeus, who sent twelve thousand drachms to Jerusalem for sacrifices and prayers to be offered in behalf of the dead, there are very few who cannot at least make the offering of the poor widow of the Gospel, who was praised by our Saviour Himself. She gave only two mites, but these two mites were of more value than all the gold of the rich, because, said Jesus, " *she of her want cast in all she had, even her whole living.*"[1] This touching example was imitated by a humble Neapolitan woman, who had the greatest difficulty in providing for the wants of her family. The resources of the house depended upon the daily earnings of the husband, who each evening brought home the fruit of his labors.

Alas! one day this poor father was imprisoned for debt, so that the responsibility of supporting the family rested upon the unhappy mother, who possessed nothing but her confidence in God. With faith she besought Divine Providence to come to her aid, and especially to deliver her husband, who languished in prison for no other crime than his poverty.

She went to a wealthy and benevolent gentleman, and, relating to him the sad story of her woes, entreated him with tears

[1] St. Mark xii. 44.

to assist her. God permitted that she should receive but a trifling alms, *a carline,* a piece of money worth about ten cents of our coin. ˙ Deeply afflicted, she entered a church to implore the God of the indigent to succor her in her distress, since she had nothing to hope from earth. She was absorbed in her prayers and tears, when, by an inspiration, no doubt, of her good angel, it occurred to her to interest the sympathy of the Holy Souls in her behalf, for she had heard much of their sufferings, and of their gratitude toward those who befriend them. Full of confidence, she went into the sacristy, offered her little piece of money, and asked if a Mass could be celebrated for the dead. The good priest, who was there, hastened to say Mass for her intention, and ascended the altar for that purpose, whilst the poor woman, prostrate on the pavement, assisted at the Holy Sacrifice, offering her prayers for the departed.

She returned quite consoled, as though she had received the assurance that God had heard her prayer. Whilst traversing the populous streets of Naples, she was accosted by a venerable old man, who inquired whence she came and whither she was going? The unfortunate woman explained her distress, and the use she had made of the small alms she had received. The old man seemed deeply touched by her misery, spoke some words of encouragement, and gave her a note enclosed in an envelope, which he directed her to take to a gentleman whom he designated, and then left her.

The woman went in all haste to deliver the note to the gentleman indicated. The latter, on opening the envelope, was seized with astonishment, and was on the point of fainting away; he recognized the handwriting of his father, who had died some time previous. " Where did you get this letter? " he cried, quite beside himself. " Sir," replied the good woman, " it was from an old man who accosted me in the street. I told him of my distress, and he sent me to give you this note in his name. As regards his features, he very much resembles that portrait which you have there over the door." More and more impressed by these circumstances, the gentleman again took up the note, and read aloud: " My son, your father has just been delivered from Purgatory, thanks to a Mass which the bearer has had celebrated this morning. She is in great distress, and I recommend her to you." He read and re-read those lines, traced by that hand so dear to him, by a father who was now among the number of the elect. Tears of joy coursed down his cheeks as he turned toward the woman. " Poor woman," he said, " by your trifling alms you have secured the eternal felicity of him who gave me life. In my turn I will secure your temporal happiness. I take upon myself to supply all the needs of yourself and your whole family."

What joy for that gentleman! what joy for that poor woman! It is difficult to say on which side was the greatest happiness. What is most important and most easy is to see the instruction to be derived from this incident; it teaches us that the smallest act of charity toward the members of the Church Suffering is precious in the sight of God, and draws down upon us miracles of mercy.

*

WE HAVE just spoken of the gratitude of the Holy Souls. This they sometimes manifest, as we have seen, in a clearly visible manner, but most frequently they exercise it invisibly by their prayers. The souls pray for us not only when, after their deliverance, they are with God in heaven, but even in their place of exile and in the midst of their sufferings. Although they cannot pray for themselves, yet, by their supplications, they obtain great grace for us. Such is the express doctrine of two eminent theologians, Bellarmine and Suarez. " These souls are holy," says Suarez, " and dear to God. Charity urges them to love us, and they know, at least in a general way, to what dangers we are exposed, and what need we have of the divine assistance. Why, then, would they not pray for their bene-factors? "

Why? But it will be answered, because they know them not. In that dismal abode, in the midst of their torments, how can they know who are those that assist them by their suffrages?

To this objection it may be replied: the souls feel at least the alleviation which they receive and the assistance which is given them; this suffices, even should they be ignorant of the source whence it came, to call down the benedictions of Heaven upon their benefactors, whosoever they may be, and who are known to God.

But in reality do they not know from whom they receive assistance in their sufferings? Their ignorance of this is nowise proved, and we have strong reason to believe that no such ignorance exists. Would their angel guardian, who dwells there with them to give them all the consolation in his power, deprive them of this consoling knowledge? Is this knowledge not conformable to the doctrine of the Communion of Saints? Would the intercourse which exists between us and the Church Suffering not be the more perfect for its being reciprocal, and that the souls know their benefactors better?

This doctrine is confirmed by a great number of particular revelations, and by the practice of several holy persons. We have already said that St. Bridget, in one of her ecstasies, heard several souls cry aloud, " Lord, God all-powerful, reward a hundredfold those who assist us by their prayers, and who offer to you their good works, in order that we may enjoy the light of your divinity."

We read in the Life of St. Catherine of Bologna that she had a most tender devotion toward the holy souls in Purgatory; that she prayed for them very frequently, and with the greatest fervor; that she recommended herself to them with the greatest confidence in her spiritual necessities, and advised others to do the same, saying, "When I wish to obtain any favor from our Father in heaven, I have recourse to the souls that are detained in Purgatory; I entreat them to present my request to the Divine Majesty in their own name, and I feel that I am heard through their intercession." A holy priest of our own day, the cause of whose beatification has been commenced in Rome, Venerable Vianney, Curé of Ars, said to an ecclesiastic who consulted him, "Oh! if it were but known how great is the power of the good souls in Purgatory with the Heart of God, and if we knew all the graces we can obtain through their intercession, they would not be so much forgotten. We must, therefore, pray much for them, that they may pray much for us."

These last words of Venerable Vianney indicate the true manner of having recourse to the souls in Purgatory; we must assist them, to obtain their prayers and the effects of their gratitude in return—*We must pray much for them that they may pray much for us.*

There is no question here of invoking them as we invoke the saints in heaven. Such is not the spirit of the Church, which, before all else, prays for the departed, and assists them by her suffrages. But it is nowise contrary to the spirit of the Church nor to Christian piety to procure relief for the souls, with the intention of obtaining in return, through the assistance of their prayers, the favors which we desire. Thus, it is a laudable and pious act to offer a Mass for the departed when we are in need of any particular grace. If, when the Holy Souls are still in their sufferings, their prayers are so powerful, we may easily conceive that they will be much more efficacious when, being entirely purified, these souls stand before the throne of God.

—Rev. F. X. Schouppe, S.J., *Purgatory.*

Chapter 7

Two Views of Purgatory

THERE have always been two views of Purgatory prevailing in the Church, not contradictory the one of the other, but rather expressive of the mind and devotion of those who have embraced them. One is the view met with in by far the greater number of the lives and revelations of Italian and Spanish saints, the works of the Germans of the Middle Ages, and the popular delineations of Purgatory in Belgium, Portugal, Brazil, Mexico, and elsewhere. The other is the view which has been made popular by St. Francis of Sales, though he drew it originally from his favorite treatise on Purgatory by St. Catherine of Genoa; and it is also borne out by many of the revelations of Sister Francesca of Pampeluna, a Teresian nun, published with a long and able *censura* by Fra Giuseppe Bonaventura Ponze, a Dominican professor at Saragossa. Each of these two views, though neither denies the other, has its own peculiar spirit of devotion.

The first view is embodied in the terrifying sermons of Italian *Quaresimali,* and in those wayside pictures which so often provoke the fastidiousness of the English traveller. It loves to represent Purgatory simply as a hell which is not eternal. Violence, confusion, wailing, horror, preside over its descriptions. It dwells, and truly, on the terribleness of the pain of sense which the soul is mysteriously permitted to endure. The fire is the same fire as that of hell, created for the single and express purpose of giving torture. Our earthly fire is as painted fire compared to it. Besides this, there is a special and indefinable horror to the unbodied soul in becoming the prey of this material agony. The sense of imprisonment, close and intolerable, and the intense palpable darkness, are additional features in the horror of the scene, which prepare us for that sensible neighborhood to hell, which many saints have spoken of as belonging to Purgatory. Angels are represented as active execution-ers of God's awful justice. Some have even held that the demons were permitted to touch and harass the spouses of Christ in those ardent fires. Then to this terribleness of the pain of sense is added the dreadful-ness of the pain of loss. The beauty of God remains in itself the same immensely de-sirable object it ever was. But the soul is changed. All that in life and in the world of sense dulled its desires after God, is gone from it, so that it seeks Him with an impetu-osity which no imagination can at all con-ceive. The very burning excess of its love becomes the measure of its intolerable pain. What love can do even on earth, we may learn from the example of Father John Baptist Sanchez, who said he was sure he should die of misery if, any morning when he rose, he should know that he was certain not to die that day. To these horrors we might add many more which depict Purga-tory simply as a hell which is not eternal.

The spirit of this view is a holy fear of offending God, a desire for bodily austerities, a great value put upon indulgences, an extreme horror of sin, and an habitual trembling before the judgments of God. Those who have led lives of unusual pen-ance, and the severer Orders in religion, have always been impregnated with this view; and it seems to have been borne out in its minutest details by the conclusions of Scholastic theologians, as may be seen at once by referring to Bellarmine, who, in each section of his treatise on Purgatory, compares the revelations of the saints with the conclusions of theology. It is remarkable also, that when the Blessed Henry Suso, through increased familiarity and love of God, began to think comparatively lightly of the pains of Purgatory, Our Lord warned him that this was very displeasing to Him. For what judgment can be light which God has prepared for sin? Many theologians have said, not only that the least pain of Purgatory was greater than the greatest pain of earth, but greater than all the pains of earth put together. This, then, is a true view of Purgatory, but not a complete one. Yet it is not one which we can safely call coarse or grotesque. It is the view of many saints and servants of God; and it is embodied in the popular celebrations of All Souls' Day in several Catholic countries.

The second view of Purgatory does not deny any one of the features of the preceding view, but it almost puts them out of sight by the other considerations which it brings more prominently forward. It goes into Purgatory with its eyes fascinated and its spirit sweetly tranquillized by the face of Jesus, its first sight of the Sacred Humanity at the particular judgment which it has undergone. That vision abides with it still, and beautifies the uneven terrors of its prison as if with perpetual silvery showers of moonlight, which seem to fall from our Saviour's loving eyes. In the sea of fire it holds fast by that image. The moment that in His sight it perceives its own unfitness for heaven, it wings its voluntary flight to Purgatory, like a dove to her proper nest in the shadows of the forest. There need no angels to convey it thither. It is its own free worship of the purity of God. This is beautifully expressed in a revelation of St. Gertrude, related by Blosius. The Saint saw in spirit the soul of a Religious who had passed her life in the exercise of the most lofty virtues. She was standing before Our Lord clothed and adorned with charity; but she did not dare to lift her eyes to look at Him. She kept them cast down as if she was ashamed to stand in His presence, and showed by some gesture her desire to be further from Him. Gertrude marvelled at this, and ventured to question Him: " Most merciful God! why dost Thou not receive this soul into the arms of Thine infinite charity? What are the strange gestures of diffidence which I behold in her? " Then Our Lord lovingly stretched out His right arm, as if He would draw the soul nearer to Himself; but she, with profound humility and great modesty, retired from Him. The Saint, lost in still greater wonder, asked why she fled from the embraces of a Spouse so worthy to be loved; and the Religious answered her: " Because I am not yet perfectly cleansed from the stains which my sins have left behind them; and even if He were to grant me in this state a free entrance into heaven, I would not accept it; for, all resplendent as I look to your eyes, I know that I am not yet a fit spouse for my Lord."

In that moment the soul loves God most tenderly, and in return is most tenderly beloved by Him. To the eyes of those who take this view, that soul seems most beautiful. How should a dear spouse of God be anything but beautiful? The soul is in punishment, true; but it is in unbroken union with God. " It has no remembrance," says St. Catherine of Genoa most positively, " no remembrance at all of its past sins or of earth." Its sweet prison, its holy sepulchre, is in the adorable will of its heavenly Father; and there it abides the term of its purification with the most perfect contentment and the most unutterable love. As it is not teased by any vision of self or sin, so neither is it harassed by an atom of fear, or by a single doubt of its own imperturbable security. It is impeccable; and there was a time on earth when that gift alone seemed as if it would contain all heaven in itself. It cannot commit the slightest imperfection. It cannot have the least movement of impatience.

It can do nothing whatever which will in the least degree displease God. It loves God above everything, and it loves Him with a pure and disinterested love. It is constantly consoled by angels, and cannot but rejoice in the confirmed assurance of its own salvation. Nay, its very bitterest agonies are accompanied by a profound unshaken peace, such as the language of this world has no words to tell.

There are revelations which speak of some who are in Purgatory, but have no fire. They languish patiently, detained from God, and that is enough chastisement for them. There are revelations, too, which tell of multitudes who are in no local prison, but abide their purification in the air, or by their graves, or near altars where the Blessed Sacrament is, or in the rooms of those who pray for them, or amid the scenes of their former vanity and frivolity. If silent suffering, sweetly, gracefully endured, is a thing so venerable on earth, what must this region of the Church be like? Compared with earth, its trials, doubts, exciting and depressing risks, how much more beautiful, how much more desirable, that still, calm, patient realm over which Mary is crowned as queen, and Michael is the perpetual ambassador of her mercy.

The spirit of this view is love, an extreme desire that God should not be offended, a yearning for the interests of Jesus. It takes

its tone from the soul's first voluntary flight
into that heritage of suffering. As it took
God's part against itself in that act, so is it
throughout. This view of Purgatory turns
on the worship of God's purity and sanctity.
It looks at things from God's point of view,
and merges its own interests in His. It is
just the view we might expect to come from
St. Francis of Sales, or the loving St. Catherine of Genoa. It is the helplessness rather
than the wretchedness of the souls detained
there, which moves those who take this view,
to compassion and devotion; but it is God's
glory and the interests of Jesus which influence them most of all.

How solemn and subduing is the thought
of that holy kingdom, that realm of pain.
There is no cry, no murmur; all is silent,
silent as Jesus before His enemies. We
shall never know we really love Mary till
we look up to her out of those deeps, those
vales of dread mysterious fire. Beautiful
region of the Church of God! Lovely troop
of the flock of Mary! What a scene is presented to our eyes when we gaze upon that
consecrated empire of sinlessness, and yet of
keenest suffering! There is the beauty of
those immaculate souls, and then the love-
liness, yea, the worshipfulness of their
patience, the majesty of their gifts, the dignity of their solemn and chaste sufferings,
the eloquence of their silence; the moonlight of Mary's throne lighting up their land

of pain and unspeechful expectation; the silver-winged angels voyaging through the deeps of that mysterious realm; and, above all, that unseen face of Jesus, which is so well remembered that it seems to be almost seen! What a sinless purity of worship is here in this liturgy of hallowed pain! O world! O weary, clamorous, sinful world! who would not break away if he could, like an uncaged dove, from thy perilous toils and unsafe pilgrimage, and fly with joy to the lowest place in that most pure, most safe, most holy land of suffering and of sinless love?—Rev. John Fitzpatrick, O.M.I., *November Leaves* from Father Faber.

Chapter 8

Union of the Two Views of Purgatory

The Sufferings and the Helplessness of the Holy Souls

BUT let us now see what is common to both these views of Purgatory. This is a more practical consideration. I suppose there are none of us who expect to be lost. We know and feel, with more or less of alarm, the greatness of the risk we are running; but to expect to be lost would be the sin of despair. Hell is only practical to us as a motive of greater diligence, greater strictness, greater circumspectness, greater fear.

But it is not so with Purgatory. I suppose
we all expect, or think ourselves sure, to go
there. If we do not think much of the mat-
ter at all, then we may have some vague
notion of going straight to heaven as soon as
we are judged. But if we seriously reflect
upon it, upon our own lives, upon God's
sanctity, upon what we read in books of
devotion and the Lives of the Saints, I can
hardly conceive any one of us expecting to
escape Purgatory, and not rather feeling
that it must be almost a stretch of the divine
mercy which will get us even there. It
would more likely be vain presumption than
heroic hope, if we thought otherwise. Now,
if we really expect that our road to heaven
will be through the punishments of Purgatory—for surely its purification is penal—it
very much concerns us to know what is common to both the views of Purgatory, which,
it appears, prevail in the Church.

First, both these views agree that the pains
are extremely severe, as well because of the
office which God intends them to fulfil, as
because of the disembodied soul being the
subject of them. Both agree also in the
length of the suffering. This requires to be
dwelt upon, as it is hard to convince people
of it, and a great deal comes of the conviction, both to ourselves and others. This
duration may be understood in two ways:
first, as of actual length of time; and,
secondly, as of seeming length from the

excess of pain. With regard to the first, if we look into the revelations of Sister Francesca of Pampeluna, we shall find among some hundreds of cases that by far the greater majority suffered thirty, forty, or sixty years. Here are some of the examples: a holy bishop, for some negligence in his high office, had been in Purgatory fifty-nine years, before he appeared to the servant of God; another bishop, so generous of his revenues that he was named the alms-giver, had been there five years because he had wished for the dignity; another bishop had been forty; a priest forty years, because through his negligence some sick persons had died without the sacraments; another, forty-five years for inconsiderateness in his ministerial functions; a gentleman fifty-nine years for worldliness; another, sixty-four for fondness for playing at cards for money; another, thirty-five years for worldliness. Bishops seem, upon the whole, according to her revelations, to remain longest there, and to be visited with the extreme of rigor.

Without multiplying instances, which it would be easy to do, these disclosures may teach us greater watchfulness over ourselves, and more unwearied perseverance in praying for the departed. The old foundations for perpetual Masses embody the same sentiment. We are apt to leave off too soon, imagining with a foolish and unenlightened fondness that our friends are freed from

Purgatory much sooner than they really are. If Sister Francesca beheld the souls of many fervent Carmelites, some of whom had wrought miracles in their lifetime, still in Purgatory ten, twenty, thirty, sixty years after their death, and still not near their deliverance, as many told her, what must become of us and ours? Then, as to seeming length from the extremity of pain, there are many instances on record in the Chronicles of the Franciscans, the Life of St. Francis Jerome, and elsewhere, of souls appearing an hour or two after death, and thinking they had been many years in Purgatory. Such may be the Purgatory of those who are caught up to meet the Lord at the last day.

Both views agree again in holding that, what we in the world call very trivial faults are most severely visited in Purgatory. St. Peter Damian gives us many instances of this, and others are collected and quoted by Bellarmine. Slight feelings of self-complacency, trifling inattentions in the recital of the Divine Office, and the like, occur frequently among them. Sister Francesca mentions the case of a girl of fourteen, in Purgatory because she was not quite conformed to the will of God in dying so young; and one soul said to her: " Ah! men little think in the world how dearly they are going to pay here for faults they hardly note there." She even saw souls that were immensely punished only for having been scrupulous in this life; either, I suppose, because there is mostly self-will in scruples, or because they did not lay them down when obedience commanded. Wrong notions about small faults may thus lead us to neglect the dead, or leave off our prayers too soon, as well as lose a lesson for ourselves.

Then, again, both views agree as to the helplessness of the Holy Souls. They lie like the paralytic at the pool. It would seem as if even the coming of the Angel were not an effectual blessing to them, unless there be some one of us to help them. Some have even thought they cannot pray. Anyhow, they have no means of making themselves heard by us on whose charity they depend. Some writers have said that our blessed Lord will not help them without our co-operation; and that our blessed Lady cannot help them, except in indirect ways, because she is no longer able to make satis- faction; though I never like to hear of any- thing our dearest Mother cannot do, and I regard such statements with susp:cion. Whatever may come of these opinions, they at least illustrate the strong way in which theologians apprehend the helplessness of the Holy Souls. Then, another feature in their helplessness is the forgetfulness of the living, or the cruel flattery of relations who will always have it that those near or dear to them die the death of saints. They would

surely have a scruple, if they knew of how
many Masses and prayers they rob the souls,
by the selfish exaggeration of their goodness.
I call it selfish, for it is nothing more than a
miserable device to console themselves in
their sorrow. The very state of the Holy
Souls is one of the most unbounded helplessness. They cannot do penance; they
cannot merit; they cannot satisfy; they
cannot gain indulgences; they have no
sacraments; they are not under the jurisdiction of God's Vicar, overflowing with the
plenitude of means of grace and manifold
benedictions. They are a portion of the
Church without either priesthood or altar at
their own command.

These are the points common to both
views of Purgatory; and how manifold are
the lessons we learn from them, on our own
behalf as well as on behalf of the Holy Souls.
For ourselves, what light does all this throw
on slovenliness, lukewarmness, and love of
ease? What does it make us think of performing our devotions out of a mere spirit
of formality, or a trick of habit? What a
change should it not work in our lives!
What diligence in our examens, confessions,
communions, and prayers! It seems as if
the grace of all graces, for which we should
ever be importuning our dear Lord, would
be to hate sin with something of the hatred
wherewith He hated it in the Garden of
Gethsemane. Oh, is not the purity of God

something awful, unspeakable, adorable? He, who is Himself a simple act, has gone on acting, multiplying acts since creation, yet He has incurred no stain! He is ever mingling with a most unutterable condescension with what is beneath Him—yet no stain! He loves His creatures with a love immeasurably more intense than the wildest passions of earth—yet no stain! He is omnipotent, yet it is beyond the limits of His power to receive a stain. He is so pure that the very vision of Him causes eternal purity and blessedness. Mary's purity is but a fair thin shadow of it. Nay, the Sacred Humanity itself cannot adequately worship the purity of the Most High; and we, even we, are to dwell in His arms for ever; we are to dwell amid the everlasting burnings of that uncreated purity! Yet, let us look at our lives; let us trace our hearts faithfully through but one day, and see of what mixed intentions, human respects, self-love, and pusillanimous temper our actions, nay, even our devotions, are made up; and does not Purgatory, heated sevenfold, and endured to the day of doom, seem but a gentle novitiate for the vision of the All-Holy?

But some persons turn in anger from the thought of Purgatory, as if it were not to be endured, that after trying all our lives long to serve God, we should accomplish the tremendous feat of a good death, only to pass from the agonies of the death-bed into fire—

long, keen, searching, triumphant, incomparable fire. Alas! my dear friends, your anger will not help you nor alter facts. But have you thought sufficiently about God? Have you tried to realize His holiness and purity in assiduous meditation? Is there a real divorce between you and the world, which you know is God's enemy? Do you take God's side? Have you wedded His interests? Do you long for His glory? Have you put sin alongside of our dear Saviour's passion, and measured the one by the other? Surely, if you had, Purgatory would but seem to you the last, unexpected, and inexpressibly tender invention of an obstinate love, which was mercifully determined to save you in spite of yourself. It would be a perpetual wonder to you—a joyous wonder, fresh every morning, a wonder that would be meat and drink to your soul— that you, being what you are, what you know yourself to be, what you may conceive God knows you to be, should be saved eternally. Remember what the suffering soul said so simply, yet with such force, to Sister Francesca: "Ah! those on that side the grave little reckon how dearly they will pay on this side for the lives they live." To be angry because you are told you will go to Purgatory! Silly, silly people! Most likely it is a great false flattery, and that you will never be good enough to go there at all. Why, positively, you do not recognize your

own good fortune. when you are told of it.
And none but the humble go there. I remember Maria Crocifissa was told that
although many of the saints while on earth
loved God more than some do even in
heaven, yet that the greatest saint on earth
was not so *humble* as are the souls in Purgatory. I do not think I ever read anything
in the Lives of the Saints which struck me
so much as that. You see it is not well to
be angry; for those only are lucky enough
to get into Purgatory who sincerely believe
themselves to be worthy of hell.

But we not only learn lessons for our own
good, but for the good of the Holy Souls.
We see that our charitable attentions toward
them must be far more vigorous and per-
severing than they have been; since men
go to Purgatory for very little matters, and
remain there an unexpectedly long time.
But their most touching appeal to us lies in
their helplessness; and our dear Lord, with
His usual loving arrangement, has made the
extent of our power to help them more than
commensurate with their inability to help
themselves. Some theologians have said
that prayer for the Holy Souls is not infallibly answered. I confess their arguments
on this head do not convince me; but, con-
ceding the point, how wonderful still is the
power which we can exercise in favor of the
departed! St. Thomas has at least taught
us that prayer for the dead is more readily

accepted with God than prayer for the living.
We can offer and apply for them all the
satisfactions of our blessed Lord. We can
do vicarious penance for them. We can
give to them all the satisfactions of our
ordinary actions, and of our sufferings. We
can make over to them, by way of suffrage,
the indulgences we gain, provided the
Church has made them applicable to the
dead. We can limit and direct upon them,
or any one of them, the intention of the
Adorable Sacrifice. The Church, which has
no jurisdiction over them, can yet make indulgences applicable or inapplicable to them
by way of suffrage; and by means of liturgy,
commemoration, incense, holy water, and
the like, can reach efficaciously to them, and
most of all by her device of privileged altars.
The Communion of Saints furnishes the
veins and channels by which all these things
reach them in Christ. Heaven itself con-
descends to act upon them through earth.
Their Queen helps them by setting us to
work for them, and the angels and the saints
bestow their gifts through us, whom they
persuade to be their almoners; nay, we are
often their almoners without knowing that
we are so. Our blessed Lord vouchsafes to
look to us, as if He would say: Here are My
weapons, work for Me! just as a father
will let his child do a portion of his work, in
spite of the risk he runs of having it spoiled.
To possess such powers, and not to use them,
₆₉

would be the height of irreverence toward God, as well as of want of charity to men. There is nothing so irreverent, because nothing so unfilial, as to shrink from God's gifts simply because of their exuberance. Men have a feeling of safety in not meddling with the supernatural; but the truth is, we cannot stand aloof on one side and be safe. Naturalism is the unsafe thing. If we do not enter the system, and humbly take our place in it, it will draw us in, only to tear us to pieces when it has done so. The dread of the supernatural is the unsafest of feelings. The jealousy of it is a prophecy of eternal loss, which far too often comes true.

All that I have said hitherto has been, indirectly at least, a plea for this devotion; but I must come now to a more direct recommendation of it.—Father Faber, *ibid*.

Chapter 9

Devotion for the Conversion of Sinners and Devotion for the Holy Souls

EVERY hour—at least, so we trust—a new soul lands in Heaven from Purgatory, or from earth, and begins its eternity of rapture and of praise. Each soul that swells the throng of worshippers, each silent voice added to the angelic choirs, is an increase to the glory of God; and so it is the interest of Jesus to make these arrivals more frequent, and that they should bring more merits and higher degrees of love with them when they come.

Look at that vast kingdom of Purgatory, with its Empress-Mother, Mary. All those countless throngs of souls are the dear and faithful spouses of Jesus. Yet in what a strange abandonment of supernatural suffering has His love left them! He longs for their deliverance; He yearns for them to be transferred from that land, perpetually overclouded with pain, to the bright sunshine of their heavenly home. Nevertheless, He has tied His own hands, or nearly so. He gives them no more grace; He allows them no more time for penance; He prevents them from meriting; nay, some have thought they could not pray. How, then, stands the case with the souls in the suffering Church? Why, it is a thing to be meditated on when we have said it—they depend almost more on earth than they do on Heaven, almost more on us than on Him; so He has willed it on whom all depend, and without whom there is no dependence. It is clear, then, that Jesus has His interests there. He wants His captives released. Those whom He has redeemed He now bids us redeem—us whom, if there be life at all in us, He has already Himself redeemed. Every satisfaction offered up to God for these suffering souls, every oblation of the precious blood to the eternal Father, every Mass heard, every communion received, every voluntary penance undergone—the scourge, the hair-shirt, the prickly chain— every indulgence gained, every jubilee whose conditions we have fulfilled, every *De Profundis* whispered, every little alms doled out to the poor who are poorer than ourselves—all these things are part of the glory of Jesus; and if they be offered for the intention of these dear prisoners, the interests of Jesus are hourly forwarded in Mary's kingdom of Purgatory. There is no fear of overworking the glorious secretary of that wide realm, the Blessed Michael, Mary's subject. See how men work at the pumps on board a ship when they are fighting for their lives with an ugly leak; oh, that we had the charity so to work, with the sweet instrumentality of indulgences, for the holy souls in Purgatory! The infinite satisfactions of Jesus are at our command, and Mary's sorrows, and the martyrs' pangs, and the Confessors' weary perseverance in well-doing. Jesus will not help Himself here, because He loves to see us helping Him, and because He thinks our love will rejoice that He still leaves us something we can do for Him. There have been saints who have devoted their whole lives to this one work, mining in Purgatory; and to those who reflect in faith it does not seem, after all, so strange. It is a foolish comparison, simply because it is so much below the mark, but, on all principles of reckoning, it is a much less work to have won the battle of Waterloo, or to have invented the steam-engine, than to have freed one soul from Purgatory.

See how far some have gone, whose praise is in all the churches. Father Ferdinand de Monroy, a most apostolic man, at the hour of death made in writing a donation and transfer to the souls in Purgatory of all the Masses that should be said for him after he was dead, of all the penances offered up for him, and all the indulgences gained for him. He might well make the donation, for little need of such things had one who loved God so tenderly, and had wedded the interests of Jesus so utterly, as this very action shows he must have done. " Love is strong as death: many waters cannot quench charity, neither can the floods drown it; if a man should give all the substance of his house for love, he shall despise it as nothing " (Cant. viii. 6, 7).

*

R OSSIGNOLI, in " Wonders of God in Purgatory," which he wrote at the request of the Blessed Sebastian Valfré, of the Turin Oratory, relates from the Dominican annals an interesting dispute between two good friars as to the respective merits of devotion for the conversion of sinners and devotion for the Holy Souls. Fra Bertrando was the great advocate of poor sinners, constantly said Mass for them, and offered up all his prayers and penances to obtain for them the grace of conversion. " Sinners," he said, " without grace are in a state of perdition. Evil spirits are continually laying snares for them, to deprive them of the beatific vision, and to carry them off to eternal torments. Our blessed Lord came down from heaven, and died a most painful death for them. What can be a higher work than to imitate Him, and to co-operate with Him in the salvation of souls? When a soul is lost, the price of its redemption is lost also. Now, the souls in Purgatory are safe. They are sure of their eternal salvation. It is most true that they are plunged into a sea of sorrows; but they are sure to come out at last. They are the friends of God; whereas sinners are His enemies, and to be God's enemy is the greatest misery in creation."

Fra Benedetto was an equally enthusiastic advocate of the Suffering Souls. He offered all his free Masses for them, as well as his prayers and penances. " Sinners," he said, " were bound with the chains of their own will. They could leave off sinning if they pleased. The yoke was of their own choosing; whereas the dead were tied hand and foot against their own will in the most atrocious sufferings. Now come, dear Fra Bertrando, tell me: Suppose there were two beggars, one well and strong, who could use his hands and work if he liked, but chose to suffer poverty rather than part with the sweets of idleness; and the other sick, and maimed, and helpless, who, in his piteous condition, could do nothing but supplicate help with cries and tears. Which of the two would deserve compassion most, especially if the sick one was suffering the most intolerable agonies? Now this is just the case between sinners and the Holy Souls. These last are suffering an excruciating martyrdom, and they have no means of helping themselves. It is true they have deserved these pains for their sins; but they are now already cleansed from those sins. They must have returned to the grace of God before they died, else they would not have been saved. They are now most dear, inexpressibly dear, to God; and surely charity, well-ordered, must follow the wise love of the divine will, and love most what He loves most."

Fra Bertrando, however, would not give way, though he did not quite see a satisfactory answer to his friend's objection. But the night following he had an apparition which, it seems, so convinced him, that from that time he changed his practice, and offered up all his Masses, prayers, and penances, for the Holy Souls. It would appear as if the authority of St. Thomas might be quoted on the side of Fra Benedetto, as he says, " Prayer for the dead is more acceptable than prayer for the living; for the dead are in the greatest need of it, and cannot help themselves as the living can."

How acceptable this devotion is to Almighty God, and how He vouchsafes to seem, as it were, impatient for the deliverance of the souls, and yet to leave it to our charity, is taught us on the unimpeachable authority of St. Teresa. In the "Book of her Foundations," she tells us that Don Bernardino di Mendoza gave her a house, garden, and vineyard for a convent at Valladolid. Two months after this, and before the foundation was effected, he was suddenly taken ill, and lost the power of speech, so that he could not make a confession, though he gave many signs of contrition. "He died," says St. Teresa, "very shortly, and far from the place where I then was. But Our Lord spoke to me and told me that he was saved, though he had run a great risk, for that He had had mercy upon him because of the gift he had given for the convent of His blessed Mother; but that his soul would not be freed from Purgatory until the first Mass was said in the new house. I felt so deeply the pains this soul was suffering, that although I was very desirous of accomplishing the foundation of Toledo, I left it at once for Valladolid. Praying one day at Medina del Campo, Our Lord told me to make haste, for that soul was suffering grievously. On this, I started at once, though I was not well prepared for it, and arrived at Valladolid on St. Lawrence's Day." She then goes on to relate that, as she received communion at the first Mass said in the house, her benefactor's soul appeared to her all glorious, and afterward entered heaven. She did not expect this, for, as she observes, " although it had been revealed to me that this would happen at the first Mass, I thought it must mean the first Mass when the Blessed Sacrament would be reserved there." We might multiply almost indefinitely the revelations of the saints which go to prove the special favor with which our blessed Lord regards this devotion wherein His interests are so nearly and dearly engaged. But it is time now to get a clear view of our subject.

There are, as we all know, two worlds, the world of sense and the world of spirit. We live in the world of sense, surrounded by the world of spirit, and as Christians we have hourly and very real communications with that world. Now it is a mere fragment of the Church which is in the world of sense. In these days the Church Triumphant in heaven, collecting its fresh multitudes in every age, and constantly beautifying itself with new saints, must necessarily far exceed the limits of the Church Militant, which does not embrace even a majority of the inhabitants of earth. Nor is it unlikely, but most likely, that the Church Suffering in Purgatory must far exceed the Church Militant in extent, as it surpasses it in beauty. Toward those countless hosts who are lost we have no duties; they have fallen away from us; we hardly know the name of one who is there, for many have thought that Solomon was saved, some have gone so far as to regard the words in the "Acts of the Apostles" about Judas as not infallibly decisive, and there is not quite a consent even against Saul. We are cut off from them; all is blackness and darkness about them; we have no relations with them.

But by the doctrine of the Communion of Saints, and of the unity of Christ's mystical body, we have most intimate relations both of duty and affection with the Church Triumphant and Suffering; and Catholic devotion furnishes us with many appointed and approved ways of discharging these duties toward them. For the present it is enough to say that God has given us such power over the dead that they seem, as I have said before, to depend almost more on earth than on Heaven; and, surely, that He has given us this power, and supernatural methods of exercising it, is not the least touching proof that His Blessed Majesty has contrived all things for love. Can we not conceive the joy of the Blessed in heaven, looking down from the bosom of God and the calmness of their eternal repose upon this scene of dimness, disquietude, doubt and fear, and rejoicing, in the plenitude of their

charity, in their vast power with the Sacred
Heart of Jesus, to obtain grace and blessing
day and night for the poor dwellers upon
earth?   It does not distract them from God;
it does not interfere with the Vision, or make
it waver and grow misty; it does not trouble
their glory or their peace.   On the contrary,
it is with them as with our guardian angels:
the affectionate ministries of their charity
increase their own accidental glory.   The
same joy in its measure may be ours even
upon earth.   If we are fully possessed with
the Catholic devotion for the Holy Souls, we
shall never be without the grateful consciousness of the immense powers which
Jesus has given us on their behalf.   We are
never so like Him, or so nearly imitate His
tender offices, as when we are devoutly
exercising these powers.   We are humbled
excessively by becoming the benefactors of
those beautiful souls who are so immeasurably our superiors, as Joseph was said to
have learned humility by commanding
Jesus.   While we are helping the Holy Souls,
we love Jesus with a love beyond words, a
love that almost makes us afraid, yet also
with a delightful fear, because in this devotion it is His hands we are moving, as we
would move the unskilful hands of a child.
Dearest Lord, is it not incredible that He
should let us do these things?   That He
should let us do with His satisfactions what
we will, and sprinkle His precious blood as

if it were so much water from the nearest well? That we should limit the efficacy of His unbloody Sacrifice, and name souls to Him, and expect Him to obey us, and that He should do so? Beautiful was the helplessness of His blessed Infancy; beautiful is His helplessness in His most dear Sacrament; beautiful is the helplessness in which for the love of us He mostly wills to be with regard to His dear spouses in Purgatory, whose entrance into glory His Heart is so impatiently awaiting! What thoughts, what feelings, what love should be ours, as we, like choirs of terrestrial angels, gaze down on the wide, silent, sinless kingdom of suffering, and then with our own venturous touch wave the sceptred hand of Jesus over its broad regions, all richly dropping with the balsam of His saving blood!

*

THERE was an old Spanish Jesuit, who could not for the life of him make up his mind whether it was better to gain an indulgence for the soul in Purgatory that was most neglected and forgotten, or for the soul that was nearest to its release and entrance into glory. There was a puzzle; both were sweet acts of charity, but which was the sweetest? which would Jesus most approve? He was such a kind-hearted man, that good Father, that he inclined very much to the poor neglected soul, just because it was so neglected: it went to his heart to pass over that forgotten soul. But at last he decided in favor of the other; and now see the reasons. Although it seems the greater mercy to offer it for the other soul, because it is most in want, seeing that it is in greater misery; notwithstanding, charity is a greater virtue than mercy, and it is a greater act of charity to offer the indulgence for the soul that was most just and loved God most, looking simply to the greater glory of the Divine Majesty as the Creator of that soul; for it is nearest to its entry into heaven, where it will at once begin to glorify God immensely by its praises and its bliss. Here was eagerness for the glory of God. Again, the soul is not properly the full conquest of Jesus till it is safely landed in heaven, and our dear Redeemer presents it to the Eternal Father as a trophy of His sacred passion; and was it not better to keep the poor neglected soul waiting in Purgatory than to keep Jesus waiting in heaven? Moreover, all this sadness about passing over the forgotten soul, would it not influence Jesus, and something would be done for that poor soul? Here was touchiness about the interests of Jesus. Furthermore, thought our good old Jesuit, the sooner this soul, that is so near heaven, gets into heaven, the sooner will it begin to gain all manner of graces from God for my soul, and for the souls of sinners upon earth. Here was anxiety for the salvation of souls. So away went the indulgence to the soul that was nearest its release, not without a very fervent sigh, and a very wistful look to Mary, and a comfortable suspicion that Jesus would do something extra for the poor forgotten soul.

The decision of the good Father seems to have high authority; for among the revelations made to Sister Francesca of the Blessed Sacrament, a Spanish Teresian nun, it was told her that immense numbers of souls issued from Purgatory on the evening of All Souls' Day; and that they were mostly those who were near to glory, among whom God distributed the suffrages of the universal Church on that day. Yet, on the other hand, we know that St. Vincent de Paul's special devotion was to the most destitute soul. But, then, destitute souls were his line; he was their property and possession.—Father Faber, *ibid.*

Chapter 10

Devotion to the Holy Souls in Relation to Other Devotions

IT IS not saying too much to call devotion to the Holy Souls a kind of centre in which all Catholic devotions meet, and which satisfies more than any other single devotion our duties in that way, because it is a devotion all of love, and of disinterested love. If we cast an eye over the chief Catholic devotions, we shall see the truth of this. Take the devotion of St. Ignatius to the glory of God. This, if we may dare to use such an expression of Him, was the special and favorite devotion of Jesus. Now, Purgatory is simply a field white for the harvest of God's glory. Not a prayer can be said for the Holy Souls but God is at once glorified, both by the faith and the charity of the mere prayer. Not an alleviation, however trifling, can befall any one of the souls, but He is forthwith glorified by the honor of His Son's precious blood, and the approach of the soul to bliss. Not a soul is delivered from its trial, but God is immensely glorified. He crowns His own gifts in that dear soul. The cross of Christ has triumphed. The decree of predestination is victoriously accomplished, and there is a new worshipper in the courts of heaven. Moreover, God's glory, His sweetest glory, the glory of His love, is sooner or later infallible in Purgatory, because there is no sin there nor possibility of sin. It is only a question of time. All that is gained is real gain. All that is reaped is true wheat, without chaff or stubble or any such thing.

Again, what devotion is justly more dear to Christians than the devotion to the Sacred Humanity of Jesus? It is rather a family of various and beautiful devotions than a devotion by itself. Yet see how they are all, as it were, fulfilled, affectionately fulfilled, in devotion to the Holy Souls. The quicker the souls are liberated from Purgatory, the more is the bountiful harvest of His blessed passion multiplied and accelerated. An early harvest is a blessing, as well as a plentiful one; for all delay of a soul's ingress into the praise of heaven is an eternal and irremediable loss of honor and glory to the Sacred Humanity of Jesus. How strangely things sound in the language of the sanctuary! yet so it is. Can the Sacred Humanity be honored more than by the adorable sacrifice of the Mass? But here is our chief action upon Purgatory. Faith in His sacraments as used for the dead is a pleasing homage to Jesus, and the same may be said of faith in indulgences and privileged altars and the like. The powers of the Church all flow from His Sacred Humanity, and are a perpetual praise and thank-offering to it. So, again, this devotion honors Him by imitating His zeal for souls. For this zeal is a badge of His people and an inheritance from Him.

Devotion to our dearest Mother is equally comprehended in this devotion to the Holy Souls, whether we look at her as the Mother of Jesus, and so sharing the honors of His Sacred Humanity, or as Mother of Mercy, and so specially worshipped by works of mercy, or, lastly, whether we regard her as, in a particular sense, the Queen of Purgatory, and so having all manner of dear interests to be promoted in the welfare and deliverance of those suffering souls.

Next to this we may rank devotion to the holy angels, and this also is satisfied in devotion to the Holy Souls. For it keeps filling the vacant thrones in the angelic choirs, those unsightly gaps which the fall of Lucifer and one-third of the heavenly host occasioned. It multiplies the companions of the blessed spirits. They may be supposed also to look with an especial interest on that part of the Church which lies in Purgatory, because it is already crowned with their own dear gift and ornament of final perseverance, and yet it has not entered at once into its inheritance as they did. Many of them also have a tender personal interest in Purgatory. Thousands, perhaps millions of them, are guardians to those souls, and their office is not over yet. Thousands have clients there who were specially devoted to them in life. Will St. Raphael, who was so faithful to Tobias, be less faithful to his clients there? Whole choirs are interested about others, either because they are finally to be aggregated to that choir, or because in lifetime they had a special devotion to it. Marie Denise, of the Visitation, used to congratulate her angel every day on the grace he had received to enable him to stand when so many around him were falling. It was, as

I have said before, the only thing she could know for certain of his past life. Could he neglect her, if by the will of God she went to Purgatory? Again, St. Michael, as prince of Purgatory, and Our Lady's regent, in fulfilment of the dear office attributed to him by the Church in the Mass for the dead, takes as homage to himself all charity to the Holy Souls; and if it be true that a zealous heart is always a proof of a grateful one, that bold and magnificent spirit will recompense us one day in his own princely style, and perhaps within the limits of that special jurisdiction.

Neither is devotion to the saints without its interests in this devotion for the dead. It fills them with the delights of charity, as it swells their numbers and beautifies their ranks and orders. Numberless patron saints are personally interested in multitudes of souls. The affectionate relation between their clients and themselves not only subsists, but a deeper tenderness has entered into it, because of the fearful suffering, and a livelier interest because of the accomplished victory. They see in the Holy Souls their own handiwork, the fruit of their example, the answer to their prayers, the success of their patronage, the beautiful and finished crown of their affectionate intercession. All this applies with peculiar force to the Founders of Orders and Congregations. Who can tell how Founders yearn over their children in the cleansing fires? Those souls honored them through life; they lived in their Father's and Founder's house; his voice was ever in their ears; his feasts there were days of song and joy and spiritual sunshine; his relics were their shield; his rule their second gospel; his sayings and doings were ever on their lips.

But there is another peculiarity in this devotion for the dead. It does not rest in words and feelings, nor does it merely lead to action indirectly and at last. It is action in itself, and thus it is a substantial devotion. It speaks and a deed is done; it loves and a pain is lessened; it sacrifices and a soul is delivered. Nothing can be more solid. We might almost dare to compare it, in its pure measure, to the efficacious voice of God, which works what it says, and effects what it utters and wills, and a creation comes. The royal devotion of the Church is the works of mercy; and see how they are all satisfied in this devotion for the dead! It feeds the hungry souls with Jesus, the Bread of Angels. It gives them to drink in their incomparable thirst His precious blood. It clothes the naked with a robe of glory. It visits the sick with mighty powers to heal, and at the least consoles them by the visit. It frees the captives, with a heavenly and eternal freedom, from a bondage dreader far than death. It takes in the strangers, and heaven is the hospice into which it receives them. It buries the dead in the bosom of Jesus in everlasting rest. When the last doom shall come, and our dearest Lord shall ask those seven questions of His judicial process, those interrogatories of the works of mercy, how happy will that man be—and it may be the poorest beggar amongst us who never gave an alms because he has had to live on alms himself—who shall hear his own defence sweetly and eloquently taken up by crowds of blessed souls, to whom he has done all these things while they waited in their prison-house of hope! Three times a day St. Francis of Sales put himself in the presence of God as before his judge, and tried to judge himself in his Saviour's way. Let us but do that, and we shall become so many servitors of Michael, so many guardian angels of that beautiful but melancholy land of suffering and expectant souls.

—Father Faber, *ibid.*

Chapter 11

Means of Assisting the Holy Souls in Purgatory

WE HAVE as many means of assisting them as we have means of gaining grace and merit for ourselves, since we can apply all our good works to the Poor Souls by way of intercession. The holy Fathers therefore advise prayer, the invocation of the Mother of God, of the angels and saints, fasting or works of penance, almsgiving or works of mercy, and the holy sacrifice of the Mass. There are many other ways of assisting them, such as offering up our merits, applying indulgences, using holy water, burning blessed candles, making pilgrimages to holy places, etc. In holy communion we have one of the greatest means of assisting them.

—Help for the Poor Souls in Purgatory.

*

1. WE READ in the Catechism of the Council of Trent (Part II., Chap. iv., Question 77) that such is the efficacy of the holy sacrifice of the Mass, "that it is profitable not only to the celebrant and communicant, but also to all the faithful, whether living with us on earth, or already numbered with those who are dead in the Lord, but whose sins have not yet been fully expiated; for, according to Apostolic Tradition, the most authentic, it is not less available when offered for them than when offered for the sins of the living, their punishments, satisfactions, calamities, and difficulties of every sort."

It must be evident to every thoughtful mind that nothing can be so surely efficacious in satisfying the justice of God and in obtaining the remission of the temporal punishment due to sin as the Holy Mass, in which Jesus Christ renews the sacrifice He once offered on Calvary, the Holy Mass, being one and the same sacrifice as that of the cross, is of an infinite value, and would, therefore, suffice to redeem a thousand worlds; hence it follows that every soul in Purgatory, however burdened with debt for sins committed, could be released by one Holy Mass, if there were no impediment in the soul to its full application. From the time of the apostles it has been the custom of the Church to make a commemoration of the faithful departed in every Mass after the Consecration, since, as St. Cyril says, "this sacrifice affords them extraordinary relief."

Another most efficacious means of delivering one individual soul from Purgatory is the offering of the holy sacrifice of the Mass at a *privileged altar.* An altar is called privileged when the Pope, by a special concession, has attached to it the favor of a plenary indulgence granted to the deceased person for whom the Holy Mass is said at that altar. It depends, it is true, on the dispensation of God's mercy how far this indulgence will benefit that soul, for there are often obstacles which prevent its full application. But even in this latter respect the Holy Mass is of special efficacy. Being a sacrifice of atonement, it appeases God's justice, and removes precisely that impediment which deprives the soul of the entire fruit of the

Mass and other good works performed in her behalf. Hence it is always advisable, and this is the practice of pious Catholics, to have several Masses said at a privileged altar.

We read in the Life of St. Nicholas of Tolentine, O.S.A., who was noted for his devotion to the Holy Souls, that after his daily Mass it was frequently revealed to him that the souls for whom he had offered the Holy Sacrifice had been released from Purgatory.

2. Besides the Holy Mass, there are numerous other ways of aiding the Holy Souls. We have the practice of fervent prayer, almsgiving, the gaining of indulgences, and the offering of holy communion on their behalf.

In addition to its power of impetration, holy communion also possesses a great power of satisfaction, since, as it is one of the most excellent acts of religion, it honors God in a special manner and makes atonement for the offences committed against Him. Moreover, in receiving holy communion, various acts of virtue, such as humility, love, sorrow for sin, etc., are exercised and they are so much the more meritorious as the soul performs them while Jesus Christ is sacramentally united to her. Now, all these acts of virtue can be offered up to the Divine Majesty for the souls in Purgatory, especially in atonement for those sins they may have committed in regard to the

Blessed Sacrament, and for which they have not yet made satisfaction.

3. Christ, Our Redeemer, as we know, has left to His Church the rich treasure of His own infinite merits and satisfactions, together with the superabundant merits and satisfactions of the Blessed Virgin and the saints. This treasure He entrusted to St. Peter, on whom He bestowed the keys of the Kingdom of Heaven, and to his successors on earth, the Sovereign Pontiffs, to be dispensed by them for the spiritual benefit of the faithful. From this inexhaustible treasure, then, the Church draws and imparts to her children, both living and dead, what are called indulgences, by means of which the temporal punishment due to sin is remitted. The Council of Trent says that "the use of indulgences is in the highest degree beneficial to Christian people"; we should, therefore, strive with holy eagerness to gain as many indulgences as possible, both for our own spiritual good and also for the relief of the faithful departed.

4. We read in the Book of Tobias (xii. 9) the following striking declaration of the Archangel Raphael:

"Alms delivereth from death, and the same is that which purgeth away sins, and makes to find mercy and life everlasting."

In another passage the Holy Ghost exhorts us: "Stretch out thy hand to the poor, that thy expiation and thy blessing may be perfected," by which He gives us to understand that there is no perfect satisfaction without almsgiving; hence St. Thomas does not hesitate to attribute to alms-deeds a greater power of satisfaction than to prayer. For the same reason St. Ambrose exhorts parents to give in alms for the repose of the souls of their deceased children that portion of their fortune which they had destined for them. St. John Chrysostom gave the same advice to his flock, and St. Jerome praises Pammachius, a Roman nobleman, because after the death of his wife he assembled all the poor of the city in the Church of St. Peter, and distributed a dole of bread among them, in order to comfort by this abundant almsgiving the soul of her for whom he mourned. "While other husbands," said the Saint, "adorn the grave of their wives with flowers, our Pammachius covers her dear remains with the balm of almsgiving."—Vy. Rev. Richard A. O'Gorman, O.S.A., *A Novena for the Holy Souls in Purgatory.*

Chapter 12

The Heroic Act

THIS heroic act of charity in behalf of the souls in Purgatory consists in a voluntary offering made in their favor to the Divine Majesty, by any one of the faithful, of all works of satisfaction done by him in his life, as well as of all the suffrages which shall be offered for him after his death. Many of the faithful, devout to the Blessed Virgin, have followed the praiseworthy practice, introduced, or at least much spread since the last century, by F. D. Gaspar Oliden, Theatine, of placing them in the hands of the Blessed Virgin, that she may distribute them in behalf of those souls whom it is her good pleasure to deliver sooner from the pains of Purgatory. By this offering he foregoes in their behalf only that special fruit which belongs to himself; so that a priest is not hindered thereby from applying the holy sacrifice of the Mass for the intention of those who give him alms.

This heroic act of charity was enriched with many indulgences: first, by Pope Benedict XIII., in a decree, August 23, 1728, confirmed by Pope Pius VI., in a decree, December 12, 1788; and lastly, these indulgences were specified by the Sovereign Pontiff, Pius IX., in a decree of the Sacred Congregation of Indulgences, September 10, 1852. They are as follows:

I. *The Indult of a Privileged Altar*, personally, every day in the year, to all priests who shall have made this offering.

II. *A Plenary Indulgence*, applicable only to the departed, to all the faithful who shall have made this offering, whenever they go to holy communion, provided they visit a church or public oratory, and pray there, for some time, for the intention of His Holiness.

III. *A Plenary Indulgence*, every Monday, to all who hear Mass in aid of the souls in Purgatory, provided they fulfil the other conditions mentioned above.

All indulgences granted or to be granted, which are to be gained by the faithful who have made this offering, may be applied to the Holy Souls in Purgatory.

Lastly, his Holiness, Pope Pius IX., having in view the young, who have not yet made their first communion, as well as the sick, those who are afflicted with chronic disorders, the aged, farm-laborers, prisoners, and others who are debarred from communion, or are unable to hear Mass on Mondays, declared, by another decree of the Sacred Congregation of Indulgences, November 20, 1854, that, for all the faithful who cannot hear Mass on Monday, the Mass heard on Sundays should be available, and that in favor of those who have not yet made their first communion, or who are hindered from receiving holy communion, he has left it to the will of their respective Ordinaries to authorize confessors to commute the works here enjoined.

And note, lastly, that, although this act of charity is called *heroic vow of charity* in some printed sheets, in which also is given a formula for making the offering, no inference is to be drawn therefrom that this offering binds under sin; neither is it necessary to make use of the said formula, or any other, since, in order to share in the said indulgences, no more is required than a heartfelt act of the will.—*The New Raccolta.*

Formula for Making This Offering

HEAVENLY Father, in union with the Sacred Hearts of Jesus and Mary, I offer Thee all the works of satisfaction of my life, as well as the prayers and good works, which will be offered for me after my death, for the poor souls in Purgatory. All these works I put into the hands of the immaculate Virgin Mary, Mother of God, that she may apply them to the souls she wishes to deliver from Purgatory. Graciously accept this my humble offering, O my God, and grant me, in return, mercy and forgiveness for my sins, a daily increase of holy charity, and Thy grace at the hour of my death. Amen.

—*Voices from Purgatory.*

Chapter 13

The Gregorian Masses

For the Release of the Souls in Purgatory

POPE St. Gregory the Great (590–60), the first Pontiff of that name, tells us in his " *Dialogues* " that he caused thirty Masses to be said on thirty consecutive days for the repose of the soul of Justus, a monk who had died in his convent of St. Andrew on Mount Coelius, where the church of St. Gregory now stands. At the end of the trental the deceased appeared to his brother Copiosus who, in quality of physician, had assisted him in his last illness, and announced to him that he had been delivered from the flames of Purgatory.

Copiosus went at once to the convent to tell the brethren. The latter having carefully counted the days, found that this had happened on exactly the thirtieth day on which the Holy Sacrifice had been offered for Justus. Now Copiosus did not know anything about these thirty Masses celebrated for his brother, nor did the monks know anything of the apparition which Copiosus had just had. On comparing notes, it was found that the thirtieth Mass and the apparition coincided, and it was evident that the deceased had been delivered from his sufferings by the merits of the Holy Sacrifice.

With regard to the foregoing fact, the Bollandists tell us that on the thirtieth day St. Gregory was assured of the deliverance of the soul of Justus. An inscription, also, in the church of Sts. Andrew and Gregory, erected in the ancient dwelling of the Holy Pontiff, on Mount Coelius, Rome, confirms the fact. St. Gregory was instructed by a revelation upon the efficacy of these thirty Masses.

The obligation of having the thirty Gregorian Masses for every deceased member may be found in the Constitutions or other writings of most Religious Orders. The Carmelites, Dominicans, and Visitandines still follow this custom. The Dominican Missal has, in a very old edition, special prayers for the Gregorian Masses.

St. Vincent Ferrer had a trental celebrated for his sister, whom he saw delivered from Purgatory by these Masses.

We subjoin a few questions put to the Sacred Congregation of Indulgences regarding the celebration of the Gregorian Masses, along with the answers given to them.

A Decree regarding these Masses was issued January 14, 1889.

Q. Is it necessary that the Masses called *Gregorian* be celebrated in memory of St. Gregory, without, however, making commemoration of the saint?

A. They need not be said in memory of St. Gregory.

Q. Must the thirty Masses, called *Gregorian*, be said by the same priest?

A. There is no obligation that they be said by the same priest.

Q. Must they be said for one soul alone, without any other special intention?

A. The Masses should be said *exclusively* for the soul whose deliverance from the pains of Purgatory is especially solicited from the divine mercy.

Q. Should they be said on thirty consecutive days without interruption?

A. Yes; for thirty days without interruption.

Q. Must they be said at the same altar?

A. No; they may be said at different altars.

Many are astonished that thirty Masses said consecutively can obtain grace which cannot be obtained by a greater number. But God alone knows the reason of this. What is certain is that the custom of offering prayer for thirty days for the dead without interruption dates back to the remotest antiquity. We read in Holy Scripture that the Jewish people wept and prayed for thirty days after the death of Moses and Aaron, respectively. St. Gregory revived this custom, and the *revelation* given him, as we have stated, confirmed him in the idea that he was acting rightly.

Pope Benedict XIII extolled the pious practice of these Masses, in one of the thirty sermons that he preached on Purgatory, in 1720, in the cathedral of Benevento, of which he was then archbishop. He says: " The reason of the special utility of this custom lies in the merits of St. Gregory who, then a monk, obtained by the great efficacy of his prayers the satisfactory virtue for these thirty Masses."

It would be very conformable to the end proposed if the thirty Gregorian Masses were celebrated at a privileged altar, when that is possible. Their efficacy would then be more highly guaranteed.

On August 24, 1888, the Sacred Congregation of Indulgences declared that these thirty Masses *cannot be said for the living*. These thirty Masses, moreover, cannot always be *Masses of Requiem*, since in the course of thirty consecutive days, Sundays and certain other days occur on which it is not permitted to say *Requiem Masses*. The only essential on this point is that, during *thirty consecutive days*, Mass be offered for the soul whose deliverance is demanded (*Ferraris*, L. c. v. *Missae Sacrificium*, art. 14, no. 27).

Even on days when a *Mass of Requiem* is permitted, the obligation of the Gregorian Masses is rigorously satisfied by saying the Mass of the day, because neither the custom introduced by St. Gregory nor the decisions of the Church already cited make a *Mass of Requiem* an essential· condition. Such a Mass, however, seems more appropriate to the end in view, by reason of its special prayers for the dead. If the *three last days of the Holy Week* fall in the course of the *trental*, they do not constitute any interruption (on account of the precept of the Church), provided that, immediately after, the celebration of the thirty Masses be continued (Benedict XIV, *Instit.* 34, No. 22).

—*The Lamp,* Nov. 1912.

Chapter 14

Voices from Purgatory

1

THE Venerable Sister Paula of St. Teresa was a Dominican nun of the Convent of St. Catherine in Naples. One day, being in prayer, she was transported in spirit to Purgatory, where she saw a great number of souls plunged in flames. Close to them she saw our divine Lord, attended by His angels, who pointed out, one after the other, several souls that He desired to take to heaven, whither they ascended in transports of delight. At this sight the servant of God, addressing herself to her Divine Spouse, said to Him: " O my beloved Lord, why this choice among such a vast multitude?" " I have released," He deigned to reply, " those who during life performed great acts of charity and mercy, and who have merited that I should fulfil My promise in their regard, *Blessed are the merciful, for they shall obtain mercy.*"

—*Forget-me-nots from Many Gardens.*

2

THERE are few souls, even of the just, who directly after this life pass immediately to the eternal joys of heaven. Even the imperfections of the saints have to be cleansed by fire. The following example, related by St. Peter Damian, will serve to prove this: St. Severinus, archbishop of Cologne, was a prelate of such extraordinary sanctity that God vouchsafed to distinguish him by remarkable miracles. After his death the Saint appeared one day to a Canon of Cologne cathedral in a small branch of the Rhine, in which he stood plunged up to the waist. The canon asked him why he stood there in the water—as on account of his extraordinary sanctity he ought to be reigning gloriously in heaven. "If you wish to know," replied the Saint, "give me your hand, in order that you may understand the pain which I suffer, not by hearing of it, but by touch." Then, having seized his hand, he dipped it gently into the water. Though he drew it rapidly out, so great was the heat that he felt from it that the flesh fell off scorched, and the bare bones held together by the joints were in great pain. Then the Saint said: "I do not suffer this great torment for anything more than for having recited the Canonical Hours hastily and with distraction. For while I was counsellor in the Emperor's Court, having a great deal of business, I did not recite the Divine Office at the proper hours or with devotion. This is my only fault." Then, begging the canon to join with him in prayer to obtain the cure of his hand, and beseeching him to obtain his own liberation from such great sufferings by the suffrage of prayers, alms, and Masses, he suddenly disappeared, leaving the priest miraculously cured and full of fear of God's judgments.—*Ibid.*

3

CANTIPRATANUS writes of a sick man who was so impatient at the length and severity of his illness that he earnestly begged of God either to restore him to health, or to take him out of the world. God sent an angel to say to him that he might choose whether he would suffer the pains of Purgatory for three days, or those of his sickness for another year. The sick man thought to himself that the three days would soon be over, while a year of illness meant a long trial of one's patience. He therefore chose the three days in Purgatory. According to his wish, he died and went to Purgatory, but was hardly an hour there when he imagined the three days and even more had expired. He grew exceedingly anxious, sighed, suffered, and wept. "Ah!" he said, "I must be more than a month here, and yet the door is not opened to let me out! I am afraid that he who gave me that choice was not an angel in reality, but one disguised as an angel, who has shamefully deceived me." While busied with these thoughts, the angel came to comfort him, and to congratulate him on having accomplished the third part of his atonement. "What!" exclaimed the suffering soul, "the third part! No more than that?" "No more. You have been here but one day; your body is not yet buried." "Ah, holy Guardian Angel!" cried the poor soul, "help me to return to my body and my former sufferings; I would rather endure them patiently for ten years than bear these pains for two days more."

St. Antoninus relates in his "Summo" (Part IV., c. x.) that a preacher of his Order appeared a month after his death to the infirmarian of the convent in which he had lived, and told him that he had been kept in Purgatory all that time for no other reason than that he had been too familiar and jocose in his conversations with seculars. A whole month he had to suffer because he had not observed that gravity of demeanor that becomes the Religious when in the society of seculars. And how many Masses and prayers had not been offered for him by his brethren in the meantime!—*Ibid.*

4

WE READ in the life of St. Monica that, feeling her last hour at hand, she sent for St. Augustine, and thus addressed him: "My son, I know that I shall soon be no more; but when I am gone pray for the repose of my soul! Do not forget me who have loved you so dearly. Especially think of me when you are at the altar and about to offer the Holy Sacrifice." St. Augustine, bathed in tears, made the required promise, and after his mother's edifying death he never ceased to intercede for her. " God of Mercy! " he exclaimed in his sorrow, "forgive my mother the faults which she may have committed; enter not into judgment with her; turn aside Thine eyes from her sins. Remember that on the point of expiring she thought not of the honors which should be paid to her lifeless corpse; she asked only that she should not be forgotten at Thine altar, in order that any stains of sin which might not have been expiated during her life should be washed away."—*Ibid.*

5

ST. MARY MAGDALENE de Pazzi had assisted in her last moments a member of her Community who died with the reputation of great sanctity. The sisterhood not only lost no time in reciting for her the usual Offices, but also applied in her behalf all the indulgences which it was in their power to gain. The body was laid in the church exposed to view, and St. Mary Magdalene from the grating gazed upon it with feelings of tenderness and devotion, whilst she offered fervent prayers for the eternal repose of the Sister. Suddenly she saw the soul of the deceased, beaming with light, arise from the cold remains and ascend to heaven, there to receive the crown of eternal glory. The Saint, at the sight, could not refrain from exclaiming: " Farewell, sister, farewell, happy soul, who enterest heaven before thy body has been committed to the tomb. What a happiness! What glory! In the bosom of the Eternal Spouse be not forgetful of us poor mortals who still pine and sigh on earth." Then Jesus Himself appeared to console her, and told her that this soul had been thus promptly delivered from Purgatory and admitted to heaven by virtue of holy indulgences. Thenceforth the zeal of the Sisters for gaining indulgences was such that each one would feel a scruple unless she tried to obtain every one she could. Let us imitate the piety of these good Religious, and if we but possess the requisite dispositions, we cannot fail to deliver many souls from Purgatory.—*Ibid.*

6

A CERTAIN mother, inconsolable at the death of her only son, wept for his loss long and bitterly, without, however, helping him by those means which religion affords. To give her affection a useful direction, God sent her a vision. She beheld a procession of youths, clad in white garments, enriched with various ornaments, and directing their joyous course toward a magnificent temple. This temple represented heaven, the white garments were the garb of faith, and the ornaments upon them were the works of charity. The bereaved mother, having her lost son unceasingly in her mind and heart, anxiously sought for him amongst this chosen band, but her searching glance could not discover him till all the rest had passed. She then beheld him, but clothed in a dark and sullied robe, and she saw that he advanced but slowly and with difficulty. This sad sight caused her tears to flow anew, and, with a voice broken with sobs, she exclaimed: "Why, O my son, are you so sad, and differ so much from your companions? Why do you remain so far behind?" The young man sorrowfully replied: "Mother, you see these mournful and sullied garments. Behold in them what your obstinate grief and tears for me produce! Your unreasonable grief weighs heavily upon me and impedes my progress. Ah! cease to abandon yourself to mere natural feelings, and, if you truly love me, if you desire to see me happy, arouse your faith, and aid me by works of faith and charity. Assist me by your pious suffrages, as is done by other mothers not less affectionate, but more wise and more religious than you. Then I shall be enabled to join the happy company you have seen, and attain to that heavenly bliss, for which I long with so much ardor."

Without saying more he disappeared, leaving his mother as eager to procure him spiritual help as before she had been remarkable for giving herself up to useless grief.

May similar sentiments of faith animate us with regard to our departed friends, and render us more mindful of aiding and consoling them by meritorious works than of abandoning ourselves to unprofitable grief and sadness for their loss.—*Ibid.*

7

SAINT MARGARET MARY, praying one day for two persons of rank in the world who had died, one of them was shown to her as condemned for several years to the pains of Purgatory, notwithstanding the solemn services and the great number of Masses that were offered for her. All these prayers and suffrages were applied by the Divine Justice to the souls of some families subject to her who had been ruined by her want of charity and equity in their regard; and as these poor people had left nothing after their death to obtain prayers for their souls, God supplied them in this way. The other person was in Purgatory for as many days as she had lived years upon earth. Our Lord made known to Saint Margaret Mary that amongst all the good works this person had performed He had had particular regard to certain humiliations she had received in the world, which she endured with a truly Christian spirit, not only without complaint, but even without mentioning them, and that in reward He had been mild and favorable in His judgment.

A gentleman, father to one of the novices, being dead, was recommended to the prayers of the Community at Paray. The charity of Saint Margaret Mary, then Mistress of Novices, induced her to pray more particularly for this person, and on the novice repeating her request for her prayers some days after, she said: "Be satisfied, my child; he is in a state to benefit us by his prayers instead of needing ours." She then added: "Ask your mother what generous action her husband performed before his death, for it is that which made the judgment of God favorable to him." The novice did not see her mother until the time of her Profession. She then asked what this act of Christian generosity was, and learned that when the Holy Viaticum was given to her father, a butcher of the town joined those who accompanied the Blessed Sacrament, and placed himself in a corner of the room. The sick man, perceiving him, called him by his name, told him to approach, and, cordially pressing his hand, asked his pardon, with a humility very unusual in persons of high rank, for some severe words he had said to him some time before, and was desirous that everyone should witness the satisfaction he made him. Saint Margaret Mary had learned from God alone what had passed, and the novice knew by this the truth of what had been revealed to her holy Mistress regarding the happy state of her father.—*Ibid.*

8

THE celebrated Father Lacordaire, in the beginning of the conferences on the immortality of the soul, which he addressed a few years before his death to the pupils of Sorèze, related to them the following incident:

The Polish Prince of X., an avowed infidel and materialist, had just composed a work against the immortality of the soul. He was on the point of sending it to press, when one day walking in his park, a woman bathed in tears threw herself at his feet, and in accents of profound grief said to him, " My good Prince, my husband has just died. . . . At this moment his soul is perhaps suffering in Purgatory. . . . I am in such poverty that I have not even the small sum required to have a Mass celebrated for the dead. In your kindness come to my assistance in behalf of my poor husband."

Although the gentleman was convinced that the woman was deceived by her credulity, he had not courage to refuse her. He slipped a gold piece into her hand, and the happy woman hastened to the church, and begged the priest to offer some Masses for the repose of her husband's soul. Five days later, toward evening, the prince, in the seclusion of his study, was reading over his manuscript and retouching some details, when, raising his eyes, he saw, close to him, a man dressed in the costume of the peasants of the country. "Prince," said the unknown visitor, "I come to thank you. I am the husband of that poor woman who besought you the other day to give her an alms, that she might have the holy sacrifice of the Mass offered for the repose of my soul. Your charity was pleasing to God: it was He who permitted me to come and thank you."

These words said, the Polish peasant disappeared like a shadow. The emotion of the prince was indescribable, and in consequence he consigned his work to the flames, and yielded himself so entirely to the conviction of truth that his conversion was complete. He persevered until death.

—Rev. F. X. Schouppe, S. J., *Purgatory.*

9

THERE were at Cologne, among the students in the higher classes of the university, two Dominican Religious of distinguished talent, one of whom was Blessed Henry Suzo. The same studies, the same kind of life, and above all the same relish for sanctity, had caused them to contract an intimate friendship, and they mutually imparted the favors which they received from Heaven.

When they had finished their studies, seeing that they were about to be separated, to return each one to his own convent, they

agreed and promised each other that the
first of the two who should die should be
assisted by the other for a whole year by the
celebration of two Masses each week—on
Monday a Mass of Requiem, as was cus-
tomary, and on Friday that of the Passion,
in so far as the rubrics would permit. They
engaged to do this, gave each other the kiss
of peace, and left Cologne.

For several years they both continued to
serve God with the most edifying fervor.
The brother whose name is not mentioned
was the first to be called away, and Suzo
received the tidings with the most perfect
sentiments of resignation to the divine will.
As to the contract they had made, time had
caused him to forget it. He prayed much
for his friend, imposing new penances upon
himself, and many other good works, but he
did not think of offering the Masses which
he had promised.

One morning, whilst meditating in retire-
ment in the chapel, he suddenly saw appear
before him the soul of his departed friend,
who, regarding him with tenderness, reproached him with having been unfaithful
to his word, given and accepted, and which
he had a perfect right to rely upon with confidence. Blessed Suzo, surprised, excused
his forgetfulness by enumerating the prayers
and mortifications which he had offered, and
still continued to offer, for his friend, whose
salvation was as dear to him as his own.

"Is it possible, my dear brother," he added, "that so many prayers and good works which I have offered to God do not suffice for you?" "Oh! no, dear brother," replied the suffering soul, "that is not sufficient. It is the blood of Jesus Christ that is needed to extinguish the flames by which I am consumed; it is the August Sacrifice which will deliver me from these frightful torments. I implore you to keep your word, and refuse me not that which in justice you owe me."

Blessed Suzo hastened to respond to the appeal of the suffering soul; and, to repair his fault, he celebrated, and caused to be celebrated, more Masses than he had promised.

On the following day several priests, at the request of Suzo, united with him in offering the Holy Sacrifice for the deceased, and continued this act of charity for several days.

After some time the friend of Suzo again appeared to him, but now in a very different condition; his countenance was joyful, and surrounded with beautiful light. "Oh! thanks, my faithful friend," said he; "behold, by the blood of my Saviour I am delivered from my sufferings. I am now going to heaven to contemplate Him whom we so often adored together under the Eucharistic veil." Suzo prostrated himself to thank the God of all mercy, and understood more than ever the inestimable value of the August Sacrifice of the Altar.[1]—*Ibid.*

[1] Rossignoli, Merv., 34, and Ferdinand de Castile.

10

THE Church advises the faithful to have prayers said for the dead, to give alms, and perform other good works, to apply indulgences to them, but especially to have Holy Mass celebrated, and to assist thereat. Whilst giving the first place to the Divine Sacrifice, she approves and makes use of various kinds of suffrages, according to the circumstances, devotion, or social condition of the deceased or his heirs.

It is a Catholic custom, religiously observed from the remotest antiquity, to have Mass celebrated for the dead with solemn ceremonies, and a funeral with as much pomp as their means will allow. The expense of this is an alms given to the Church, an alms which, in the eyes of God, greatly enhances the price of the Holy Sacrifice, and its satisfactory value for the deceased.

It is well, however, so to regulate the funeral expenses, that a sufficient sum be left for a certain number of Masses, and also to give alms to the poor.

That which must be avoided is, to lose sight of the Christian character of funerals, and to look upon the funeral service less as a great act of religion than a display of worldly vanity.

What must be further avoided are the profane mourning emblems which are not conformable to Christian tradition, such as

the wreaths of flowers, with which, at a great
expense, they load the coffins of the dead.
This is an innovation justly disapproved by
the Church, to which Jesus Christ has in-
trusted the care of religious rites and ceremonies, not excepting funeral ceremonies.
Those of which she makes use at the death
of her children are venerable by their antiquity, full of meaning and consolation. All
that presents itself to the eyes of the faithful
on such occasions, the cross and the holy
water, the lights and the incense, the tears
and prayers, breathe compassion for the
Poor Souls, faith in the Divine Mercy, and
the hope of immortality.

What is there of all this in the cold wreaths
of violet?   They say nothing to the Christian
soul; they are but profane emblems of this
mortal life, that contrast strangely with the
cross, and which are foreign to the rites of
the Catholic Church.—*Ibid.*

*

Spiritual Bouquets for the Dead

THE early Christians were distinguished
for their love and remembrance of the
dead.   Their devotion consisted not so much
in tears and gifts of flowers, but in prayers,
communions, and the offering of the sacrifice of the Mass. We would do well to
model our devotion to the faithful departed
on that of our predecessors in the Faith.

There is a custom fast becoming common

of sending cards of condolence to the parents or members of the family of the deceased. These cards, besides extending sympathy, also express the intention of having Masses said, communions offered up, and Rosaries and other indulgenced prayers recited for the repose of the soul of the deceased. This custom is thoroughly Catholic and expresses our sympathy in a more efficacious way than do offerings of flowers. If the deceased was at all known to us, we should certainly prefer to aid his soul in this way than to parade our generosity by a pompous display of expensive flowers, which cannot aid the dead.—Rev. Thomas S. McGrath, *Prayers for Our Dead.*

Chapter 15

The Blessed Virgin Mary, the Angels and the Saints, in Relation to the Holy Souls

1

All Saints—All Souls

IT WAS well done to place thus close together these two beautiful solemnities. There is a fitness, too, in this reason of the fall of the leaf for such a commemoration of the departed. The flowers and green leaves of May, the yellow harvests and the warm glow of August, would be out of place upon

All Souls' Day. Better to sing this universal Requiem when Nature herself has laid aside the garments of her gladness, when the warm blood of youth is no longer coursing through the earth's veins, when the very sunshine seems chill and sad, and the wind through the naked branches is a dirge. But at whatever period they come, All Saints' and All Souls' should come together. And they come together, though one might be tempted, in all reverence, to wish that the order of their coming were reversed. If the commemoration of All Souls came first, we might hope that the suffrages of all the Church Militant on that day, joined with the prayers of all the Church Triumphant, might avail much to the relief of the Suffering Church; might procure the discharge of many, perhaps, amongst the patient victims detained in that prison-house of mercy, and so increase the hosts of those honored in the festival of All Saints. Or is it only by a tender after-thought, as it were, that the Church, having rejoiced in the glory of those of her children who have secured their crown in heaven, turns with affectionate compassion to those others who are not yet *there*, though they are no longer *here*, whose earthly fight is over, but whose heavenly happiness is not yet attained? Would that all who are gone were gone to join that multitude which no man can number, thronging the Courts of Heaven! But so many disappoint the yearnings of the Heart of Jesus. So many live and die as if Jesus had not lived and died for them. And even of those who die in the grace of Our Lord Jesus Christ, how few are found " with the perfect sheen of Heaven upon them "! How few are pure enough, at once, after closing their eyes upon this sinful world, to open them to the full piercing light of glory, to meet, without shrinking, the all-discerning eye of the God of infinite purity! And we are living under that same eye, and we are laboring for that heaven which the saints have not earned too dearly, and for which the Holy Souls are not undergoing too severe a preparation. Have we worked and prayed during the past year as if we believed this?

Before the month closes which is opening now may our hearts have grown more pleasing to the Heart of Jesus and the Heart of Mary—more dear to them because more like to them; and, as all belongs to Jesus, let us give to Mary a mother's share in all the days of our lives, especially in these two sacred days which invite us to love and honor her as Queen of All Saints and Compassionate Mother of the Suffering Souls.

> " Ah! turn to Jesus, Mother! turn,
> And call Him by His tenderest names.
> Pray for the holy souls that burn
> This hour amid the cleansing flames."
> —Rev. Matthew Russell, S.J.
> –*Forget-me-nots from Many Gardens.*

2

Our Lady

THE souls in Purgatory receive great consolation from the Blessed Virgin. Is she not the *Consolation of the Afflicted?* And what affliction can be compared to that of the Poor Souls? Is she not the *Mother of Mercy?* And is it not toward these holy Suffering Souls that she must show all the mercy of her heart? We must not, therefore, be astonished that in the " Revelations of St. Bridget " the Queen of Heaven gives herself the beautiful name of *Mother of the Souls in Purgatory.* " I am," she said to that Saint, " the Mother of all those who are in the place of expiation; my prayers mitigate the chastisements which are inflicted upon them for their faults."[1]

On October 25, 1604, in the College of the Society of Jesus at Coimbra, Father Jerome Carvalho died in the odor of sanctity, at the age of fifty years. This admirable and humble servant of God felt a lively apprehension of the sufferings of Purgatory. Neither the cruel macerations which he inflicted upon himself several times every day, not counting those prompted each week by the remembrance of the passion, nor the six hours which he devoted morning and evening to the meditation of holy subjects, seemed suf-

[1] Revel. S. Brig., lib. iv. c. 50.

119

ficient, in his estimation, to shield him from the chastisement which he imagined awaited him after death. But one day the Queen of Heaven, to whom he had a tender devotion, condescended herself to console her servant by the simple assurance that she was a *Mother of Mercy* to her dear children in Purgatory as well as to those upon earth. Seeking, later, to spread this consoling doctrine, the holy man accidentally let fall, in the ardor of his discourse, these words: *" She told me this herself."*

It is related that a great servant of Mary, Blessed Renier of Citeaux, trembled at the thought of his sins and the terrible justice of God after death. In his fear, addressing himself to his great Protectress, who calls herself Mother of Mercy, he was rapt in spirit, and saw the Mother of God supplicating her Son in his favor. " My Son," she said, " deal mercifully with him in Purgatory, because he humbly repents of his sins." " My Mother," replied Jesus, " I place his cause in your hands," which is to say, be it done to your client according to your desire. Blessed Renier understood with unutterable joy that Mary had obtained his exemption from Purgatory.

It is especially on certain days that the Queen of Heaven exercises her mercy in Purgatory. These privileged days are, first, all Saturdays, then the different feast-days of the Blessed Virgin, which thus become as festivals in Purgatory. We see in the revelations of the saints that on Saturday, the day specially consecrated to the Blessed Virgin, the sweet Mother of Mercy descends into the dungeons of Purgatory to visit and console her devoted servants. Then, according to the pious belief of the faithful, she delivers those souls who, having worn the holy scapular, enjoy this Sabbatine Privilege, and afterward gives relief and consolation to other souls who had been particularly devout to her. A witness to this was the Venerable Sister Paula of St. Teresa, a Dominican Religious of the Convent of St. Catherine in Naples.[1]

Being rapt in ecstasy one Saturday, and transported in spirit into Purgatory, she was quite surprised to find it transformed into a paradise of delights, illuminated by a bright light, instead of the darkness which at other times prevailed. Whilst she was wondering what could be the cause of this change, she perceived the Queen of Heaven surrounded by a multitude of angels, to whom she gave orders to liberate those souls who had honored her in a special manner, and conduct them to heaven.

If such takes place on an ordinary Saturday, we can scarcely doubt that the same occurs on feast-days consecrated to the Mother of God. Among all her festivals, that of the glorious Assumption of Mary

[1] Rossign., Merv., 50; Marchese, tom. i. p. 56.

seems to be the chief day of deliverance. St. Peter Damian [1] tells us that each year, on the day of the Assumption, the Blessed Virgin delivers several thousands of souls.

The following account of a miraculous vision illustrates this subject: " It is a pious custom," he says, " which exists among the people of Rome, to visit the churches, carrying a candle in the hand, during the night preceding the feast of the Assumption of Our Lady." Now it happened that a person of rank, being on her knees in the basilica of the Ara-Cœli in the Capital, saw before her, prostrate in prayer, another lady, her godmother, who had died several months previous. Surprised, and not being able to believe her eyes, she wished to solve the mystery, and for this purpose placed herself near the door of the church. As soon as she saw the lady go out, she took her by the hand and drew her aside. " Are you not," she said to her, " my godmother, who held me at the baptismal font? " " Yes," replied the apparition immediately, " it is I." " And how comes it that I find you among the living, since you have been dead more than a year? " " Until this day I have been plunged in a dreadful fire, on account of the many sins of vanity which I committed in my youth, but during this great solemnity the Queen of Heaven descended into the midst of the Purgatorial flames and delivered me,

[1] Opusc. xxxiv. c. 3, o. 1.

together with a large number of other souls, that we might enter heaven on the feast of her Assumption. She exercises this great act of clemency each year; and, on this occasion alone, the number of those whom she has delivered equals the population of Rome."

Seeing that her goddaughter remained stupefied and seemed still to doubt the evidence of her senses, the apparition added, "In proof of the truth of my words, know that you yourself will die a year hence, on the feast of the Assumption; if you outlive that period, believe that this was an illusion."

St. Peter Damian concluded this recital by saying that the young lady passed the year in the exercise of good works, in order to prepare herself to appear before God. The year following, on the Vigil of the Assumption, she fell sick, and died on the day of the feast itself, as had been predicted.

The feast of the Assumption is, then, the great day of Mary's mercy toward the Poor Souls; she delights to introduce her children into the glory of heaven on the anniversary of the day on which she herself first entered its blessed portals. This pious belief, adds Father Louvet, is founded on a great number of particular revelations; it is for this reason that in Rome the Church of St. Mary in Montorio, which is the centre of the arch-confraternity of *suffrages for the dead,* is dedicated under the title of the Assumption.

—Rev. F. X. Schouppe, S.J., *Purgatory.*

3

The Angels

BESIDES the consolations which the souls receive from the Blessed Virgin, they are also assisted and consoled by the holy angels, and especially by their guardian angels. The Doctors of the Church teach that the tutelary mission of the guardian angels terminates only on the entrance of their clients into paradise. If, at the moment of death, a soul in the state of grace is not yet worthy to see the face of the Most High, the angel guardian conducts it to the place of expiation, and remains there with her to procure for her all the assistance and consolations in his power.

It is an opinion common among the holy Doctors, says Father Rossignoli, that God, who will one day send forth His angels to assemble the elect, also sends them from time to time into Purgatory, there to visit and console the Suffering Souls. No doubt there cannot be any relief more precious than the sight of the inhabitants of heaven, that blessed abode whither they will one day go to enjoy its glorious and eternal felicity. The Revelations of St. Bridget are filled with examples of this nature, and the Lives of several saints also furnish a great number. . . .

If the holy angels interest themselves in

124

behalf of the souls of Purgatory in general, it is easy to understand that they have particular zeal for those of their clients. . . .

It may be here asked how the saints and blessed already crowned in heaven can assist them. It is certain, says Father Rossignoli, and such is the teaching of all masters in theology, St. Augustine and St. Thomas, that the saints are very powerful in this respect by way of supplication, or as we say, by *impetration*, but not by *satisfaction*. In other words, the saints in heaven may pray for the souls, and thus *obtain* from divine mercy a diminution of their suffering; but they cannot *satisfy* for them, nor pay their debts to divine justice; that is a privilege which God reserves to the Church Militant.—*Ibid*.

4

St. Joseph

IF WE reflect on the close alliance St. Joseph has with the Incarnate Word and His Immaculate Mother, we must surely acknowledge him worthy of our deepest love and veneration. One of the best modes of honoring him is to supplicate the Most High for souls who were devout to him during life and are now suffering in Purgatory.

St. Joseph may be regarded as the special Patron of Purgatory, because he is, after our blessed Lady, the most powerful and charitable of all the saints. The Prime

Minister of Egypt had authority to open or shut the gates of the prison at will, which has always been considered a privilege of the highest order. Thus it is with St. Joseph, of whom the first Joseph was a true type. Assured of the power of our holy Patriarch, can we doubt his good will? Who can express his burning zeal in favor of the poor sufferers in Purgatory, who are in his eyes all-beautiful by sanctifying grace, beloved by God, and destined soon to enjoy the beatific vision in the realms of bliss? St. Joseph, before entering into heaven, passed through Limbo, which, doubtless, was not a place of torments like Purgatory; still, it was not paradise. Here eager souls sighed for the coming of the Messias, and saluted Him from afar. This great Saint mingled his desires with theirs. In consoling the souls in Purgatory, St. Joseph continues the merciful avocation Divine Providence assigned him in Limbo. . . .

The beautiful mission of Consoler of the Dead is too glorious, too dear to God and to the saints, not to have it still continued to St. Joseph after the ascension of our divine Redeemer. A venerable writer says that the Son of God, having the keys of paradise, has given one to His Immaculate Mother and the other to St. Joseph. Oh, then you who so much love the dear departed ones, you who still weep at the remembrance of a cherished parent, a beloved brother or sister, or dear friend, have recourse to St. Joseph! You who dread the flames of Purgatory invoke St. Joseph, for though he is the mediator of all who are detained in those cleansing fires, he exercises special influence in behalf of persons who during life have been distinguished for their zeal in honoring him. Lastly, after the example of St. Joseph, let us be messengers of joy to those helpless souls detained captive in the fiery prison by offering fervent prayers and gaining indulgences for their relief.

—*Forget-me-nots from Many Gardens.*

5

St. Thomas Aquinas

ST. THOMAS AQUINAS showed a most tender devotion to the Poor Souls, making frequent commemoration of them in Mass, in his prayers and penances. When he was Professor of Theology at the University of Paris, his sister—who was Abbess of the Convent of St. Mary of Capua, and had lately died—appeared to him, and told him she was suffering great torments in Purgatory. St. Thomas immediately began to pray and fast and mortify himself for her; he also asked several of his friends to join him in prayer. He obtained the release of his sister's soul. She appeared to him again in Rome, whither he had been sent; but this time overflowing with heavenly joy and radiant with glory, and told him of her deliverance, and happy entrance into heaven. And she added: " Thou, my brother, hasten and finish those writings and works which thou hast begun, for thou wilt soon be called away to eternal life." .

Gemminger, *All Souls' Forget-me-not.*

6

St. Catherine of Ricci

ST. CATHERINE of Ricci cultivated a special devotion to the passion of Christ and in union with the sufferings of Our Lord endured many pains and torments and offered many prayers and mortifications for the relief of the holy souls in Purgatory. Her charity on behalf of the Holy Souls became so famous, as we read in the " Miniature Lives of the Saints," that whenever a death occurred in the vicinity of her convent (or indeed anywhere throughout Tuscany) the friends of the deceased invariably hastened to Catherine to secure her prayers. She knew by revelation the arrival of a soul in Purgatory and the hour of its release. She died, amid angels' songs, in 1589.

7

St. Philip Neri

THIS Saint was animated with the most tender love for the poor suffering souls in Purgatory. He prayed constantly for them, and bestowed on them the merits of his good works. He was particularly anxious to help those souls who during life had been under his spiritual care. He considered he owed more to them because, as a priest, he had labored for the salvation of their souls. Many dead appeared to him, because they hoped to be delivered from Purgatory by his prayers, and indeed he never failed to pray for them forthwith. His biographer assures us that the results of his prayers were most wonderful. The Saint was all the more anxious to pray for the dead, as they often obtained wonderful graces for him.

This devoted love to the souls in Purgatory has passed from the founder on to the whole Congregation of the Oratorians. Father Magnanti scarcely ever ceased praying for the dead, and like St. Philip Neri, was often made aware of the happy results of his prayers. This zealous priest spent the alms which pious Christians gave him, partly in alms to the poor, and partly for Masses in behalf of the Suffering Souls. He himself loved and practised poverty, but he kept in his cell an alms-box, which he called the " box of the souls." He thus followed the example of the divine Saviour, who, according to the Ven. Bede, gathered the gifts of the faithful in a box in order to distribute them among the poor and sick. To the treasury of his alms Father Magnanti added his prayers, fasts, vigils, and complete retire-

ment from the vain and idle joys of this
world. His burning love for the Poor Souls
carried him so far, that he asked Our Lord to
lay on him some of their sufferings in order
to give them relief. His heroic prayer was
heard and accepted; he became a prey to the
most cruel pains, which hardly allowed him
to change from one position to another, and
yet, from zeal for salvation of souls, he
undertook several long journeys. We may
well apply to him the words which a Roman
historian pronounced upon a victorious
soldier, who, in consequence of a wound
received in battle, returned with a limping
leg: "His every step is a mark of his
glory."

The souls of the faithful departed were not
ungrateful to him. A great part of the many
wonderful graces he had received Father
Magnanti ascribed to their intercession.
He had the gift of knowing the future, of
discovering hidden sins, and of frustrating
and escaping the numerous snares of the
enemy.

—Gemminger, *All Souls' Forget-me-not.*

8

St. Bridget

IN THE revelations of St. Bridget, we have
wonderful accounts of the appearances
of the poor departed souls. Nor are they
untrustworthy, because they have been ex-

amined by learned divines, and recognized
by them as authentic, so that the words
spoken of Judith, "All things which thou
hast spoken are true, and there is nothing to
be reprehended in thy words" (Judith viii.
28), might fitly be applied to St. Bridget, and
put at the foot of her portrait.

Once, St. Bridget saw in a vision the souls
of the faithful departed being purified, as it
were, in a crucible before they reached their
place of eternal rest. And at the same time
she heard the voice of an angel saying,
"Blessed are those who dwell upon earth,
and who by their prayers and other good
works hasten to the relief of the souls in
Purgatory. For the justice of God demands
that their sins be atoned for either by their
sufferings or else by the prayers and good
works of their friends on earth." Then
the Saint heard a great number of voices
praying in piteous tones, "O Lord Jesus
Christ! O great and just Judge! We implore Thee in Thine infinite mercy to regard
not the number and magnitude of our offences, but to look on the merits of Thy most
precious passion and death. Oh, let the
streams of Thy great charity flow into the
hearts of all Thy priests, monks, and all the
faithful, that by their Masses, prayers and
alms, they may come to our relief. If they
wish, they can help us greatly by their
prayers and indulgences, and can shorten
the term of our awful sufferings. They can

hasten our happy reunion with Thee, O God." At other times, St. Bridget heard appeals from Purgatory like the following: " O Lord, send down Thy grace a thousand-fold to those charitable Christians, who have helped us in our affliction by their prayers! "

Then she saw a certain light, half clear, half obscure, coming down, as it were, like the dawn of day, whereby she knew was meant, that the day of deliverance had dawned for some. And she heard new voices singing, " O God, whose power is infinite, we beg of Thee to reward a thousand-fold all those, who pray for our deliverance, and help us to come to Thine everlasting light."

From all this we can easily see, what great rewards all those will receive, who pray for the dead and obtain their release, and what grateful friends they make for themselves near the throne of God. God grant, that there may be instilled into the hearts of a great many Christians even a small portion of the love and sympathy which St. Bridget, in consequence of her visions, felt for the Poor Souls as long as she lived.—*Ibid*.

9

St. Margaret of Cortona

MARGARET was a great sinner in her youth. She lost her mother when quite young, and so was mostly left to herself. Her extraordinary beauty and lively temperament soon led her away from the right path into a frivolous and sinful life, which lasted for some considerable time. Amongst the many virtues which she practised after her conversion, the most striking was her love and devotion for the poor suffering souls in Purgatory, for whose deliverance she sacrificed time and rest, and everything. Great was her reward for it! As she lay on her death-bed, she saw a crowd of souls, released by her, hastening to her side, to form, as it were, a guard of honor, escorting her to the heavenly kingdom.

An intelligent love of the dead will, above all and in the first place, embrace one's own parents. Margaret always remembered her parents first, in all her supplications for the dead. Her father and mother were both dead, and for their repose she offered up communions, Masses, and other good works. God revealed to her, that she had very much shortened their term of punishment by her fervor, and delivered their souls from Purgatory much sooner than it was at first determined. With like affection, Margaret also remembered a faithful servant of the name of Julia. She prayed for her with such intense zeal, that she delivered her, as was told her by revelation. In the next place, Margaret prayed with great ardor for all the dead, whether known or unknown to her.

In fact, we might say that praying for the dead was her special daily occupation. Her every thought and desire was tending toward the deliverance of the souls in Purgatory: to hasten the day of their deliverance, to shorten the term of their punishment, to soothe their pains, was her one aim and object. She seemed to completely forget her own self, for all the merits which she gained by her virtuous, penitential life, she bestowed with heroic and most unselfish love on her poor suffering brethren in Purgatory.—*Ibid.*

10

St. Gertrude

ST. GERTRUDE had great zeal in praying for the Suffering Souls. On one occasion while Mass was being offered for a person of her acquaintance who had died a short time before, the Saint recited five *Paters* in honor of Our Lord's five wounds for the repose of her soul; and, moved by divine inspiration, she offered all her good works for the increase of the beatitude of this person. When she had made this offering she immediately beheld the soul in heaven in the place destined for her, and the throne prepared for her was elevated as far above the place where she had been as the highest throne of the seraphim is above that of the lowest angel. The Saint then asked Our Lord how this soul had been worthy to obtain such advantage from her prayers, and He replied: " She has merited this grace in three ways: First, because she always had a sincere will and perfect desire of serving Me in religion, if it had been possible; secondly, because she had a special regard for all Religious and all good people; thirdly, because she was always ready to honor Me by performing any service she could for them." He added: " You may judge by the sublime rank to which she is elevated how agreeable these practices are to Me."

—*Forget-me-nots from Many Gardens.*

11

St. Magdalene of Pazzi

AS REGARDS indulgences; I shall tell you how St. Magdalene of Pazzi and her Religious were encouraged to persevere in their great zeal for the souls of the dead. Shortly after the death of one of the Sisters, the holy Superioress went into the church in order to take a last farewell of her dear daughter, for the respose of whose soul she had offered up all her indulgences. She had scarcely advanced as far as the communion rails, when she saw the soul of the dead Sister ascending toward heaven. Overcome with joy, St. Magdalene exclaimed: " Farewell, dear Sister! farewell, happy soul! Your body has not yet been deposited into the grave, and you have already taken possession of heaven." As Our Lord revealed to St. Magdalene afterward, this soul was detained but fifteen hours in Purgatory, because, during her life, she had endeavored to gain and offer up holy indulgences for the dead. Such is the power of indulgences.

—*Voices from Purgatory.*

12

St. Dominic

THE VENERABLE ALANUS stated that the Blessed Virgin, when appearing to St. Dominic, declared that the redemption of the Holy Souls from Purgatory was one of the principal effects of the Rosary. The following illustration proves this also: "A woman named Catherine, having been converted by the sermons of St. Dominic at Rome, devoted herself most zealously to the recitation of the holy Rosary, which she usually applied to the Holy Souls in Purgatory. In an apparition St. Dominic saw Our Lord displaying fifty-five fountains, from which refreshing waters flowed into Purgatory." The Venerable Alanus writes that many of the brethren had assured him that numerous souls had appeared to them whilst reciting the Rosary and had declared that next to the holy sacrifice of the Mass there was no more powerful means than the Rosary to help the Poor Souls. Also, that numerous souls were daily redeemed thereby who otherwise would have been obliged to remain there for years. St. Liguori therefore says: "If we wish to be of material assistance to the souls in Purgatory we must always recommend them in our prayers to the Blessed Virgin Mary, and especially offer up the holy Rosary for them." (*Glories of Mary.*)—Ackermann, *Help for the Poor Souls in Purgatory.*

13

St. Augustine

ST. AUGUSTINE writes the following in his treatise on the Solicitude for the Dead: "The souls in Purgatory have a knowledge of what is going on in this world through the medium of their angels, and in so far as Almighty God permits it. If there were no angels who could be present at the places of sojourn of the living as well as of the dead, Our Lord would not have said: 'And it came to pass that the beggar died and was carried by the angels into Abraham's bosom'" (Luke xvi, 22). . . .

It is certain, as St. Augustine and St. Thomas teach, that the saints in heaven have great power by their intercession to redeem souls from Purgatory; and we cannot doubt but that they extend this love to their suffering brethren in the greatest measure possible, as they know well the extent of their suffering. Their being in heaven does not change their sentiments in this regard, but rather increases their charity; and if they were zealous and successful while on earth in obtaining God's help and grace for their sinful fellow men, why should they not in heaven exercise a greater charity for these souls, who are adorned with the grace of sanctification and are destined to share their eternal bliss? They cannot suffer themselves, but they sympathize with the suffering, and, standing before the throne of the all-merciful God, are necessarily imbued with sentiments of mercy. If the Church urges us to have recourse to the saints of God in all our necessities, and if we often experience their actual assistance, it naturally follows that the devout invocation of saints for the souls in Purgatory is a most salutary work.—*Ibid.*

14

The Saints in Reference to Works of Penance for the Holy Souls

THE saints have always had recourse to works of penance as the best means of obtaining extraordinary graces from God either for themselves or for others. There is no doubt that these works of mortification have a great efficacy for the departed, as numerous examples will show. Boudon says: "If we had but a little faith, fasting, scourging, and other works of penance and mortification would be our usual means of assisting the Poor Souls." Although such zeal is not expected of every one, yet there is no one who could not occasionally deny himself a part of some favorite dish or some amusement, mortify his eyes, ears, or tongue, preserve silence for a short time, bear in patience the pains of sickness, heat, or cold, or any other adversity, or curb his self-will or inclinations; in fact, bear with submission and gratitude to God everything that causes pain or distress. Thus the husbandman, the tradesman, the servant, and all others who have corporal and spiritual suffering to bear, possess much that can be offered for the Holy Souls. At the same time this Christian charity will draw the greatest blessings down upon themselves and give them strength in their own suffering. Boudon relates that persons who had offered up all the hardships of a journey for the Poor Souls had been rescued from great dangers in a miraculous manner, as God chose to reward their charity for the Holy Souls by a special protection of His loving providence.—*Ibid.*

15

St. Ludwina's Spirit of Penance for the Holy Souls

THOMAS À KEMPIS, the author of the *Following of Christ*, writes the following in the biography of this holy virgin, who was a contemporary of his and lived in his neighborhood: "This patient sufferer was afflicted throughout thirty-four years with the most painful diseases. In her repeated ecstasies she often saw her guardian angel, who led her to Purgatory, where she saw the Poor Souls tortured in many different ways, according to the variety of their guilt. Among them she recognized many of her friends. Moved by this sight, she not only bore with the greatest patience her own excruciating pains, but took upon herself many other painful works of penance. She constantly implored the infinite mercy of God for these Poor Souls, and often wept very bitterly over their misery." Her biographer states also that although she always redeemed a great number of souls by her penances, she increased this number largely on the principal feasts. Another biographer writes of her that she once formed the heroic resolution rather to suffer the most terrible pains for the Poor Souls till doomsday, if it were permitted, than to be received immediately into heaven, and that she had redeemed thereby the souls of her parents and of all her relatives and friends.—*Ibid.*

16
St. Cæsarius of Arles

ST. CÆSARIUS of Arles writes: "Some one may say, I care little for the time that I shall suffer in Purgatory if I only attain to eternal happiness. Such a sentiment, however, is not pleasing to God. All the sufferings of this life cannot compare with those of Purgatory. And who knows how many days, months, or years he is to remain there? We fear to hold our finger above the fire and do not fear to remain a long time in these devouring flames." In a similar sense St. Bernard says: "Purge out the old leaven, brethren, whilst you still have time to do so. The days that are given us for our purification pass by, whether we will it or not; but woe to us, if, when the days are ended, the purification is not completed, so that it will be necessary for us to be cleansed by that fire, than which nothing more painful, more severe, or violent can be imagined." (Serm. 6, de Purific.)—*Ibid.*

17
St. Bernard and St. Malachias

IN THE life of St. Malachias, St. Bernard commends the great zeal this Saint had for the Holy Souls, and blames his sister, who was of an entirely different disposition. Already before Malachias was raised to the holy priesthood, he assisted frequently at burials, and at the recitation of the prayers for the dead. Often he buried them with his own hands, to practise Christian charity, and, above all, the virtue of humility. His worldly-minded sister was very much displeased at his performing such mean actions, because she considered them as degrading the rank of her family; but the Saint continued in all humility, and God rewarded his perseverence with many interior consolations. The sister, on the contrary, was severely punished. She died young, and her brother, solicitous for a soul who was so soon called upon to render a strict account of herself to the Eternal Judge, prayed much and fervently for her. A long time after her death he saw her. She appeared sad, was dressed in black, and standing in the porch of the church, she implored him to have pity on her, because for thirty days she had experienced no alleviation of her sufferings. The Saint remembered then that, for a whole month, he had not offered up the Holy Sacrifice for her. No doubt, God had allowed this to happen in order to punish her indifference toward the Poor Souls. Malachias offered up the Holy Mass for his sister on the next morning, and saw her again a short time after. She was standing sighing and weeping at the threshold of the church, as if some one was preventing her from crossing it. The Saint continued to pray and say Mass for her, and at last he saw her in a third apparition. This time she was, with many other souls, standing at the foot of the altar, resplendent in heavenly glory.

St. Malachias was beautifully rewarded for his love and zeal for the Poor Souls. He had wished to die in the monastery of Clairvaux, which St. Bernard had founded, because directly after his death he knew there would be so many holy Masses said for him. And the day he desired to depart this life was All Souls' Day, because this was the day the Holy Church had set apart for special prayers for the dead. His wish was granted; he died at Clairvaux, on the 2d day of November, and went to receive in heaven the reward for his zeal in behalf of the souls in Purgatory.

—*Voices from Purgatory.*

Chapter 16

The Origin of All Souls' Day

THE great historian, P. Surius, of the Carthusian Order, traces the origin of this anniversary of the Poor Souls to the following occurrence, which St. Peter Damian relates in the Life of the holy Abbot of Clugny. A pious Religious from France, who, on his return from a pilgrimage to the Holy Land, was cast by a storm upon an unknown island, there met a devout hermit. This hermit informed the Religious that near his cell he frequently heard an awful and terrific howling of the evil spirits, crying out that the prayers and good works for the departed wrought much damage to themselves, as they released, or at least greatly relieved, the souls that had been given over to them for torture. They expressed an especial hatred against the Abbot Odilo of Clugny and his monks. Upon his return, the Religious, in accordance with the wishes of the hermit, communicated this information to the Abbot of Clugny, who was the more incited thereby to continue this work of charity; and to spread it more widely, he introduced in the year 1030, on the 2d day of November, in all the monasteries of his Order an annual commemoration of all the faithful departed. Pope John XIX, after conferring with Abbot Odilo, extended the practice to the whole Church. Tertullian, even in the third century, mentions that the Christians of his time celebrated an annual commemoration of the departed; and Bishop Amalarius of Treves had introduced an All Souls' Day in his diocese two centuries before Odilo.

—*Help for the Poor Souls in Purgatory.*

*

TO THE truly fervent Catholic, the Church's calendar is ever replete with the most beautiful symbolism. He who unconsciously classifies the successive seasons of the year in accordance with the ecclesiastical rather than the civil division; he who habitually thinks of Advent and Lent instead of winter and spring, and in whose vocabulary May, June, and October are not more familiar terms than are the months of Mary, of the Sacred Heart, and of the Holy Rosary—such a one discovers in the physical characteristics of each season much that harmonizes wonderfully with the special devotion which Holy Church has associated therewith.

And if ever such symbolism becomes strikingly manifest, it is assuredly during the month of November, when the age-stricken year is being hurried to its dissolution. A spirit of sadness and gloom invests the leafless trees, the bare brown fields, and sodden meadows; ashen clouds sweep across the unlovely firmament, and the desolate soughing of the November winds is incessantly wailing the sad plaint of each suffering soul in Purgatory: " *Miseremini mei, miseremini mei, saltem vos amici mei.*"— " Have pity on me, have pity on me, at least you my friends." The depressing aspect of the physical world during this dreary month must typify to every sympathetic child of the Church the cheerless and wretched condition of hosts of our brethren detained in sad and lonely exile from the heavenly home they long to enter, doomed to wear out a tedious probation of keenest pain and keenest sense of loss before they may hope to stand " before the throne, clothed with white robes, and palms in their hands " (Apoc. vii.). . . .

If ever we entertained for some of those hapless Prisoners of the King sentiments of tender affection; if ever we rejoiced in their presence and experienced the bliss of their unfailing sympathy; if ever we vowed undying remembrance of their manifold kindnesses, and proffered them the tribute of our enduring gratitude—now is the time to make good our protestations, now the time to prove the genuineness of our love.—Rev. A. B. O'Neill, C.S.C., in the *Ave Maria.*

" As you measure to others," says our blessed Saviour, " it shall be measured to you again." Now, what would you wish to be done for you if in Purgatory? Surely you you would not like to be forgotten—to have no longer a share in the prayers of the faithful. To escape so great a misery, which is often an effect of Divine Justice on such as have had no charity for the deceased, be very earnest to-day in your supplications for those poor souls who have none to pray for them.

—*Forget-me-nots from Many Gardens.*

Chapter 17

The Happiness of Purgatory

1. THE happiness of Purgatory is a happiness of prospect, not of actual enjoyment. It is *in spe* and not *in re*, hoped for, not already possessed. But the hope is something more than hope, it is a certain expectation which the Holy Souls know cannot be disappointed. This is their support and strength, their joy and consolation, amid their unspeakable anguish. They can look forward to the long years of eternal bliss when they will repose in the bosom of God. O happy prospect, to us always uncertain, so certain to those Holy Souls!

2. Happiness consists in union with God. If the soul is united to God by supernatural charity, beneath every kind of sorrow and misery there is an underlying joy. Now the Holy Souls are perfect in their charity. They have made an act of fervent charity at their judgment, and the habit of charity is in them as strong as ever. Hence in spite of all their sufferings they are intensely happy, and cry out, "I know that my Redeemer liveth."

3. Happiness is not incompatible with intense suffering. A man may be light-hearted while he is shrieking with physical pain; he may be light-hearted even when

separated from one whom he loves better than all the world beside. He is happy by reason of his internal dispositions, and in spite of the bitterness of the separation or the fierceness of the physical pain. So it is with most Holy Souls. Their dispositions are perfect, their will is God's. They are full of hope and love; how can they fail to be happy?

Pray for an unceasing union with God by charity.

—Richard F. Clarke, S.J., *The Devout Year.*

Chapter 18

The Alleviations of Purgatory

1. OUR LORD does not forget the souls that He loves. As at the time of His death He visited Limbo, so He from time to time manifests Himself to the holy souls in Purgatory, to comfort and cheer them. What a day of joy must it be for the Holy Souls when their Lord and King vouchsafes, if it be but for a moment, to illumine the dark prison-house with the light of His divine presence! How they must sigh after Him when He departs! for what joy is there like the joy that comes of the presence of Jesus?

2. Our Lady, too, comes also with the same merciful design, especially on a Saturday, on her great feasts, and, above all, on the feast of the Assumption, when she re-

leases not a few holy souls every year, and carries them with her to heaven. What a delight it must be to them to be thus comforted by the holy Mother of God! How they must rejoice in having gained this privilege by their devotion to her while they were yet alive!

3. The angels, too, are often sent by God to assuage the pains of the Suffering Souls. Our Lord does not forget the angel who consoled Him during His sacred agony, when He took upon Himself the intolerable weight of the sins of the whole world, and He knows what it is to be suffering for sin that has no hold on the soul, but nevertheless drags it down, like some heavy weight attached to it by the divine justice. Hence there are angels appointed to comfort the Holy Souls, to refresh them amid the devouring flames.

Ask your guardian angel never to let you fall into sin, that so you may not need his help after life is done.

—*Ibid*

Chapter 19

Means of Avoiding Purgatory

1. A GREAT devotion to the sacred passion of Christ is one of the surest methods of escaping the penalty due to our sins. He is always touched by any compassion shown Him in His sacred sufferings. He is said to have revealed to

some saint that He would remit the temporal punishment due after death to any one who for fifteen years should say every day seven *Paters,* seven *Aves,* and one *Gloria* in honor of His sacred passion.   It seems very likely that such perseverence in honoring Him in what He suffered for us would exempt from Purgatory altogether.   What do I do in this respect?

2. We may also hope to avoid Purgatory if we pray God to give us our purgatory in this life.   It requires some courage to do so, as, if God hears our prayer, we must expect to suffer greatly before we die, and perhaps to spend our lives in intense pain.   How small will be the price paid in comparison with the advantage gained!   All the sufferings of this life are small compared with the sufferings after death;   and moreover here we can merit, we can go on increasing our eternal reward, but not in Purgatory.

3. Purity of intention in all our actions is another of the most efficacious means of attaining the same end.   Any one who does all his actions purely for God's sake will have nothing for the searching fire to lay hold of. It is self that has to be burnt out of us; self-will, self-love, self-indulgence. He who is rid of these may hope to go straight to heaven.

Pray that by one or other of these means you may avoid separation from God after your death.

—Ibid.

Chapter 20

How to Help the Holy Souls in Purgatory

1. WE SHOULD make it our practice to offer each day some special prayer or work for the Holy Souls. We may not do much, but by constancy in laboring on their behalf we shall gradually accumulate a treasure for their benefit. We should never miss saying a *De Profundis* for them every night, and we should offer up holy communion for them from time to time. In our morning oblation we should pray that God may accept our labors, our sufferings, our penances for them.

2. We should also be careful to say as many indulgenced prayers as we can for them. Every prayer offered for them benefits them; every indulgenced prayer has a double efficacy. It has a satisfactory value in itself, and has a further power to obtain relief for them by reason of the indulgence attached to it. In this way how much we may do for the Holy Souls!

3. There are some whom God inspires to make what is called the *Heroic Act*, by which they offer up all the satisfactions of all their works, of the prayers and Masses said for them, and the indulgences gained for them after their own death, to be bestowed on the

Holy Souls according to Our Lady's pleasure. This supreme act of self-sacrifice is indeed heroic, for it includes a willingness to remain in Purgatory as long as God shall please for the sake of helping others out. What a great reward this will obtain in heaven! What gratitude it will earn from the Holy Souls!

Think how many there are that need your help.

—*Ibid.*

Chapter 21

Purgatory

THE object of this meditation is to excite in us a desire to make satisfaction for past sin and at the same time to help with our prayers the suffering souls in Purgatory, with whom we shall some day be numbered.

History.—"It is therefore a holy and wholesome thought to pray for the dead, that they may be loosed from sins "(II Mach. xii. 46). Men, as a rule, when they die, are not fit to go straight into the presence of the All-Holy God. Common sense, as well as Scripture and Tradition, tells us that there must be a Purgatory.

Mental Picture.—A land of sadness and suffering where the souls of the just are cleansed from their sins.

Petition.—Grace to satisfy God's justice in this life, that so my purgatory may be shortened.

FIRST POINT

THE guilt of sin must be forgiven before we pass out of this world; yet even then its debt remains upon the soul. This debt must be cleared off before we can find admittance into the heavenly city; for it is written: "There shall not enter into it any thing defiled" (Apoc. xxi. 27). Now the sufferings of this life borne humbly and patiently, as also punishments voluntarily inflicted on ourselves, are accepted by God in atonement for sin. They are also meritorious, whereas the pains of Purgatory are not. How much better, then, to clear off our debt now, seeing that we can do it at far less cost to ourselves and at the same time increase our eternal reward.

SECOND POINT

WE CALL the souls in Purgatory the *Poor Souls*. They are in truth very much to be pitied, and that for three reasons:

1. Because they are *suffering*. What their sufferings are we do not know; but the mere fact of their being shut out of heaven is enough. They realize now, as they never did before, the blessedness of possessing God, and, as they cannot attain it, they have to endure the bitterness of "hope deferred that afflicted the soul" (Prov. xiii. 12).

2. Because they are *helpless*. They can do nothing to shorten their banishment, nor

to ease their pain; for that they depend entirely on our charity.

3. Because they are often *forgotten*. "Out of sight out of mind." Even their dearest friends think of them only occasionally; and some, were it not for the prayers of the Church for all her dead, would not be thought of at all.

Let us resolve, then, to pray often for the dead, above all for those who have any special claim upon us and for those who are most forgotten. This is a great act of mercy which draws down God's mercy on us and earns the gratitude of the Poor Souls themselves, who will pray in return for those that help them, and, when they get to heaven, will not be like Pharao's cup-bearer, who forgot Joseph.

THIRD POINT

WE ALSO call them the *Holy Souls* and holy indeed they are.

1. Because they are *confirmed in grace*. What a joy it must be amid their sufferings to know that they can never again fall away from God!

2. Because they are free from all affection to sin and everything that leads to it. Sin is now the one thing they hate; its cruel consequences still clinging to them are a source of intense loathing and anguish.

3. They love God with a perfect love, with their whole heart, with their whole soul, with

their whole mind, with their whole strength;
and they are unspeakably dear to Him.

So, whereas in hell there is neither joy nor
love nor hope, in Purgatory we find all three,
mingled nevertheless with heart-breaking
sorrow, which love and longing only increase.
It will be well for us if we learn to love God
now; for love will teach us to do penance
for our offences against Him, and then we
shall not have for such a weary while to
lament: " Woe is me, that my sojourning is
prolonged! " (Ps. cxix. 5).—Rev. C. W.
Barraud, S.J., *Meditations on the Mysteries
of Our Holy Faith.*

Intercession for the Departed

YE SOULS of the faithful,
  Who sleep in the Lord
But as yet are shut out
  From your final reward!
Oh! would I could lend you
  Assistance to fly
From your prison below
  To your palace on high!

O Father of mercies!
  Thine anger withhold;
These works of Thine hand
  In Thy mercy behold;
Too oft from Thy path
  They have wandered aside;
But Thee, their creator,
  They never denied.

O tender Redeemer!
Their misery see;
Deliver the souls
That were ransomed by Thee;
Behold how they love Thee
Despite of their pain;
Restore them, restore them
To favor again.

O spirit of grace!
O Consoler divine!
See how for Thy presence
They longingly pine;
Ah then, to enliven
Their sadness, descend!
And fill them with peace,
And with joy in the end.

O Mother of mercy!
Dear Mother in grief!
Lend thou to their torments
A balmy relief;
Attemper the rigor
Of justice severe;
And soften their flame
With a pitying tear.

Ye patrons! who watched
O'er their safety below;
Oh! think how they need
Your fidelity now;
And stir all the angels
And saints of the sky
To plead for the souls
That upon you rely.

Ye friends, who once sharing
   Their pleasures and pain,
Now haply already
   In paradise reign!
Oh, comfort their hearts
   With a whisper of love;
And call them to share
   In your pleasures above!

O fountain of goodness!
   Accept our sighs;
Let Thy mercy bestow
   What Thy justice denies;
So may Thy poor captives,
   Released from their woes,
Thy praises proclaim
   While eternity flows.

All ye, who would honor
   The saints and their Head,
Remember, remember,
   To pray for the dead;
And they, in return,
   From their misery freed,
To you will be friends
   In the hour of need.

—Anon.

*

MAY we all meet merrily in heaven!
   —Blessed Thomas More.

PART TWO

Prayers and Devotions

Mary, Mother of God and Mother of mercy,
pray for us, and for the departed.

Indulgence: 100 days, once a day.

Holy-Days of Obligation in the United States

All the Sundays of the year.
Jan. 1. The Circumcision.
Ascension Day.
Aug. 15. The Assumption.
Nov. 1. All Saints.
Dec. 8. Immaculate Conception.
Dec. 25. Christmas.

The Church Law of Abstinence and Fast

1. The Law of Abstinence forbids the use of flesh meat and of the juice thereof (soup, etc.). Eggs, cheese, butter and seasonings of food are permitted. The Law of Fasting forbids more than one full meal a day, but does not forbid a small amount of food in the morning and in the evening.

2. All Catholics seven years old and over are obliged to abstain. All Catholics from the completion of their twenty-first to the beginning of their sixtieth year, unless lawfully excused, are bound to fast.

3. Abstinence alone is prescribed every Friday, unless a holy-day falls thereon. Fasting and abstinence are prescribed in the

163

United States on the Wednesdays and Fridays of Lent and Holy Saturday forenoon (on all other days of Lent fasting alone is prescribed and meat is allowed once a day), the Ember days, viz.: the Wednesday, Friday and Saturday following the first Sunday of Lent, Pentecost or Whitsunday, the 14th of September, and the third Sunday of Advent; the vigils of Pentecost, Assumption, All Saints and Christmas. There is no fast or abstinence if a vigil falls on a Sunday. Whenever meat is permitted, fish may be taken at the same meal. A dispensation is granted to the laboring classes and their families on all days of fast and abstinence except Fridays, Ash Wednesday, Wednesday in Holy Week, Holy Saturday forenoon, and the vigil of Christmas. When any member of such a family lawfully uses this privilege all the other members may avail themselves of it also; but those who fast may not eat meat more than once a day.

The Manner in which a Lay Person is to Baptize in Case of Necessity

Pour common water on the head or face of the person to be baptized, and say while pouring it:

" I baptize thee in the name of the Father, and of the Son, and of the Holy Ghost."

N.B. Any person of either sex who has reached the use of reason can baptize in case of necessity.

The Blessing before Meals

✠ Bless us, O Lord! and these Thy gifts, which we are about to receive from Thy bounty, through Christ our Lord.   Amen.

Grace after Meals

✠ We give Thee thanks for all Thy benefits, O Almighty God, Who livest and reignest forever, and may the souls of the faithful departed through the mercy of God, rest in peace.   Amen.

The Most Necessary Prayers

The Sign of the Cross

IN THE name of the Father, and of the Son, and of the Holy Ghost. Amen.

The Lord's Prayer

OUR Father, Who art in heaven, hallowed be Thy name; Thy kingdom come; Thy will be done on earth as it is in heaven. Give us this day our daily bread; and forgive us our trespasses as we forgive those who trespass against us: and lead us not into temptation, but deliver us from evil. Amen.

The Angelical Salutation

HAIL Mary, full of grace! the Lord is with thee: blessed art thou among women, and blessed is the fruit of thy womb, Jesus. Holy Mary, Mother of God, pray for us sinners, now and at the hour of our death. Amen.

The Apostles' Creed

I BELIEVE in God, the Father Almighty, Creator of heaven and earth; and in Jesus Christ, His only Son, our Lord; Who was conceived by the Holy Ghost, born of the Virgin Mary, suffered under Pontius Pilate, was crucified: died, and was buried.

He descended into hell: the third day He arose again from the dead: He ascended into heaven, sitteth at the right hand of God, the Father Almighty; from thence He shall come to judge the living and the dead. I believe in the Holy Ghost, the Holy Catholic Church, the communion of Saints, the forgiveness of sins, the resurrection of the body, and the life everlasting. Amen.

The Confiteor

I CONFESS to Almighty God, to blessed Mary, ever Virgin, to blessed Michael the Archangel, to blessed John the Baptist, to the holy Apostles Peter and Paul, and to all the Saints, that I have sinned exceedingly in thought, word and deed, through my fault, through my fault, through my most grievous fault. Therefore, I beseech blessed Mary, ever Virgin, blessed Michael the Archangel, blessed John the Baptist, the holy Apostles Peter and Paul, and all the Saints, to pray to the Lord our God for me.

May Almighty God have mercy on me, and forgive me my sins, and bring me to everlasting life. Amen.

May the Almighty and merciful Lord grant me pardon, absolution, and remission of all my sins. Amen.

An Act of Faith

O MY God! I firmly believe that Thou art one God in three divine Persons,

Father, Son, and Holy Ghost; I believe that Thy divine Son became man, and died for our sins, and that He will come to judge the living and the dead. I believe these and all the truths which the Holy Catholic Church teaches, because Thou hast revealed them, Who canst neither deceive nor be deceived.

An Act of Hope

O MY God! relying on Thy infinite goodness and promises, I hope to obtain pardon of my sins, the help of Thy grace, and life everlasting, through the merits of Jesus Christ, my Lord and Redeemer.

An Act of Love

O MY God! I love Thee above all things, with my whole heart and soul, because Thou art all-good and worthy of all love. I love my neighbor as myself for love of Thee. I forgive all who have injured me, and ask pardon of all whom I have injured.

An Act of Contrition

O MY God! I am heartily sorry for having offended Thee, and I detest all my sins, because I dread the loss of heaven and the pains of hell, but most of all because they offend Thee, my God, Who art all good and deserving of all my love. I firmly resolve, with the help of Thy grace, to confess my sins, to do penance, and to amend my life.

Morning Prayers

IN THE name of the Father, ✠ and of the Son, and of the Holy Ghost. Amen.

ALMIGHTY and eternal God, I adore Thee, and I *thank* Thee for all the benefits which Thou, in Thy infinite goodness, hast conferred upon me. I thank Thee especially for having preserved and protected me this night.

I *believe* in Thee, because Thou art Truth itself.

I *hope* in Thee, because Thou art merciful and faithful to Thy promises.

I *love* Thee, because Thou art all good, and for Thy sake I love my neighbor as myself.

O MY God, I offer Thee all my prayers, works, and sufferings of this day in union with the Sacred Heart of Jesus, for the intentions for which He pleads and offers Himself in the holy sacrifice of the Mass, in thanksgiving for Thy favors, in reparation for my offences, and in humble supplication for my temporal and eternal welfare, for the wants of our holy Mother the Church, and for the relief of the poor souls in Purgatory.

I have the intention to gain all the indulgences that are attached to the prayers I shall say and the good works I shall perform this day.

Our Father, Hail Mary, I believe, Glory.

O SWEETEST Heart of Jesus! I implore That I may ever love Thee more and more.

Indulgence: 300 days, each time.—Pius IX, Nov. 26, 1876.

All for Thee, most Sacred Heart of Jesus!

Indulgence: 300 days, each time.—Pius X, Nov. 26, 1908.

MY LADY and my Mother, remember I am thine; protect and defend me as thy property and possession.

Indulgence: 40 days, each time.—Pius IX, Aug. 5, 1851.

ST. JOSEPH, model and patron of those who love the Sacred Heart of Jesus, pray for us!

Indulgence: 100 days, once a day.—Leo XIII, Dec. 19, 1891.

ANGEL of God, my guardian dear, To whom His love commits me here, Ever this day be at my side, To light and guard, to rule and guide. Amen.

Indulgence: 100 days, each time.—Pius VI, Oct. 2, 1795.

ALL ye holy angels and saints of God, and especially you, my dear patron saint, pray for me! May Our Lord bless us and preserve us from all evil, and bring us to life everlasting.

May the souls of the faithful departed,

through the mercy of God, rest in peace.
Amen.

IN THE name of the Father, ✠ and of the
Son, and of the Holy Ghost. Amen.

Morning Offering of the Apostleship of Prayer

O JESUS, through the Immaculate Heart
of Mary, I offer Thee my prayers,
works, and sufferings of this day for all the
intentions of Thy Sacred Heart, in union
with the holy sacrifice of the Mass throughout the world, in reparation for my sins, for
the intentions of all our Associates, and in
particular for the general intention recommended this month.

*A short offering which may be made each
morning for the souls in Purgatory:*

O MY God! Deign to accept my every
thought, word, and action, as a loving
petition to Thy mercy in behalf of the suffering souls in Purgatory, particularly ——.
I unite to Thy Sacred Passion the trials and
contradictions of this day, which I purpose to
bear with patience in expiation for the sins
and infidelities which retain Thy children
in the purifying flames of Purgatory.

—Forget-me-nots from Many Gardens.

*Resolve to gain many indulgences this day
in behalf of the holy souls in Purgatory.*

Evening Prayers

IN THE name of the Father, ✠ and of the Son, and of the Holy Ghost. Amen.

O MY God, I believe that Thou art here present; I adore Thee, and I love Thee with all my heart.

I return Thee thanks for all the benefits which I have received from Thee. Give me light, O my God, to see what sins I have committed this day, and grant me grace to be truly sorry for them.

[Here examine your conscience; then make an act of contrition.]

O MY God, I beg pardon from my heart for all my offences against Thee; I am truly sorry that I have sinned, because Thou art infinitely good and sin displeases Thee. I am firmly resolved, with the help of Thy grace, never more to offend Thee, and to avoid the occasions of sin.

Our Father, Hail Mary, Glory.

JESUS, Mary, Joseph, I give you my heart and my soul.

Jesus, Mary, Joseph, assist me in my last agony.

Jesus, Mary, Joseph, may I breathe forth my soul in peace with you. Amen.

Indulgence: 300 days, each time.—Pius VII, Aug. 26, 1814.

INTO Thy hands, O Lord, I commend my spirit. Holy Mary, be a mother to me.

O MY good angel, whom God has appointed to be my guardian, watch over me during this night.

All ye angels and saints of God, pray for me.

May Our Lord bless us and preserve us from all evil and bring us to life everlasting.

May the souls of the faithful departed, through the mercy of God, rest in peace. Amen.

Bless yourself with Holy Water.

In the name of the Father, ✠ and of the Son, and of the Holy Ghost. Amen.

A Night Prayer, by St. Alphonsus Liguori

JESUS CHRIST, my God, I adore Thee and I thank Thee for all the graces Thou hast bestowed on me this day. I offer Thee my sleep and every moment of this night, and I beseech Thee to keep me free from sin. Therefore I place myself in Thy most sacred side and under the protecting mantle of our Lady, my Mother. May Thy holy angels help me and keep me in peace, and may Thy blessing be upon me.

Indulgence: 60 days, once a day.—Leo XIII, June 30, 1893.

Indulgenced Prayers Arranged for Use at Mass

Note.—The use of indulgenced prayers is highly recommended. Let us bear in mind, however, that it is far better to say a few of these prayers during Mass with attention and devotion than to recite many of them hurriedly and indevoutly.

Preparatory Prayers and Offerings

The sign of the cross

IN THE name of the Father, ✠ and of the Son, and of the Holy Ghost.

Indulgence: 50 days, each time.—Pius IX, July 28, 1863.

Offering to Be Made at the Beginning of Mass

ETERNAL Father, I unite myself with the intentions and affections of Our Lady of Sorrows on Calvary, and I offer Thee the sacrifice which Thy beloved Son Jesus made of Himself on the cross, and now renews on this holy altar: 1. To adore Thee and give Thee the honor which is due to Thee, confessing Thy supreme dominion over all things, and the absolute dependence of everything upon Thee, Who art our one and last end. 2. To thank Thee for innumerable benefits received. 3. To appease Thy justice, irritated against us by so many sins, and to make satisfaction for them. 4. To implore grace and mercy for myself, for . . ., for all afflicted and sorrowing, for poor sinners, for all the world, and for the holy souls in Purgatory.

Indulgence: 300 days.—Pius X, July 8, 1904.

Ejaculations

WE ADORE Thee, most holy Lord Jesus Christ, we bless Thee; because by Thy holy cross Thou hast redeemed the world.

Indulgence: 100 days, once a day.—Leo XIII, March 4, 1882.

Jesus, my God, I adore Thee here present in the Sacrament of Thy love.

Indulgence: 100 days, each time, before the tabernacle; 300 days, each time, at exposition of the Blessed Sacrament.—Pius X, July 3, 1908.

At the Confiteor

Prayer

LOOSEN, O Lord, we pray Thee, in Thy pity, the bonds of our sins, and by the intercession of the blessed and ever virgin Mary, mother of God, St. Joseph, the blessed apostles Peter and Paul, and all the saints, keep us, Thy servants, and our abodes in all holiness; cleanse us, our relations, kinsfolk, and acquaintances, from all stain of sin; adorn us with all virtue; grant us peace and health; drive far off all our enemies, visible and invisible; bridle our carnal appetites; give us healthful seasons; bestow Thy love upon our friends and our enemies; guard Thy holy city; preserve our Sovereign Pontiff, N., and defend all our prelates, princes, and all Thy Christian people, from all adversity. Let Thy blessing be ever upon us, and grant to all the faithful departed eternal rest. Through Christ our Lord. Amen.

Indulgence: 40 days, each time.—Leo XII, July 9, 1828.

At the Introit
Prayer to the Most Holy Trinity

OMNIPOTENCE of the Father, help my weakness, and deliver me from the death of misery.

Wisdom of the Son, direct all my thoughts, words, and actions.

Love of the Holy Ghost, be thou the source and beginning of all the operations of my soul, whereby they may be always conformable to the divine will.

Indulgence: 200 days, once a day.— Leo XIII, March 15, 1890.

Ejaculations

MY GOD and my all!

Indulgence: 50 days, each time.—Leo XIII, May 4, 1888.

My God, unite all minds in the truth, and all hearts in charity.

Indulgence: 300 days, each time.—Pius X, May 30, 1908.

At the Kyrie Eleison

Ejaculations

1. **MY** JESUS, mercy!

Indulgence: 100 days, each time.—Pius IX, Sept. 24, 1846.

2. My sweetest Jesus, be not my judge, but my saviour!

Indulgence: 50 days, each time.—Pius IX, Aug. 11, 1851.

3. Eucharistic Heart of Jesus, have mercy on us.

Indulgence: 300 days, each time.—Pius X, Dec. 26, 1907.

At the Gloria

GLORY to God in the highest and on earth peace to men of good will. (Luke ii. 14.)

Therefore, whether you eat or drink, or whatsoever else you do—do all to the glory of God.   (I Cor. x. 31.)

Now to the King of ages, immortal, invisible, the only God, be honor and glory for ever and ever.   Amen.   (I Tim. i. 17.)

Ejaculation

MAY the most just, most high, and most adorable will of God be in all things done, praised, and magnified forever.

Indulgence: 100 days, once a day.—Pius VII, May 19, 1818.

At the Collects

Let us pray

OMNIPOTENT Lord, Who dost permit
evil that good may spring from it, listen
to the humble prayers by which we ask of
Thee the grace of remaining faithful to Thee,
even unto death. Grant us also, through
the intercession of Mary ever blessed, that
we may always conform ourselves to Thy
most holy will.

*Indulgence: 100 days, once a day.—Leo XIII, July
19, 1879.*

Prayer

O MOST compassionate Jesus! Thou
alone art our salvation, our life, and our
resurrection. We implore Thee, therefore,
do not forsake us in our needs and afflictions,
but, by the agony of Thy most Sacred Heart,
and by the sorrows of Thy immaculate
mother, succor Thy servants whom Thou
hast redeemed by Thy most precious blood.

*Indulgence: 100 days, once a day.—Pius IX, Oct. 6,
1870.*

Prayer

DIVINE Jesus, incarnate Son of God,
Who for our salvation didst vouchsafe
to be born in a stable, to pass Thy life in
poverty, trials, and misery, and to die amid
the sufferings of the cross, I entreat Thee,
say to Thy divine Father at the hour of my
death: *Father, forgive him;* say to Thy

beloved mother: *Behold thy son;* say to my soul: *This day thou shalt be with Me in paradise.* My God, my God, forsake me not in that hour. *I thirst:* yes, my God, my soul thirsts after Thee, Who art the fountain of living waters. My life passes like a shadow; yet a little while, and all will be consummated. Wherefore, O my adorable Saviour, from this moment, for all eternity, *into thy hands I commend my spirit.* Lord Jesus, receive my soul. Amen.

Indulgence: 300 days, each time.—Pius IX, June 10, 1856.

At the Epistle

THIS is the will of God—your sanctification. (I Thess. iv. 3.)

Pursue justice, godliness, faith, charity, patience, mildness. (I Tim. vi. 11.)

Follow peace with all men, and holiness, without which no man shall see God. (Heb. xii. 14.)

According to Him that hath called you, Who is holy, be you also in all manner of conversation holy. Because it is written: you shall be holy, for I (the Lord your God) am holy. (I Peter i. 15, 16.)

The grace of God our Saviour hath appeared to all men; instructing us that, denying ungodliness and worldly desires, we should live soberly and justly and godly in this world.

Looking for the blessed hope and coming

of the glory of the great God and our Saviour Jesus Christ. (Titus ii. 11–13.)

Ejaculations

JESUS, my God, I love Thee above all things.

Indulgence: 50 days, every time.—Pius IX, May 7, 1854.

Jesus, meek and humble of heart, make my heart like unto Thine.

Indulgence: 300 days, every time.—Pius X, Sept. 15, 1905.

May the Sacred Heart of Jesus be loved everywhere!

Indulgence: 100 days, once a day.—Pius IX, Sept. 23, 1860.

At the Gospel

JESUS said to His disciples: " If you love Me, keep My commandments." (John xiv. 15.)

" This is charity, that we walk according to His commandments." (II John i. 6.)

" For not the hearers of the law are just before God, but the *doers* of the law shall be justified." (Rom. ii. 13.)

" What shall it profit, my brethren, if a man say he hath faith, but hath not works? Shall faith be able to save him? " . . . " Faith without works is dead." (James ii. 14, 26.)

" Do good to thy friend before thou die and according to thy ability; stretching out thy hand, give to the poor." (Ecclus. xiv. 13.)

"Wherefore be you also ready, because at what hour you know not the Son of man will come." (Matt. xxiv. 44.)

"O that they would be wise and would understand and would provide for their last end." (Deut. xxxii. 29.)

"For what shall it profit a man, if he gain the whole world, and suffer the loss of his soul?" (Mark viii. 36.)

Prayer to the Holy Spirit for the Church

O HOLY Spirit, Creator, propitiously help the Catholic Church, and by Thy heavenly power strengthen and confirm it against the assaults of the enemy; by Thy charity and grace renew the spirit of Thy servants whom Thou hast anointed, that in Thee they may glorify the Father and His only-begotten Son, Jesus Christ our Lord. Amen.

Indulgence: 300 days, once a day.—Leo XIII, Aug. 26, 1889.

Prayer for the Propagation of the Faith

O HOLY Spirit, spirit of truth, come into our hearts; shed the brightness of Thy light on all nations, that they may be one in faith and pleasing to Thee.

Indulgence: 100 days, once a day.—Leo XIII, July 31, 1897.

Veni, Sancte Spiritus

VENI, Sancte Spiritus, reple tuorum corda fidelium, et tui amoris in eis ignem accende.

COME, O Holy Ghost, fill the hearts of Thy faithful, and kindle in them the fire of Thy love.

Indulgence: 300 days, each time.—Pius X, May 8, 1907.

At the Credo

An Act of Faith

O MY God! I believe in Thee; I believe all that Thou hast revealed, and that the holy Catholic Church proposes to my belief. I believe that the most blessed Virgin is truly the mother of God; I believe firmly and with all certainty, that she is at the same time mother and virgin, and that she is free from even the least actual sin. I also believe most firmly, and with all certainty, that, by a singular grace and privilege of almighty God, in view of the merits of Jesus Christ, the Saviour of the human race, Mary was, in the first instant of her conception, preserved free from all stain of original sin. I believe most firmly, and with all certainty, that when the Roman Pontiff speaks *ex cathedra*—that is, when, in quality of the chief pastor and teacher of all Christians, he in virtue of his supreme and apostolic authority defines the doctrine to be held by the universal Church concerning faith or morals—by the divine assistance, promised him in the person of St. Peter, he enjoys that infallibility with which the divine Redeemer wished His Church to be endowed when defining matters of faith or morals; and, therefore, that such definitions of the Roman Pontiff are, of themselves, and not from the consent of the Church, irreformable. I believe all this, because Thy holy Church, which is the pillar and ground of truth, which has never erred and can never err, proposes it to be believed.

Indulgence: 100 days, once a day.—Pius IX, Jan. 10, 1871.

At the Offertory and Secret Prayers

Offering and Prayer of St. Ignatius Loyola

SUSCIPE, Domine, universam meam libertatem. Accipe memoriam, intellectum atque voluntatem omnem. Quidquid habeo vel possideo, mihi largitus es; id tibi totum restituo ac tuæ prorsus voluntati trado gubernandum. Amorem tui solum cum gratia tua mihi dones et dives sum satis, nec aliud

TAKE, O Lord, and receive all my liberty, my memory, my understanding, and my whole will. Thou hast given me all that I am and all that I possess; I surrender it all to Thee that Thou mayest dispose of it according to Thy will. Give me only Thy love and Thy grace; with these I will be rich enough, and will

quidquam ultra pos- co.

have no more to de- sire.

Indulgence: 300 days, once a day.—Leo XIII, May 26, 1883.

An Offering to Jesus

MY LOVING Jesus, I, N. N., give Thee my heart, and I consecrate myself wholly to Thee, out of the grateful love I bear Thee, and as a reparation for all my unfaithfulness; and with Thy aid I purpose never to sin again.

Indulgence: 100 days, once a day, to all who shall, with at least contrite heart and devotion, make this offering before a picture of the Sacred Heart.—Pius VII, June 9, 1807.

An Offering to the Eternal Father

ETERNAL Father, we offer Thee the blood, the passion, and the death of Jesus Christ, the sorrows of Mary most holy, and of St. Joseph, in satisfaction for our sins, in aid of the Holy Souls in Purgatory, for the needs of holy Mother Church, and for the conversion of sinners.

Indulgence: 100 days, once a day.—Pius IX, April 30, 1860.

A Daily Act of Oblation

O LORD Jesus Christ, in union with that divine intention with which Thou didst on earth offer praises to God through Thy Sacred Heart, and now dost continue to offer them in all places in the sacrament of the Eucharist, and wilt do so to the end of the world, I most willingly offer Thee, throughout this entire day without the smallest exception, all my intentions and thoughts, all my affections and desires, all my words and actions, that they may be conformed to the most sacred heart of the blessed Virgin Mary, ever immaculate.

Indulgence: 100 days, once a day.—Leo XIII, Dec. 19, 1885.

Ejaculation

SWEETEST Jesus, grant me an increase of faith, hope, and charity, a contrite and humble heart.

Indulgence: 100 days, once a day.—Leo XIII, Sept. 13, 1893.

At the Preface

Prayer to the Most Holy Trinity

I ADORE Thee, O my God, one God in three Persons; I annihilate myself before Thy majesty. Thou alone art being, life, truth, beauty, and goodness. I glorify Thee, I praise Thee, I thank Thee, and I love Thee, all incapable and unworthy as I am, in union with Thy dear Son Jesus Christ, our Saviour and our Father, in the mercifulness of His Heart and through His infinite merits. I wish to serve Thee, to please Thee, to obey Thee, and to love Thee always, in union with Mary immaculate, mother of God and our mother, loving also and serving my neighbor for Thy sake. Therefore, give me Thy holy Spirit to enlighten, correct, and guide me in the way of

Thy commandments, and in all perfection, until we come to the happiness of heaven, where we shall glorify Thee forever. Amen.

Indulgence: 300 days, each time.—Pius X, April 18, 1906.

At the Sanctus

SANCTUS, sanctus, sanctus, Dominus Deus exercituum: plena est terra gloria tua. Gloria Patri, gloria Filio, gloria Spiritui Sancto.

HOLY, holy, holy, Lord God of hosts: the earth is full of Thy glory. Glory be to the Father, glory be to the Son, glory be to the Holy Ghost.

Indulgence: 100 days, once a day, and 100 days, three times each Sunday, as well as on the feast of the Most Holy Trinity, and during its octave.—Clement XIV, June 6, 1769.

Ejaculation

MAY the Heart of Jesus in the Most Blessed Sacrament be praised, adored, and loved with grateful affection, at every moment, in all the tabernacles of the world, even to the end of time. Amen.

Indulgence: 100 days, once a day.—Pius IX, Feb. 29, 1868.

During the Canon

An Offering to the Eternal Father

To be made during Mass

ETERNAL Father, I offer to Thee the sacrifice which Thy beloved Son Jesus made of Himself upon the cross, and which

He now renews upon this altar; I offer it to Thee in the name of all creatures, together with the Masses which have been celebrated, and which shall be celebrated in the whole world in order to adore Thee, and to give Thee the honor which Thou dost deserve, to render to Thee due thanks for Thy innumerable benefits, to appease Thy anger, which our many sins have provoked, and to give Thee due satisfaction for them; to entreat Thee also for myself, for the Church, for the whole world, and for the blessed souls in Purgatory. Amen.

Indulgence: 3 years, once a day.—Pius IX, April 11, 1860.

At the Commemoration of the Living

Prayer to the Most Sacred Heart of Jesus

MOST Sacred Heart of Jesus, pour down Thy blessings abundantly upon Thy Church, upon the Supreme Pontiff, and upon all the clergy; grant perseverance to the just, convert sinners, enlighten infidels, bless our parents, friends, and benefactors; assist the dying, liberate the souls in Purgatory, and extend over all hearts the sweet empire of Thy love.

Indulgence: 300 days, once a day.—Pius X, June 16, 1906.

Prayer for the Conversion of Sinners

O LORD Jesus, most merciful Saviour of the world, we beg and beseech Thee, through Thy most Sacred Heart, that all wandering sheep may now return to Thee, the Shepherd and Bishop of their souls. Who livest and reignest with God the Father and the Holy Spirit, God, for ever and ever. Amen.

Indulgence: 300 days, each time.—Pius X, Nov. 22, 1905.

Prayer to Our Lord on the Cross

JESU mi crucifixe, suscipe benignus precem quam nunc pro meæ mortis articulo tibi fundo, quando illa jam appente, omnes. mei sensus deficient.

MY CRUCIFIED Jesus, mercifully accept the prayer which I now make to Thee for help in the moment of my death, when at its approach all my senses shall fail me.

Indulgence: 300 days, once a day.—Pius X, Sept. 4, 1903.

Prayer for a Happy Death

O JESUS, while adoring Thy last breath, I pray Thee to receive mine. In the uncertainty whether I shall have the command of my senses when I shall depart out of this world, I offer Thee from this moment my agony and all the pains of my passing away. Thou art my Father and my Saviour, and I give back my soul into Thy hands. I desire that my last moment may be united to the moment of Thy death, and that the last beat of my heart may be an act of pure love of Thee. Amen.

Indulgence: 100 days, once a day.—Leo XIII, July 16, 1902.

Aspiration at the Elevation of the Sacred Host

MY LORD AND MY GOD!

His Holiness, Pope Pius X, on May 18, 1907, granted an indulgence of seven years and seven quarantines, to all the faithful who, at the Elevation during Mass, or at public exposition of the Blessed Sacrament, look upon the Sacred Host and say: " My Lord and my God! "

O SACRAMENT most holy!
O Sacrament divine
All praise and all thanksgiving
Be every moment Thine.

Indulgence: 300 days, each time.—Pius X, April 10, 1913.

At the Elevation of the Sacred Chalice

HAIL, saving victim offered upon the scaffold of the cross for me and for the whole human race! Hail, precious blood flowing from the wounds of our crucified Lord Jesus Christ and washing away the sins of the whole world! Remember, O Lord, Thy servant, the work of Thy hands, whom Thou hast redeemed by Thy precious blood.

His Holiness, Leo XIII, by a rescript of the Sacred Congregation of Indulgences, June 30, 1893, granted to the faithful who shall recite the above prayer at the Elevation during Holy Mass, an indulgence of 60 days, once a day.

Ejaculations

ETERNAL Father! I offer Thee the precious blood of Jesus in satisfaction for my sins and for the wants of holy Church.

Indulgence: 100 days, each time.—Pius VII, Sept. 22, 1817.

WE ADORE Thee, O most blessed Lord, Jesus Christ, we bless Thee; because by Thy holy cross Thou hast redeemed the world.

Indulgence: 100 days, once a day.—Leo XIII, March 4, 1882.

Saviour of the world, have mercy on us!

Indulgence: 50 days, once a day.—Leo XIII, Feb. 21, 1891.

Continuation of the Canon

Prayer for Those in Their Agony

O MOST merciful Jesus, lover of souls, I pray Thee by the agony of Thy most Sacred Heart and by the sorrows of Thy immaculate mother, wash in Thy blood the sinners of the whole world who are now in their agony, and are to die this day. Amen.

P. Heart of Jesus, once in agony, pity the dying.

Indulgence: 100 days, each time.—Pius IX, Feb. 2, 1850.

At the Commemoration of the Dead

O FATHER of mercies, in the name of Jesus, Thy beloved Son, in memory of His bitter passion and cruel death, in virtue of the wound of His Sacred Heart, and in consideration also of the sorrows of the Immaculate Heart of Mary, of the heroic deeds of all the saints, and of the torments of all the martyrs, I implore Thee to have pity on the souls of the faithful departed now suffering in Purgatory.

To Thy mercy I recommend especially the souls of my relatives, friends, and benefactors, and of all those for whom I have promised to pray.

Versicles in Aid of the Holy Souls in Purgatory

P. Eternal rest grant unto them, O Lord;
R. And let perpetual light shine upon them. Amen.

May they rest in peace. Amen.

Indulgence: 300 days, each time.—Pius X, Feb. 4, 1908.

Prayer to the Divine and Most Compassionate Heart of Jesus

O DIVINE Heart of Jesus, grant, we beseech Thee, eternal rest to the souls in Purgatory, the final grace to those who shall die to-day, true repentance to sinners, the light of the Faith to pagans, and Thy blessing to me and mine. To Thee, O most compassionate Heart of Jesus, I commend all these souls, and I offer to Thee on their behalf all Thy merits, together with the merits of Thy most holy mother and of all the saints and angels, and all the sacrifices of the holy Mass, communions, prayers, and good works, which shall be accomplished to-day throughout the Christian world.

Indulgence: 100 days, once a day.—Leo XIII, March 13, 1901.

Ejaculations

EUCHARISTIC Heart of Jesus, have mercy on us!

Indulgence: 300 days, each time.—Pius X, Dec. 26, 1907.

Divine Heart of Jesus, convert sinners, save the dying, set free the holy souls in Purgatory.

Indulgence: 300 days, each time.—Pius X, Nov. 6, 1906.

At the Pater Noster

PATER noster, qui es in cœlis, sanctificetur nomen tuum: adveniat regnum tuum: fiat voluntas tua sicut in cœlo, et in terra. Panem nostrum quotidianum da nobis hodie: et dimitte nobis debita nostra, sicut et nos dimittimus debitoribus nostris. Et ne nos inducas in tentationem. *R.* Sed libera nos a malo.

P. Amen.

OUR Father, Who art in heaven, hallowed be Thy name: Thy kingdom come: Thy will be done on earth, as it is in heaven. Give us this day our daily bread: and forgive us our trespasses, as we forgive those who trespass against us. And lead us not into temptation. *R.* But deliver us from evil.

P. Amen.

At the Libera

A Prayer for Peace

DELIVER us, we beseech Thee, O Lord, from all evils, past, present, and to come; and by the intercession of the blessed and glorious Mary, ever a virgin, mother of God, and of Thy holy apostles Peter and Paul, of Andrew, and of all the saints, graciously grant peace in our days, that through the help of Thy bountiful mercy we may always be free from sin, and secure from all disturbance.

At the Agnus Dei

LAMB of God, Who takest away the sins of the world, have mercy on us.

Lamb of God, Who takest away the sins of the world, have mercy on us.

Lamb of God, Who takest away the sins of the world, grant us peace.

Prayers for Peace

Ant. DA PACEM, Domine, in diebus nostris, quia non est alius qui pugnet pro nobis, nisi tu, Deus noster.

V. Fiat pax in virtute tua.

R. Et abundantia in turribus tuis.

Ant. GIVE peace, O Lord, in our days; for there is none other that fighteth for us, but only Thou, our God.

V. Peace be in Thy strength, O Lord!

R. And plenty in Thy strong places.

Oremus

DEUS, a quo sancta desideria, recta consilia, et justa sunt opera: da servis tuis illam, quam

Let us pray

O GOD, from Whom proceed all holy desires, all right counsels and just works: grant un-

mundus dare non potest, pacem: ut et corda nostra mandatis tuis dedita, et hostium sublata formidine, tempora sint tua protectione tranquilla. Per Christum Dominum nostrum. Amen.

to us, Thy servants, that peace which the world cannot give, that our hearts may be devoted to Thy service, and that, delivered from the fear of our enemies, we may pass our time in peace under Thy protection. Through Christ our Lord. Amen.

Indulgence: 100 days, each time.—Pius IX, May 18, 1848.

Ejaculation

MY GOD, unite all minds in the truth and all hearts in charity.

Indulgence: 300 days, each time.—Pius X, May 30, 1908.

At Holy Communion

An Act of Spiritual Communion, by St. Alphonsus Liguori

MY JESUS, I believe that Thou art in the Most Holy Sacrament. I love Thee above all things, and I long for Thee in my soul. Since I cannot receive Thee now sacramentally, come at least spiritually into my heart. I embrace Thee as already there and unite myself wholly to Thee; never permit me to be separated from Thee.

Jesus, my good, my sweet love,
Wound, inflame this heart of mine.
So that it may be always and all on fire
for Thee!

*Indulgence: 60 days, once a day.—Leo XIII, June 30,
1893.*

O JESUS, sweetest love, come Thou to me;
Come down in all Thy beauty unto me;
Thou Who didst die for longing love of me;
And never, never more depart from me.
Free me, O beauteous God, from all but
Thee;
Sever the chain that holds me back from
Thee;   .
Call me, O tender love, I cry to Thee;
Thou art my all!   O bind me close to Thee.
—Shapcote.

Ejaculations

SWEET Heart of Jesus, be my love.

*Indulgence: 300 days, once a day.—Leo XIII, May
21, 1892.*

O SWEETEST Heart of Jesus! I implore
That I may ever love Thee more and
more.

*Indulgence: 300 days, each time.—Pius IX, Nov. 26,
1876.*

Prayers after Holy Communion

SOUL of Christ, be my sanctification.
Body of Christ, be my salvation.
Blood of Christ, fill all my veins.
Water of Christ's side, wash out my stains.
Passion of Christ, my comfort be.
O good Jesu, listen to me.

In Thy wounds I fain would hide,
Ne'er to be parted from Thy side.
Guard me should the foe assail me.
Call me when my life shall fail me.
Bid me come to Thee above.
With Thy saints to sing Thy love.
World without end.   Amen.

Indulgences: 300 days, each time.   Seven years, if said after communion.   Plenary, once a month.—Pius IX, Jan. 9, 1854.

Prayer to Overcome Evil Passions and to Become a Saint

DEAR Jesus, in the Sacrament of the Altar, be forever thanked and praised. Love, worthy of all celestial and terrestrial love! Who, out of infinite love for me, ungrateful sinner, didst assume our human nature, didst shed Thy most precious blood in the cruel scourging, and didst expire on a shameful cross for our eternal welfare! Now, illumined with lively faith, with the outpouring of my whole soul and the fervor of my heart, I humbly beseech Thee, through the infinite merits of Thy painful sufferings, give me strength and courage to destroy every evil passion which sways my heart, to bless Thee in my greatest afflictions, to glorify Thee by the exact fulfilment of my duties, supremely to hate all sin, and thus to become a saint.

Indulgence: 100 days, once a day.—Pius IX, Jan. 1, 1866.

At the Blessing

IN THE name of the Father, ✠ and of the Son, and of the Holy Ghost.

Indulgence: 50 days, each time.—Pius IX, July 28, 1863.

Act of Oblation in Thanksgiving for Blessings Received

ETERNAL Father, we offer Thee the most precious blood of Jesus, shed for us with such great love and bitter pain from His right hand; and through the merits and the efficacy of that blood we entreat Thy divine majesty to grant us Thy holy benediction, in order that we may be defended thereby from all our enemies, and be set free from every ill; whilst we say, May the blessing of almighty God, Father, Son, and Holy Spirit, descend upon us and remain with us forever. Amen. Pater, Ave, and Gloria.

The Sovereign Pontiff, Leo XII, by a rescript, Oct. 25, 1823, granted to all the faithful, each time that, with at least contrite heart and devotion, they shall say this offering, with the Our Father, the Hail Mary, and the Glory be to the Father, to the Most Holy Trinity, in thanksgiving for blessings received, an indulgence of 100 days, and a plenary indulgence to those who shall have said it daily, for a month, on any day, when, after confession and communion, they shall pray for the intention of the Sovereign Pontiff.

At the Last Gospel

Prayer

O LORD, Who, in the mystery of the glorious Transfiguration of Thy Divine

Son, didst deign to make resplendent the truth of the holy Catholic Faith, and to confirm miraculously, by Thy very word, spoken from a cloud, our perfect adoption as Thy sons; we humbly beg of Thee to grant that we may in truth become coheirs of this same King of Glory, and share in Thy everlasting happiness. Amen.

Indulgence: 100 days, once a day.—Leo XIII, Dec. 14, 1889.

Ejaculation

O JESUS CHRIST, Son of the living God, light of the world, I adore Thee; for Thee I live, for Thee I die.

Indulgence: 100 days, once a day.—Pius X, July 1, 1909.

At the End of the Mass

Ejaculation

SACRED Heart of Jesus, I trust in Thee!

Indulgence: 300 days, each time.—Pius X, June 27, 1906.

Ejaculations

MARY, our hope, have pity on us!

Indulgence: 300 days, each time.—Pius X, Jan. 8, 1906.

Mother of love, of sorrow, and of mercy, pray for us.

Indulgence: 300 days, each time.—Pius X, May 30. 1908.

Prayer to St. Joseph

O JOSEPH, virgin father of Jesus, most pure spouse of the Virgin Mary, pray for us daily to the Son of God, that, armed with the weapons of His grace, we may fight as we ought in life, and be crowned by Him in death.

Indulgence: 100 days, twice a day.—Pius X, Nov. 26, 1906.

Prayer in Honor of the Holy Family

GRANT us, O Lord Jesus, faithfully to imitate the examples of Thy holy family, so that in the hour of our death, in the company of Thy glorious Virgin Mother and St. Joseph, we may deserve to be received by Thee into eternal tabernacles.

Indulgence: 200 days, once a day.—Leo XIII, March 25, 1897.

Prayers ordered by Pope Leo XIII, to be Said after Every Low Mass in All the Churches of the World

The priest with the people recites the Hail Mary thrice, then the Salve Regina:

HAIL, holy Queen, Mother of mercy, our life, our sweetness and our hope! To thee do we cry, poor banished children of Eve; to thee do we send up our sighs, mourning and weeping in this valley of tears. Turn, then, most gracious advocate, thine eyes of mercy towards us, and after this our exile show unto us the blessed fruit of thy womb, Jesus. O clement, O loving, O sweet Virgin Mary!

V. Pray for us, O holy Mother of God.

R. That we may be made worthy of the promises of Christ.

Let us pray

O GOD, our refuge and our strength, look down with favor upon Thy people, who cry to Thee; and through the intercession of the glorious and immaculate Virgin Mary, Mother of God, of her spouse, blessed Joseph, of Thy holy apostles Peter and Paul, and of all the saints, mercifully and graciously hear the prayers which we pour forth to Thee, for the conversion of sinners and the liberty and exaltation of holy mother Church. Through Christ our Lord. Amen.

St. Michael the archangel, defend us in battle; be our protection against the malice and snares of the devil. Rebuke him, O God, we humbly pray; and do thou, O prince of the heavenly host, by the divine power, thrust into hell Satan and the other evil spirits who roam through the world seeking the ruin of souls. Amen.

Indulgence: 300 days.—Leo XIII, Sept. 25, 1888.

Add the Invocation thrice

V. Most sacred Heart of Jesus,

R. Have mercy on us.

Indulgence: 7 years and 5 quarantines.—Pius X, June 17, 1904.

Mass of the Holy Cross
And
Of the Passion of Our Lord

Offering of the Mass

ETERNAL Father, I offer Thee the sacrifice which Thy beloved Son made of Himself on the cross, and which He now renews on this altar. I offer it in union with all the Masses which have been said and which shall be said throughout the world, to adore Thee and to render Thee all possible honor and glory; to thank Thee for Thy innumerable benefits; to make atonement for my offences; and to supplicate Thee for myself, for my friends, relatives, and benefactors, for the Holy Father, for the Church, for the whole world, and for the souls in Purgatory.

At the Confiteor

Represent to yourself Jesus Christ retiring to the Garden of Gethsemane to pray: unite your sentiments with the divine dispositions of the Son of God, and prepare for this divine Sacrifice of the Mass by acts of sincere contrition:

Act of Contrition

O MY God, I love Thee above all things and with my whole heart. I hope and pray by the merits of Christ's passion to

201

obtain pardon for my sins. I grieve with all my heart that I have sinned, because Thou art infinitely good and sin displeases Thee. I unite my grief for my sins to the sorrow and suffering by which Jesus, my Saviour, was oppressed in the Garden of Olives. I firmly resolve by the assistance of Thy grace never more to offend Thee.

At the Introit

Gal. vi.

BUT it behooves us to glory in the cross of Our Lord Jesus Christ, in Whom is our salvation, life, and resurrection: by Whom we are saved and delivered. Ps. lxvi. May God have mercy on us, and bless us; may He cause the light of His countenance to shine upon us, and may He have mercy on us. *P.* Glory.

At the Kyrie Eleison

Represent Jesus taken and bound with cords, and say:

MAY those bonds which confined Thy hands burst the fetters of my sins, and restore me to the sweet liberty of Thy children! I cast myself at Thy sacred feet, O my king and my God; and since Thou hast undergone the humiliation of allowing Thyself to be bound by Thy creatures, may I place all my happiness in sharing Thy humiliations, and carrying Thy cross.

LORD, have mercy on us.
Christ, have mercy on us.
Lord, have mercy on us.

At the Collects

O GOD, Who hast been pleased to hallow the standard of the life-giving cross with the precious blood of Thine only-begotten Son; grant, we beseech Thee, that all who happily hold that same cross in honor, may, in all places, likewise rejoice in Thy protection.

O GOD, Who, by the passion of Thine only-begotten Son, and by the blood shed through His five most sacred wounds, hast raised up mankind, lost because of sin; grant, we beseech Thee, that we who on earth adore the wounds our Saviour received may in heaven rejoice in the glory He, at the price of His precious blood, hath bought back for us.

At the Epistle

Philipp. ii. 8–11

BRETHREN: Christ became for us obedient unto death, even the death of the cross. Wherefore God also hath exalted Him, and hath given Him a name which is above every name: that in the name of Jesus every knee should bow, of those that are in heaven, on earth, and under the earth; and that every tongue should confess

that the Lord Jesus Christ is in the glory of
God the Father.

At the Gospel

Matt. xx. 17-19

AT THAT time: Jesus took the twelve
disciples apart, and said to them:
Behold we go up to Jerusalem, and the Son
of man shall be betrayed to the chief priests
and the scribes, and they shall condemn
Him to death. And shall deliver Him to the
Gentiles to be mocked, and scourged, and
crucified, and the third day He shall rise
again.

*Reflect on the patience and benignity of Jesus
in allowing Himself to be dragged from
tribunal to tribunal, and say:*

O SPOTLESS Lamb of God! while Thy
judges proclaim Thee an impostor, I
rise without fear or shame to declare, in the
face of heaven and earth, that Thou art
Christ the Son of the living God, and that I
unreservedly assent to every article proposed by Thy holy Church to my belief:
but, O divine Lord, give me grace to profess
by my actions as well as by my words the
faith that is in me. Have mercy on all who
are involved in the dreadful night of in-
fidelity: may the light of Thy grace shine
upon them, and so penetrate their hearts
that they may embrace the truth, and be
admitted to the communion of Thy holy
Church.

At the Offertory

Represent Jesus bound to the pillar and cruelly scourged:

JESUS, in His cruel scourging, shed His blood most painfully and abundantly, offering it to His eternal Father in atonement for our impatience and our wantonness. How is it, then, that we do not curb our wrath and self-love? Oh! let us henceforth try to be more patient in our trials, and to bear in peace the injuries men do us.

O Jesus, Thou art the love and life of my soul. I find true peace and real happiness only in Thy love, in Thy service, and in the imitation of Thy virtues. I offer myself to Thee; do what Thou willest with me; henceforth my motto shall be, "All for Jesus."

Jesus, meek and humble of heart, make my heart like unto Thine.

Sweet Heart of Jesus, be my love!

At the Secret Prayers

MAY this oblation, we beseech thee, O Lord, wash away all our offences: for it is the very same offering which on the altar of the cross took away the sins of the whole world.

O LORD Jesus Christ, Who didst come down to earth from heaven, from the bosom of the Father, and didst pour out Thy precious blood for the remission of sins, we humbly beseech Thee, that, on the day of judgment, standing on Thy right hand, we may be considered worthy to hear: Come, ye blessed.

At the Preface

Contemplate thy Saviour crowned with thorns; reflect on the words " Behold the man," and say:

BEHOLD me, O most merciful Jesus: A poor sinner; I cast myself at Thy sacred feet, penetrated with sorrow for my sins. Oh! let not pride any longer rule my soul, which Thou, my Saviour, hast so tenderly loved and redeemed at so great a price; cleanse my poor soul, O Jesus, from all offensive stains, and drown my imperfections in the boundless ocean of Thy mercy.

WE ADORE Thee, O Christ, and bless Thee, because by Thy cross Thou didst redeem the world. *V.* We adore Thy cross, O Lord, we commemorate Thy glorious passion; have mercy on us, Thou Who didst suffer for us. *V.* O blessed cross, that alone wast worthy to bear the Lord and king of the heavens.

At the Sanctus

SANCTUS, sanctus, sanctus, Dominus Deus Sabaoth.

HOLY, holy, holy, Lord God of hosts.

Pleni sunt cœli et terra gloria tua.	The heavens and the earth are full of Thy glory.
Hosanna in excelsis.	Hosanna in the highest.
Benedictus qui venit in nomine Domini.	Blessed is He Who cometh in the name of the Lord.
Hosanna in excelsis.	Hosanna in the highest.

During the Canon

Commemoration of the Living in Honor of the Five Wounds

O JESUS, dying on the cross for love of poor sinners, through *Thy sacred head* crowned with thorns I beg Thee to have mercy on the Pope; on all bishops; on all priests, and on all our superiors.

Through the wound in *Thy right hand* I recommend to Thee my father, mother, brothers, sisters, relatives, friends, and benefactors.

And through the wound in *Thy left hand* my enemies, all poor sinners, and those who have never been baptized. Help Thy servants who are trying to convert them.

Through the wound in *Thy right foot* I pray for the poor, the sick, and the dying, and for all who are in any kind of pain, temptation, or trouble.

Through the wound in *Thy left foot* I beg of Thee mercifully to grant eternal rest to the

souls of the faithful departed, especially
N. N.

Through *Thy Sacred Heart*, O Jesus, I offer myself to do and suffer all things for Thy love. Give me all the graces I stand in need of, and especially the grace which I am seeking to obtain through this holy Mass.

✳

HEART of Jesus, praying and suffering, I adore Thee, and beseech Thee to unite my prayers with Thine.

Heart of Jesus, lamenting and agonizing, I adore Thee, and beseech Thee to fill my heart with sorrow for my sins.

Heart of Jesus, offering Thyself in sacrifice to the eternal Father, I adore Thee, and beseech Thee to offer me in sacrifice with Thyself.

ETERNAL Father, I offer Thee the precious blood of Jesus Christ in satisfaction for my sins, for the wants of Holy Church, and for the needs of all who have asked me to pray for them.

At the Elevation

Contemplate Jesus hanging on the cross, and adore the same Jesus here present on the altar; say with the utmost reverence and devotion: " My Lord and My God! "

Ave Verum

AVE Verum Corpus, na-
tum

HAIL to Thee! true body sprung

Ex Maria virgine !	From the Virgin Mary's womb !
Vere passum, immolatum, In cruce pro homine !	The same that on the cross was hung, And bore for man the bitter doom !
Cujus latus perforatum	Thou Whose side was pierced and flowed
Unda fluxit et sanguine ; Esto nobis prægustatum, Mortis in examine.	Both with water and with blood ; Suffer us to taste of Thee, In our life's last agony.
O clemens, O pie ! O dulcis Jesu, Fili Mariæ !	O kind, O loving one ! O sweet Jesus, Mary's Son !

An Offering

ETERNAL Father, we offer Thee the blood, the passion, and the death of Jesus Christ, the sorrows of Mary most holy, and of St. Joseph, in satisfaction for our sins, in aid of the holy souls in Purgatory, for the needs of holy Mother Church, and for the conversion of sinners.

Indulgence: 100 days, once a day.

Prayer for a Happy Death

O JESUS, while adoring Thy last breath, I pray Thee to receive mine. In the uncertainty whether I shall have command of my senses, when I shall depart out of this world, I offer Thee from this moment my agony and all the pains of my passing away. Thou art my Father and my Saviour, and I give back my soul into Thy hands. I desire that my last moment may be united to the moment of Thy death, and that the last beat of my heart may be an act of pure love of Thee. Amen.

Indulgence: 100 days, once a day.

Commemoration of the Dead

Prayers for the Holy Souls in Purgatory

Addressed to our blessed Lord, through the pains which He suffered in His bitter passion. (St. Alphonsus Liguori.)

O MOST sweet Jesus, through that sweat of blood, which Thou didst suffer in the Garden of Gethsemane, have mercy on these holy souls.

R. Have mercy on them, O Lord, have mercy on them.

O most sweet Jesus, through the pains which Thou didst suffer during Thy most cruel scourging, have mercy on them.

R. Have mercy on them, etc.

O most sweet Jesus, through the pains which Thou didst suffer in Thy most terrible crowning with thorns, have mercy on them.

R. Have mercy on them, etc.

O most sweet Jesus, through the pains which Thou didst suffer in carrying Thy cross to Calvary, have mercy on them.

R. Have mercy on them, etc.

O most sweet Jesus, through the pains which Thou didst suffer during Thy most cruel crucifixion, have mercy on them.

R. Have mercy on them, etc.

O most sweet Jesus, through the pains which Thou didst suffer in Thy most bitter agony on the cross, have mercy on them.

R. Have mercy on them, etc.

O most sweet Jesus, through the pains which Thou didst suffer in breathing forth Thy blessed soul, have mercy on them.

R. Have mercy on them, O Lord, have mercy on them.

Versicle and Responses for the Dead

REQUIEM æternam dona eis, Domine.

R. Et lux perpetua luceat eis.

V. Requiescant in pace.

R. Amen.

ETERNAL rest give unto them, O Lord.

R. And let perpetual light shine upon them.

V. May they rest in peace.

R. Amen.

Indulgence: 300 days, each time, applicable only to the dead.—Pius X, Feb. 13, 1908.

At Communion

Make an act of contrition, a renewal of good resolutions, and casting yourself in spirit into the bleeding Heart of Jesus, pray that you may love Him more and more, be more like Him in the imitation of His virtues, and be united with Him forever more. If you do not actually communicate, make at least a spiritual communion.

An Act of Spiritual Communion

MY JESUS, I believe that Thou art in the Most Holy Sacrament. I love Thee above all things, and I long for Thee in my soul. Since I cannot receive Thee now sacramentally, come at least spiritually into my heart. I embrace Thee as already there and unite myself wholly to Thee: never permit me to be separated from Thee.

O JESUS, sweetest love, come Thou to me;
Come down in all Thy beauty unto me;
Thou Who didst die for longing love of me;
And never, never more depart from me.

Free me, O beauteous God, from all but
Thee;
Sever the chain that holds me back from
Thee;
Call me, O tender love, I cry to Thee;
Thou art my all! O bind me close to Thee.
—Shapcote.

Ejaculations

HEART of Jesus, burning with love of us, inflame our hearts with love of Thee.

Indulgence: 100 days, once a day.—Leo XIII, June 16, 1893.

Sweet Heart of Jesus, be my love.

Indulgence: 300 days, once a day.—Leo XIII, May 21, 1892.

O sweetest Heart of Jesus! I implore
That I may ever love Thee more and more.

Indulgence: 300 days, every time.—Pius IX, Nov. 26, 1876.

✠ Jesu, Vivens in Maria

O JESU, vivens in Maria, veni et vive in famulis tuis, in spiritu sanctitatis tuæ, in plenitudine virtutis tuæ, in veritate virtutum tuarum, in perfectione viarum tuarum, in communione mysteriorum tuorum; dominare omni adversæ potestati in Spiritu tuo ad gloriam Patris. Amen.

O JESUS, Who dost live in Mary, come and live in Thy servants, in the spirit of Thine own holiness, in the fulness of Thy power, in the reality of Thy virtues, in the perfection of Thy ways, in the communion of Thy mysteries; have Thou dominion over every adverse power, in Thine own spirit, to the glory of Thy Father. Amen.

Indulgence: 300 days, once a day.—Pius IX, Oct. 14, 1859.

"✠ Sacrum Convivium"

O SACRED banquet, wherein Christ is received; the memory of His passion is renewed, the mind is filled with grace, and the pledge of future glory is given unto us.

V. Thou hast given them bread from heaven;

R. Which containeth in itself all sweetness.

Let us pray

O GOD, Who in this wonderful sacrament hast left us a memorial of Thy passion; grant us the grace so to venerate the sacred mysteries of Thy body and blood, that we may ever experience within ourselves the fruit of Thy redemption; who livest and reignest with God the Father, in the unity of the Holy Spirit, one God, world without end. Amen.

At the Postcommunion

BE THOU with us, O Lord, our God; and defend, with Thine abiding help, those Whom Thou inspirest joyfully to do honor to Thy holy cross.

O LORD Jesus Christ, Son of the living God, Who at the sixth hour didst mount the tree of the cross to redeem the world, and didst shed Thy precious blood for the washing away of our sins; we humbly beseech Thee, that summoned one day by Thee from this life, it may be ours with joy and gladness to pass through the gates of paradise.

At the Blessing

An Indulgenced Prayer

ETERNAL Father! we offer Thee the most precious blood of Jesus, shed for us with such great love and bitter pain from the wound in His right hand; and, through its merits and its might, we entreat Thy divine majesty to grant us Thy holy benediction, that, by its power, we may be defended against all our enemies and freed from every ill; whilst we say,

Benedictio Dei omnipotentis, Patris et Filii et Spiritus Sancti, descendat super nos, et maneat semper. Amen.	May the blessing of God Almighty, Father, and Son, and Holy Ghost, descend upon us, and remain forever. Amen.

Our Father, Hail Mary, Glory be to the Father

The Sovereign Pontiff, Leo XII, by a rescript, Oct. 25, 1823, granted to all the faithful, every time that, with at least contrite heart and devotion, they shall say this offering, with the Our Father, the Hail Mary, and the Glory be to the Father, to the most Holy Trinity, in thanksgiving for blessings received:
An indulgence of 100 days.—The New Raccolta.

Prayer to the Blessed Virgin Mary, Our Lady of Sorrows

O MOST holy and afflicted Virgin Mary, queen of martyrs! thou who didst stand beneath the cross, witnessing the agony of thy divine Son—through the unceasing sufferings of thy life of sorrow, and the bliss which now more than amply repays thee for thy past trials, look down with a mother's tenderness and pity on me, who kneel before thee to venerate thy dolors, and place my requests, with filial confidence, in the sanctuary of thy wounded heart; present them, I beseech thee, on my behalf, to Jesus Christ, Thy Son. Through the merits of His most sacred passion and death, and through thy sufferings at the foot of the cross, I hope to obtain the grant of my present petition. To whom shall I recur in my trials and my wants if not to thee, O mother of mercy, O mother of sorrows? Great as the sea was the anguish of thy heart; unfathomably deep was the agony of thy soul; hence, thou canst compassionate the woes of those who still sigh in the land of exile. Holy Mary, mother of sorrows, pray for us.

Show that thou art indeed our Mother bequeathed to us by thy divine Son in His agony on the cross, and obtain for me, O help of Christians, the favor I desire, and the grace to use it for the glory of God and for the salvation of my soul.

Obtain for me, through thy powerful intercession, the grace that I may live a holy life, die a happy death, and eventually attain to the everlasting bliss of heaven. Amen.

Ejaculation

MARY, sorrowful Mother of all Christians, pray for us.

Indulgence: 300 days, each time.—Pius X, June 27, 1906.

✳

O THOU mother! fount of love!
Touch my spirit from above,
Make my heart with thine accord;
Make me feel as thou hast felt,
Make my soul to glow and melt
With the love of Christ my Lord.

Holy mother! pierce me through;
In my heart each wound renew
Of my Saviour crucified;
Let me share with thee His pain,
Who for all my sins was slain,
Who for me in torments died.

Christ, when Thou shalt call me hence,
Be Thy mother my defense,
Be Thy cross my victory;
While my body here decays,
May my soul Thy goodness praise,
Safe in paradise with Thee.

Mass for the Faithful Departed [1]

Prayer before Mass

HEAVENLY Father, Thy beloved Son, Jesus Christ, has instituted the Sacrifice of His body and blood as well for the dead as for the living. In union with the most Holy Sacrifice I offer Thee my humble prayers, and beseech Thee to have mercy upon our brethren suffering in Purgatory. I particularly recommend to Thine infinite mercy the souls of my parents, my relations, N., N., friends, N., N., and all those for whom it is my duty to pray; as well as for those who suffer the most intense pains, are forgotten by everyone, or for whom Thou wishest me to pray.

All ye angels and saints in heaven, but above all, thou, Blessed Virgin Mary, compassionate Mother of the Poor Souls, assist me with your powerful intercession.

From the Beginning to the Offertory

O HEAVENLY *Father*, whose mercy fills heaven and earth, have mercy on the poor souls in Purgatory. Thou hast created them to Thine own image and likeness, and hast given up Thine only-begotten Son for their salvation. Behold, in this Holy Sacri-

[1] From Voices from Purgatory.

fice, this Thy Son offers Thee His precious blood in atonement for their sins. Oh, have mercy, therefore, upon Thy suffering children. Amen.

O Jesus, source of bounty and mercy, how couldst Thou, who art present in this most Holy Sacrament out of love to us, poor sinners, forget the souls of Thy redeemed, suffering in the flames of Purgatory? Oh, remember that Thou hast become man and shed Thy precious blood for them. O Jesus, faithful lover of souls, apply Thine infinite merits, Thy passion and death to the faithful departed, particularly to the souls of N., N. Amen.

O Holy Ghost, Spirit of love and Father of the poor, have pity upon the Poor Souls! Friend and comforter of the afflicted, these souls are Thine from the time they have become Thy temples in holy Baptism. We beseech Thee, therefore, to console and comfort them, and to bring them to joy everlasting. Amen.

O Mary, Mother of Mercy, behold thy children, the redeemed of thy Son, from the depths of their misery call to thee. Oh, show them the fruit of thy womb, Jesus, O clement, O loving, O sweet Virgin Mary!

Holy Angels of God, guardians of man, and all ye saints, friends of God, remember that the Poor Souls are your brethren in Christ, that they are destined to be partakers of a happy eternity with you; and pray for them that they may be delivered from their sufferings, and praise and thank God forever.   Amen.

From the Offertory to the Consecration

In behalf of the Poor Souls offer to God the Father the merits of the Passion and Death of His Divine Son.

O HOLY and just God, the souls to whom we beseech Thee to extend Thy mercy have sinned, and not satisfied Thy justice for the sins committed, it is true; but, O my God, remember no longer their manifold transgressions, but graciously look down upon Thy Son offering Himself on this altar, and receive His most precious blood in atonement for all their failings.

O merciful Father, behold the cruel crown of thorns planted on the sacred head of Thy Son, drooping in death, and have pity on the Poor Souls, particularly upon those who suffer on my account.   O my God, bountiful in forgiving, behold the pierced hands and feet and the wounded heart of Thy Son Jesus, and have, for His sake, pity upon the Poor Souls, particularly upon those for whom it is my duty to pray.

Behold, most tender Father, Thy beloved Son hanging on the tree of the cross for three hours, and have compassion upon the sufferers in Purgatory, especially upon the souls who are forgotten by every one, and for whom no one prays.

Look down, O merciful Father, into that fiery prison, and behold there the unspeakable torments of Thy dear children. O hear our prayers which, in union with Thy Son, we offer Thee in their behalf. Amen.

At the Elevation of the Sacred Host

O JESUS, my Saviour, I believe that Thou art truly present, as both God and man, in this blessed Sacrament, where Thou offerest Thyself for the sins of mankind. I adore Thee, and beseech Thee to comfort and deliver the Poor Souls suffering in Purgatory.

At the Elevation of the Chalice

O JESUS, I adore Thy sacred Blood which Thou hast shed on the cross. Have pity upon the souls of the faithful departed, O most sweet Jesus, and give them eternal bliss in the kingdom of Thy glory.

After the Consecration

Beseech Jesus, through His precious blood shed on the cross, to have pity upon the Poor Souls.

HAIL, divine and adorable blood, which my Saviour has shed for us in the excess of His love in the Garden of Olives! Through Thy bitter agony, O Jesus, I beseech Thee to cleanse from every stain of sin the souls of Thy dead, particularly the souls of N., N.

Hail, divine and adorable blood, which my Saviour has shed in His cruel scourging! Oh, into what a state have our sins brought Thee, my loving Redeemer! Thy sacred body is but one wound, from which there flows an abundance of blood. Apply this Thy most precious blood to the poor souls suffering in Purgatory, and deliver them from their pains, particularly N., N.

Hail, divine and adorable blood, shed by my sweet Jesus in His most painful crowning! Oh, Saviour and King, one drop of Thy sacred blood is sufficient to extinguish the flames in which the Poor Souls are suffering, and to open the gates of heaven to them. Hear my humble prayer and have mercy upon them, especially upon the souls of N., N.

O my crucified Saviour, through the blood of Thy sacred five wounds, which Thou hast shed out of love for us, sinners, I beseech Thee, open the gates of Purgatory to the souls suffering there; and give them the happiness they so ardently desire, namely, to be with Thee, the Beloved of their soul, for ever and ever. Amen.

From the Pater Noster until the Communion

Recommend the Poor Souls to the five sacred wounds of Jesus.

O MY crucified Jesus, I adore the most sacred wound of Thy right hand, and recommend to Thy mercy the souls of my dead parents, brothers and sisters, relations, benefactors, friends, and enemies. Through the blood, which flowed from this sacred wound, and the sufferings Thou didst endure, I pray Thee to comfort them with Thy grace, and to lead them into eternal joy.

O most bountiful Saviour, I humbly adore the sacred wound of Thy left hand, and recommend to Thy mercy the souls of those, who particularly wish me to pray for them. Through Thy great sufferings and Thy most precious blood, I beseech Thee to extend Thy hand to them and to deliver them from their pains.

O most tender Redeemer, I adore the most sacred wound of Thy right foot, and earnestly recommend to Thy clemency those souls for whom Thou desirest me to pray. Through Thy precious blood and sacred passion, I beseech Thee speak to them the consoling words: " To-day, thou shalt be with Me in paradise."

O my Jesus, most lovingly I adore the sacred wound of Thy left foot, and recommend to Thine infinite mercy the souls who during their life have had a great devotion to Thy sacred passion, and have loved and honored Thy blessed Mother. Have pity upon them and remit them the punishment due to their sins, because they have believed in Thee and have loved Thee on earth.

O most merciful Jesus, with the deepest veneration I adore the most sacred wound of

Thy side, and most earnestly recommend to Thy mercy the souls for whom I particularly intended to hear this holy Mass. Have pity upon them, O Jesus, my dearest Saviour, extinguish with the blood and water, which flow from Thy sacred side, the flames in which they are burning, and give them eternal rest.

From the Communion until the End of the Mass

Recommend the Poor Souls to the Sacred Heart of Jesus.

O MOST sweet Jesus, in the greatness of Thy love to us, Thou wast not content to be the food of our souls in the most adorable Sacrament of the Altar, and thus to unite our poor sinful hearts with Thy Sacred Heart; but Thou didst allow this Thy Heart to be pierced with a lance after Thy death, and Thou hast kept the mark of this sacred wound even after Thy glorious resurrection, so that all the faithful, whether dead or living, might take refuge in Thy loving Heart and enter, through this true gate of heaven, into eternal bliss. O Jesus, open Thy Heart to the Poor Souls, particularly to the souls of N., N., and lead them into joy everlasting.

I beseech Thee through the desolation and the agony which Thy Sacred Heart has endured during Thy bitter passion, but especially on the tree of the cross, and through the sufferings of the Immaculate Heart of Mary, Thy Mother, to open to them the gates of heaven.

Grant to me, through their intercession, the grace to live a good life, to die a happy death, and to enter, without obstacle, into the joy of heaven through Thy own sweet Heart. Amen.

✳

Versicle and Responses for the Dead

REQUIEM æternam dona eis, Domine.

R. Et lux perpetua luceat eis.

V. Requiescant in pace.

R. Amen.

ETERNAL rest give unto them, O Lord.

R. And let perpetual light shine upon them.

V. May they rest in peace.

R. Amen.

Indulgence: 300 days, each time, applicable only to the dead.—Pius X, Feb. 13, 1908.

Burial Service for Adults

At the House

The corpse is sprinkled with Holy Water; then the following Psalm is recited:

Ant. Si iniquitates.

Ant. If Thou, O Lord.

Psalmus cxxix

DE PROFUNDIS clamavi ad te, Domine: * Domine, exaudi vocem meam.

Fiant aures tuæ intendentes, * in vocem deprecationis meæ.

Si iniquitates observaveris, Domine; * Domine, quis sustinebit?

Quia apud te propitiatio est: * et propter legem tuam sustinui te, Domine.

Sustinuit anima mea in verbo ejus: * speravit anima mea in Domino.

Psalm cxxix

OUT of the depths have I cried unto Thee, O Lord: Lord, hear my voice.

Let Thine ears be attentive to the voice of my supplication.

If Thou, O Lord, wilt mark iniquities; Lord, who shall stand it?

For with Thee there is merciful forgiveness: and by reason of Thy law have I waited for Thee, O Lord.

My soul hath relied on His word: my soul hath hoped in the Lord.

226

A custodia matutina usque ad noctem: * speret Israel in Domino.

From the morning watch even until night; let Israel hope in the Lord.

Quia apud Dominum misericordia: * et copiosa apud eum redemptio.

Because with the Lord there is mercy: and with Him plenteous redemption.

Et ipse redimet Israel, * ex omnibus iniquitatibus ejus.

And He shall redeem Israel from all his iniquities.

Requiem æternam * dona ei, Domine.

Eternal rest grant unto him [her], O Lord.

Et lux perpetua * luceat ei.

And let perpetual light shine upon him [her].

Ant. Si iniquitates observaveris, Domine: Domine, quis sustinebit?

Ant. If Thou, O Lord, wilt mark iniquities, Lord, who shall stand it?

On the Way to the Church

The following Psalm is recited:

Ant. Exultabunt Domino.

Ant. The bones that are humbled.

Psalmus l

MISERERE mei, Deus; * secundum magnam misericordiam tuam.
Et secundum mul-

Psalm l

HAVE mercy on me, O God, according to Thy great mercy.
And according to

titudinem miserationum tuarum: * dele iniquitatem meam.`

Amplius lava me ab iniquitate mea: * et a peccato meo munda me.

Quoniam iniquitatem meam ego cognosco: * et peccatum meum contra me est semper.

Tibi soli peccavi, et malum coram te feci: * ut justificeris in sermonibus tuis, et vincas cum judicaris.

Ecce enim in iniquitatibus conceptus sum: * et in peccatis concepit me mater mea.

Ecce enim veritatem dilexisti: * incerta et occulta sapientiæ tuæ manifestasti mihi.

Asperges me hyssopo et mundabor: * lavabis me et super

the multitude of Thy tender mercies, blot out mine iniquity.

Wash me yet more from mine iniquity; and cleanse me from my sin.

For I know mine iniquity, and my sin is always before me.

To Thee only have I sinned, and have done evil before Thee: that Thou mayest be justified in Thy words, and mayest overcome when Thou art judged.

For behold I was conceived in iniquities; and in sin did my mother conceive me.

For behold Thou hast loved truth: the uncertain and hidden things of Thy wisdom Thou hast made manifest to me.

Thou shalt sprinkle me with hyssop, and I shall be cleansed; Thou shalt wash me,

nivem dealbabor.

and I shall be made whiter than snow.

Auditui meo dabis gaudium et lætitiam: * et exultabunt ossa humiliata.

To my hearing Thou shalt give joy and gladness; and the bones that have been humbled shall rejoice.

. Averte faciem tuam a peccatis meis: * et omnes iniquitates meas dele.

Turn away Thy face from my sins, and blot out all mine iniquities.

Cor mundum crea in me, Deus: * et spiritum rectum innova in visceribus meis.

Create a clean heart in me, O God: and renew a right spirit within my bowels.

Ne projicias me a facie tua: * et spiritum sanctum tuum ne auferas a me.

Cast me not away from Thy face; and take not Thy Holy Spirit from me.

Redde mihi lætitiam salutaris tui: * et spiritu principali confirma me.

Restore unto me the joy of Thy salvation, and strengthen me with a perfect spirit.

Docebo iniquos vias tuas: * et impii ad te convertentur.

I will teach the unjust Thy ways: and the wicked shall be converted unto Thee.

Libera me de sanguinibus, Deus, Deus salutis meæ: * et exultabit lingua mea justitiam tuam.

Deliver me from blood, O God, Thou God of my salvation; and my tongue shall extol Thy justice.

Domine, labia mea

O Lord, Thou wilt

aperies: * et os meum annuntiabit laudem tuam.

Quoniam si voluisses sacrificium, dedissem utique: * holocaustis non delectaberis.

Sacrificium Deo spiritus contribulatus: * cor contritum et humiliatum, Deus, non despicies.

Benigne fac, Domine, in bona voluntate tua Sion: * ut ædificentur muri Jerusalem.

Tunc acceptabis sacrificium justitiæ, oblationes, et holocausta: * tunc imponent super altare tuum vitulos.

Requiem æternam, etc.

Ant. Exultabunt Domino ossa humiliata.

open my lips: and my mouth shall declare Thy praise.

For if Thou hadst desired sacrifice, I would indeed have given it: with burnt-offerings Thou wilt not be delighted.

A sacrifice to God is an afflicted spirit; a contrite and humble heart, O God, Thou wilt not despise.

Deal favorably, O Lord, in Thy good will with Sion, that the walls of Jerusalem may be built up.

Then shalt Thou accept the sacrifice of justice, oblations, and whole burnt-offerings; then shall they lay calves upon Thy altar.

Eternal rest, etc.

Ant. The bones that are humbled shall rejoice in the Lord.

At the Entrance of the Church

(Inside) is said the following:

SUBVENITE Sancti Dei, occurrite Angeli Domini, suscipientes animam ejus, offerentes eam in conspectu Altissimi.

V. Suscipiat te Christus qui vocavit te, et in sinum Abrahæ Angeli deducant te.

R. Suscipientes animam ejus, offerentes eam in conspectu Altissimi.

V. Requiem æternam dona ei, Domine, et lux perpetua luceat ei.

R. Offerentes eam in conspectu Altissimi.

COME to his [her] assistance, ye saints of God! Meet him [her], ye Angels of the Lord. Receive his [her] soul, and present it to the Most High.

V. May Christ who called thee, receive thee; and may the Angels lead thee into the bosom of Abraham.

R. Receive his [her] soul, and present it to the Most High.

V. Eternal rest give unto him [her], O Lord, and let perpetual light shine upon him [her].

R. Present it to the Most High.

The body having been deposited before the sanctuary, Mass is celebrated

✳

Mass for the Dead on the Day of Death or Burial

Prayers at the Foot of the Altar

IN NOMINE Patris, ✠ et Filii, et Spiritus Sancti. Amen.

P. Introibo ad altare Dei.

R. Ad Deum qui lætificat juventutem meam.

P. Adjutorium nostrum in nomine Domini.

R. Qui fecit cœlum et terram.

IN THE name of the Father, ✠ and of the Son, and of the Holy Ghost. Amen.

P. I will go in to the altar of God.

R. To God, Who giveth joy to my youth.

P. Our help is in the name of the Lord.

R. Who made heaven and earth.

Humbly bowing down, the priest says:

CONFITEOR Deo omnipotenti, beatæ Mariæ semper virgini, beato Michaeli archangelo, beato Joanni Baptistæ, sanctis apostolis Petro et Paulo, omnibus sanctis et vobis, fratres, quia peccavi nimis cogita-

I CONFESS to almighty God, to blessed Mary ever virgin, to blessed Michael the archangel, to blessed John the Baptist, to the holy apostles Peter and Paul, to all the saints and to you, brethren, that I have sinned ex-

tione, verbo, et opere: mea culpa, mea culpa, mea maxima culpa. Ideo precor beatam Mariam semper virginem, beatum Michaelem archangelum, beatum Joannem Baptistam, sanctos apostolos Petrum et Paulum, omnes sanctos, et vos, fratres, orare pro me ad Dominum Deum nostrum.

R. Misereatur tui omnipotens Deus, et dimissis peccatis tuis, perducat te ad vitam æternam.
  - *P*. Amen.

ceedingly in thought, word, and deed: through my fault, through my fault, through my most grievous fault. Therefore I beseech the blessed Mary ever virgin, blessed Michael the archangel, blessed John the Baptist, the holy apostles Peter and Paul, all the saints and you, brethren, to pray to the Lord our God for me.

R. May almighty God have mercy on thee and, having forgiven thee thy sins, bring thee to life everlasting.
P. Amen.

The acolytes repeat the Confiteor:

CONFITEOR Deo omnipotenti, beatæ Mariæ semper virgini, beato Michaeli archangelo, beato Joanni Baptistæ, sanctis apostolis Petro et Paulo, omnibus sanctis, et tibi, Pater, quia peccavi nimis cogitatione,

I CONFESS to almighty God, to blessed Mary ever virgin, to blessed Michael the archangel, to blessed John the Baptist, to the holy apostles Peter and Paul, to all the saints, and to thee, Father, that I have

verbo, et opere: mea culpa, mea culpa, mea maxima culpa. Ideo precor beatam Mariam semper virginem, beatum Michaelem archangelum, beatum Joannem Baptistam, sanctos apostolos Petrum et Paulum, omnes sanctos, et te, Pater, orare pro me ad Dominum Deum nostrum.

sinned exceedingly in thought, word, and deed: through my fault, through my fault, through my most grievous fault. Therefore I beseech the blessed Mary ever virgin, blessed Michael the archangel, blessed John the Baptist, the holy apostles Peter and Paul, all the saints, and thee, Father, to pray to the Lord our God for me.

P. Misereatur vestri omnipotens Deus, et dimissis peccatis vestris, perducat vos ad vitam æternam.

P. May almighty God have mercy on you and, having forgiven you your sins, bring you to life everlasting.

R. Amen.

R. Amen.

P. Indulgentiam, absolutionem, et remissionem peccatorum nostrorum, tribuat nobis omnipotens et misericors Dominus.

P. May the almighty and merciful God grant us pardon, absolution, and remission of our sins.

R. Amen.

R. Amen.

Again bowing down, the priest goes on:

P. Deus, tu conversus vivificabis nos.

P. Thou wilt turn again, O God, and quicken us.

R. Et plebs tua læ-tabitur in te.

R. And Thy people will rejoice in Thee.

P. Ostende nobis, Domine, misericordi-am tuam.

P. Show us, O Lord, Thy mercy.

R. Et salutare tu-um da nobis.

R. And grant us Thy salvation.

P. Domine, exau-di orationem meam.

P. O Lord, hear my prayer.

R. Et clamor meus ad te veniat.

R. And let my cry come unto Thee.

P. Dominus vobis-cum.

P. The Lord be with you.

R. Et cum spiritu tuo.

R. And with thy spirit.

P. Oremus.

P. Let us pray.

Going up to the altar the priest prays silently:

AUFER a nobis, quæsumus, Domine, iniquitates nostras: ut ad Sancta Sanctorum puris me-reamur mentibus in-troire. Per Christum Dominum nostrum. Amen.

TAKE away from us our iniqui-ties, we beseech Thee, O Lord; that, being made pure in heart we may be worthy to enter into the Holy of Holies. Through Christ our Lord. Amen.

He bows down over the altar, which he kisses, saying:

ORAMUS te, Do-mine, per merita sanctorum tuorum, quorum reliquiæ hic sunt, et omnium sanctorum: ut indul-

WE BESEECH Thee, O Lord, by the merits of those of Thy saints whose relics are here, and of all the saints, that

gere digneris omnia peccata mea. Amen.

Thou wouldst vouchsafe to pardon me all my sins. Amen.

The Introit

REQUIEM æternam dona eis, Domine, et lux perpetua luceat eis.

ETERNAL rest grant unto them, O Lord, and let perpetual light shine upon them.

Te decet hymnus, Deus, in Sion; et tibi reddetur votum in Jerusalem: exaudi orationem meam; ad te omnis caro veniet.

A hymn, O God, becometh Thee in Sion; and shall be paid unto Thee in Jerusalem: O hear my prayer; all flesh shall come unto Thee.

Requiem æternam, etc.

Eternal rest, etc.

Kyrie Eleison

P. KYRIE, eleison.
R. Kyrie, eleison.

P. Kyrie, eleison.

R. Christe, eleison.

P. Christe, eleison.

R. Christe, eleison.

P. Kyrie, eleison.

R. Kyrie, eleison.

P. LORD, have mercy on us.
R. Lord, have mercy on us.

P. Lord, have mercy on us.

R. Christ, have mercy on us.

P. Christ, have mercy on us.

R. Christ, have mercy on us.

P. Lord, have mercy on us.

R. Lord, have mercy on us.

P. Kyrie, eleison.

P. Dominus vobis-
cum.

R. Et cum spiritu
tuo.

P. Lord, have mer-
cy on us.

P. The Lord be
with you.

R. And with thy
spirit.

The Collect

DEUS, cui propri-
um est misereri
semper et parcere, te
supplices exoramus
pro anima famuli tui
N., quam hodie de
hoc sæculo migrare
jussisti: ut non tra-
das eam in manus
inimici, neque obli-
viscaris in finem, sed
jubeas eam a sanctis
Angelis suscipi, et ad
patriam paradisi per-
duci; ut, quia in te
speravit et credidit,
non pœnas inferni
sustineat, sed gaudia
æterna possideat. Per
Dominum, etc.

O GOD, Whose
property is ever
to have mercy and to
spare, we humbly
supplicate Thee for
the soul of Thy ser-
vant, N., which Thou
hast this day called
out of this world, that
Thou deliver it not to
the hands of the en-
emy, nor forget it for-
ever, but command
it to be received by
the holy angels and
taken to paradise, its
home; so that, since
it hath hoped and be-
lieved in Thee, it
may not bear the
pains of hell, but pos-
sess everlasting joys.
Through Our Lord.

The Epistle
I Thess. iv. 12–17

FRATRES, Nolu-
mus vos igno-
rare de dormientibus,

BRETHREN, We
will not have
you ignorant con-

ut non contristemini, sicut et cæteri qui spem non habent. Si enim credimus quod Jesus mortuus est et resurrexit, ita et Deus eos, qui dormierunt per Jesum, adducet cum eo. Hoc enim vobis dicimus in verbo Domini, quia nos, qui vivimus, qui residui sumus in adventum Domini, non præveniemus eos qui dormierunt. Quoniam ipse Dominus in jussu, et in voce Archangeli, et in tuba Dei descendet de cœlo: et mortui, qui in Christo sunt, resurgent primi. Deinde nos, qui vivimus, qui relinquimur, simul rapiemur cum illis in nubibus obviam Christo in aëra, et sic semper cum Domino

cerning them that are asleep, that you be not sorrowful, even as others who have no hope. For if we believe that Jesus died and rose again, even so them who have slept through Jesus Christ will God bring with Him. For this we say unto you in the word of the Lord, that we who are alive, who remain unto the coming of the Lord, shall not prevent them who have slept. For the Lord Himself shall come down from heaven, with commandment, and with the voice of an archangel, and with the trumpet of God; and the dead who are in Christ shall rise first. Then we who are alive, who are left, shall be taken up together with them in the clouds to meet Christ, into the air, and so shall we be always with the Lord.

erimus. Itaque con-
solamini invicem in
verbis istis.

Wherefore, comfort
ye one another with
these words.

The Gradual

REQUIEM æter-
nam dona eis,
Domine, et lux per-
petua luceat eis.

ETERNAL rest
grant unto them,
O Lord, and let per-
petual light shine up-
on them.

V. In memoria
æterna erit justus;
ab auditione mala
non timebit.

V. The just shall
be in everlasting re-
membrance; he shall
not fear the evil hear-
ing.

The Tract

ABSOLVE, Do-
mine, animas
omnium fidelium de-
functorum ab omni
vinculo delictorum.

ABSOLVE, O
Lord, the souls
of all the faithful de-
parted from every
bond of sin.

V. Et gratia tua il-
lis succurrente me-
reantur evadere judi-
cium ultionis.

V. And by the help
of Thy grace may
they be worthy to es-
cape the sentence of
vengeance.

V. Et lucis æternæ
beatitudine perfrui.

V. And to enjoy
the beatitude of the
light eternal.

The Sequence
(*Dies Iræ*)

DIES iræ, dies illa
Solvet sæclum
in favilla,
Teste David cum Si-
bylla.

DREADED day,
that day of ire,
When the world shall
melt in fire,
Told by Sibyl and
David's lyre.

Quantus tremor est futurus,
Quando Judex est venturus,
Cuncta stricte discussurus!

Fright men's hearts shall rudely shift,
As the Judge through gleaming rift
Comes each soul to closely sift.

Tuba mirum spargens sonum
Per sepulchra regionum,
Coget omnes ante thronum.

Then, the trumpet's shrill refrain,
Piercing tombs by hill and plain,
Souls to judgment shall arraign.

Mors stupebit et natura,
Cum resurget creatura,
Judicanti responsura.

Death and nature stand aghast,
As the bodies rising fast,
Hie to hear the sentence passed.

Liber scriptus proferetur,
In quo totum continetur,
Unde mundus judicetur.

Then, before Him shall be placed
That whereon the verdict's based,
Book wherein each deed is traced.

Judex ergo cum sedebit,
Quidquid latet apparebit:
Nil inultum remanebit.

When the Judge His seat shall gain,
All that's hidden shall be plain,
Nothing shall unjudged remain.

Quid sum miser tunc dicturus?

Wretched man, what can I plead?

Quem patronum rogaturus,
Cum vix justus sit securus?

Whom to ask to intercede,
When the just much mercy need.

Rex tremendæ majestatis,
Qui salvandos salvas gratis,
Salva me, fons pietatis.

Thou, O awe-inspiring Lord,
Saving e'en when unimplored,
Save me, mercy's fount adored.

Recordare, Jesu pie,
Quod sum causa tuæ viæ:
Ne me perdas illa die.

Ah! Sweet Jesus, mindful be,
That Thou cam'st on earth for me:
Cast me not this day from Thee.

Quærens me, sedisti lassus;
Redemisti, crucem passus:
Tantus labor non sit cassus.

Seeking me Thy strength was spent,
Ransoming, Thy limbs were rent:
Is this toil to no intent?

Juste Judex ultionis,
Donum fac remissionis
Ante diem rationis.

Thou, awarding pains condign,
Mercy's ear to me incline,
Ere the reckoning Thou assign.

Ingemisco, tamquam reus,
Culpa rubet vultus meus;

I, felon like, my lot bewail,
Suffused cheeks my shame unveil:

Supplicanti parce, Deus.	God, O let my prayer prevail!
Qui Mariam absolvisti,	Mary's soul Thou madest white,
Et latronem exaudisti,	Didst to heaven the thief invite;
Mihi quoque spem dedisti.	Hope in me these now excite.
Preces meæ non sunt dignæ:	Prayers of mine in vain ascend:
Sed tu bonus fac benigne,	Thou art good and wilt forefend,
Ne perenni cremer igne.	In quenchless fire my life to end.
Inter oves locum præsta,	When the cursed by shame opprest,
Et ab hœdis me sequestra,	Enter flames at Thy behest,
Statuens in parte dextra.	Call me then to join the blest.
Confutatis maledictis,	Place amid Thy sheep accord,
Flammis acribus addictis,	Keep me from the tainted horde,
Voca me cum benedictis.	Set me in Thy sight, O Lord.
Oro supplex et acclinis,	Prostrate, suppliant, now no more
Cor contritum quasi cinis:	Unrepenting, as of yore,
Gere curam mei finis.	Save me dying, I implore.

Lacrymosa dies illa,
Qua resurget ex fa-
  villa

Mournful day! that
  day of sighs,
When from dust shall
  man arise,

Judicandus homo
  reus.
Huic ergo parce,
  Deus:

Stained with guilt his
  doom to know,
Mercy, Lord, on him
  bestow.

Pie Jesu Domine,
Dona eis requiem.
  Amen.

Jesus, kind! Thy
  souls release,
Lead them thence to
  realms of peace.
  Amen.

The Munda Cor Meum

MUNDA cor me-
um, ac labia
mea, omnipotens De-
us, qui labia Isaiæ
prophetæ calculo
mundasti ignito: ita
me tua grata misera-
tione dignare mun-
dare, ut sanctum
Evangelium tuum
digne valeam nun-
tiare. Per Christum
Dominum nostrum.
Amen.

CLEANSE my
heart and my
lips, O almighty God,
Who didst cleanse
with a burning coal
the lips of the prophet
Isaias; and vouchsafe
in Thy loving-kind-
ness so to purify me
that I may be en-
abled worthily to an-
nounce Thy holy
Gospel. Through
Christ our Lord.
Amen.

The Gospel

P. Dominus vobis-
cum.
R. Et cum spiritu
tuo.

P. The Lord be
with you.
R. And with thy
spirit.

P. ✠ Sequentia sancti Evangelii secundum Joannem (xi. 21–27).

R. Gloria tibi, Domine.

IN ILLO tempore: Dixit Martha ad Jesum: Domine, si fuisses hic, frater meus non fuisset mortuus. Sed et nunc scio, quia quæcumque poposceris a Deo, dabit tibi Deus. Dicit illi Jesus: Resurget frater tuus. Dicit ei Martha: Scio, quia resurget in resurrectione in novissimo die. Dixit ei Jesus: Ego sum resurrectio et vita: qui credit in me, etiam si mortuus fuerit, vivet: et omnis qui vivit, et credit in me, non morietur in æternum. Credis hoc? Ait illi: Utique Domine, ego credidi, quia tu es Christus, Filius Dei vivi, qui in

P. ✠ The following is taken from the Holy Gospel according to St. John (xi. 21–27).

R. Glory be to Thee, O Lord.

AT THAT time, Martha said to Jesus: Lord, if Thou hadst been here, my brother had not died. But now also I know that whatever Thou wilt ask of God, God will give Thee. Jesus saith to her: Thy brother will rise again. Martha saith to Him: I know that he will rise again in the resurrection at the last day. Jesus said to her: I am the Resurrection and the Life: He that believeth in Me, although he be dead, shall live: and every one who liveth and believeth in Me shall never die. Believest thou this? She saith to Him: Yea, Lord, I

hunc mundum ve-
nisti.

believe that Thou art
the Christ, the Son of
the living God, Who
art come into this
world.

R. Laus tibi,
Christe.

R. Praise be to
Thee, O Christ.

P. Dominus vobis-
cum.

P. The Lord be
with you.

R. Et cum spiritu
tuo.

R. And with thy
spirit.

P. Oremus.

P. Let us pray.

The Offertory

DOMINE Jesu Christe, Rex gloriæ, libera animas omnium fidelium defunctorum de pœnas inferni, et de profundo lacu: libera eas de ore leonis, ne absorbeat eas tartarus, ne cadant in obscurum; sed signifer sanctus Michael repræsentet eas in lucem sanctam: Quam olim Abrahæ promisisti, et semini ejus.

O LORD Jesus Christ, King of glory, deliver the souls of all the faithful departed from the pains of hell and from the deep pit; deliver them from the lion's mouth, that hell engulf them not, nor they fall into darkness, but that Michael, the holy standard-bearer, bring them into the holy light which Thou once didst promise to Abraham and his seed.

V. Hostias et preces tibi, Domine, laudis offerimus: tu sus-

V. We offer Thee, O Lord, sacrifices and prayers of praise; do

cipe pro animabus illis, quarum hodie memoriam facimus: iac eas, Domine, de morte transire ad vitam.

Quam olim Abrahæ promisisti, et semini ejus.

Thou accept them for those souls whom we this day commemorate; grant them, O Lord, to pass from death to the life which Thou once didst promise to Abraham and his seed.

Offering of the Host

SUSCIPE, sancte Pater, omnipotens æterne Deus, hanc immaculatam hostiam, quam ego indignus famulus tuus offero tibi, Deo meo vivo et vero, pro innumerabilibus peccatis, et offensionibus, et negligentiis meis, et pro omnibus circumstantibus, sed et pro omnibus fidelibus Christianis vivis atque defunctis: ut mihi et illis proficiat ad salutem in vitam æternam. Amen.

RECEIVE, O Holy Father, almighty and eternal God, this spotless host, which I, Thine unworthy servant, offer unto Thee, my living and true God, for my countless sins, trespasses, and omissions; likewise for all here present, and for all faithful Christians, whether living or dead, that it may avail both me and them to salvation, unto life everlasting. Amen.

The priest pours wine and water into the chalice

DEUS, qui humanæ substantiæ dignitatem mira-

O GOD, Who in creating man didst exalt his nature

biliter condidisti, et mirabilius reformasti: da nobis per hujus aquæ et vini mysterium, ejus divinitatis esse consortes, qui humanitatis nostræ fieri dignatus est particeps, Jesus Christus Filius tuus Dominus noster: Qui tecum vivit et regnat in unitate Spiritus Sancti Deus: per omnia sæcula sæculorum. Amen.

very wonderfully and yet more wonderfully didst establish it anew: by the mystery signified in the mingling of this water and wine, grant us to have part in the Godhead of Him Who hath vouchsafed to share our manhood, Jesus Christ, Thy Son, Our Lord, Who liveth and reigneth with Thee in the unity of the Holy Ghost; world without end. Amen.

Offering of the Chalice

OFFERIMUS tibi, Domine, calicem salutaris, tuam deprecantes clementiam: ut in conspectu divinæ majestatis tuæ, pro nostra et totius mundi salute cum odore suavitatis ascendat. Amen.

WE OFFER unto Thee, O Lord, the chalice of salvation, beseeching Thy clemency that it may ascend as a sweet odor before Thy divine majesty, for our own salvation, and for that of the whole world. Amen.

IN SPIRITU humilitatis, et in animo contrito suscipiamur a te, Do-

HUMBLED in mind, and contrite of heart, may we find favor with Thee,

mine: et sic fiat sacrificium nostrum in conspectu tuo hodie, ut placeat tibi, Domine Deus.

O Lord; and may the sacrifice we this day offer up be well pleasing to Thee, Who art our Lord and our God.

VENI, sanctificator omnipotens æterne Deus, et benedic hoc sacrificium tuo sancto nomini præparatum.

COME, Thou the Sanctifier, God, almighty and everlasting: bless this sacrifice which is prepared for the glory of Thy holy name.

The Lavabo

The priest washes his fingers

LAVABO inter innocentes manus meas: et circumdabo altare tuum, Domine.

Ut audiam vocem laudis: et enarrem universa mirabilia tua.

Domine, dilexi decorem domus tuæ: et locum habitationis gloriæ tuæ.

Ne perdas cum impiis, Deus, animam meam: et cum viris sanguinum vitam meam.

I WILL wash my hands among the innocent, and will compass Thine altar, O Lord.

That I may hear the voice of praise, and tell of all Thy wondrous works.

I have loved, O Lord, the beauty of Thy house, and the place where Thy glory dwelleth.

Take not away my soul, O God, with the wicked: nor my life with men of blood.

In quorum manibus iniquitates sunt: dextera eorum repleta est muneribus.

Ego autem in innocentia mea ingressus sum: redime me, et miserere mei.

Pes meus stetit in directo: in ecclesiis benedicam te, Domine.

SUSCIPE, sancta Trinitas, hanc oblationem, quam tibi offerimus ob memoriam passionis, resurrectionis, et ascensionis Jesu Christi Domini nostri: et in honorem beatæ Mariæ semper virginis, et beati Joannis Baptistæ, et sanctorum apostolorum Petri, et Pauli, et istorum, et omnium sanctorum: ut illis proficiat ad honorem, nobis autem ad salutem: et illi pro nobis intercedere dignentur in cœlis, quorum memoriam agimus in terris.

In whose hands are iniquities: their right hand is filled with gifts.

But as for me, I have walked in my innocence; redeem me, and have mercy on me.

My foot hath stood in the right way; in the churches I will bless Thee, O Lord. `

RECEIVE, O holy Trinity, this oblation offered up by us to Thee, in memory of the passion, resurrection, and ascension of Our Lord Jesus Christ, and in honor of blessed Mary, ever a virgin, of blessed John the Baptist, of the holy apostles Peter and Paul, of these, and of all the saints, that it may be available to their honor and to our salvation; and may they whose memory we celebrate on earth vouchsafe to intercede for us in

Per eumdem Christum Dominum nostrum. Amen.

heaven. Through the same Christ our Lord. Amen.

The Orate Fratres

ORATE, fratres, ut meum ac vestrum sacrificium acceptabile fiat apud Deum Patrem omnipotentem.

BRETHREN, pray that my sacrifice and yours may be well pleasing to God the Father Almighty.

SUSCIPIAT Dominus sacrificium de manibus tuis, ad laudem et gloriam nominis sui, ad utilitatem, quoque nostram, totiusque Ecclesiæ suæ sanctæ. Amen.

MAY the Lord receive this sacrifice at thy hands, to the praise and glory of His name, to our own benefit, and to that of all His holy Church. Amen.

The Secret

PROPITIARE, quaesumus, Domine, animæ famuli tui N., pro qua hostiam laudis tibi immolamus; majestatem tuam suppliciter deprecantes, ut, per hæc piæ placationis officia, pervenire mereatur ad requiem sempiternam. Per Dominum, etc.

BE MERCIFUL, we beseech Thee, O Lord, to the soul of Thy servant N., for which we offer to Thee the sacrifice of praise, supplicating Thy majesty that, through these offices of pious propitiation it may be worthy to enter into everlasting rest. Through our Lord Jesus Christ, etc.

The Preface

P. Per omnia sæcula sæculorum.

R. Amen.

P. Dominus vobiscum.

R. Et cum spiritu tuo.

P. Sursum corda.

R. Habemus ad Dominum.

P. Gratias agamus Domino Deo nostro.

R. Dignum et justum est.

P. World without end.

R. Amen.

P. The Lord be with you.

R. And with thy spirit.

P. Lift up your hearts.

R. We have them lifted up unto the Lord.

P. Let us give thanks to the Lord our God.

R. It is meet and just.

The following Preface is said in all Masses for the Dead.

VERE dignum et justum est, æquum et salutare, nos tibi semper, et ubique gratias agere: Domine sancte, Pater omnipotens, æterne Deus: per Christum Dominum nostrum. In quo nobis spes beatæ resurrectionis effulsit, ut quos contristat certa moriendi conditio, eosdem consoletur

IT IS truly meet and just, right and salutary, that we should always, and in all places, give thanks to Thee, O holy Lord, Father almighty, eternal God. Through Christ our Lord: in Whom the hope of a happy resurrection has shone on us, so that those whom the certain fate of dying renders sad, may be

futuræ immortalitatis promissio. Tuis enim fidelibus, Domine, vita mutatur, non tollitur, et dissoluta terrestris hujus incolatus domo, æterna in cœlis habitatio comparatur. Et ideo cum Angelis et Archangelis, cum Thronis et Dominationibus, cumque omni militia cœlestis exercitus, hymnum gloriæ tuæ canimus, sine fine dicentes.

consoled by the promise of future immortality. For with regard to Thy Faithful, O Lord, life is changed, not taken away, and the house of their earthly dwelling being destroyed, an eternal dwelling in heaven is obtained. And therefore with angels and archangels, with thrones and dominations, and with all the army of heaven, we sing a hymn to Thy glory, saying without ceasing:

The Sanctus

SANCTUS, sanctus, sanctus, Dominus Deus Sabaoth.

Pleni sunt cœli et terra gloria tua.

Hosanna in excelsis.

Benedictus qui venit in nomine Domini.

Hosanna in excelsis.

HOLY, holy, holy, Lord God of hosts.

The heavens and the earth are full of Thy glory.

Hosanna in the highest.

Blessed is He Who cometh in the name of the Lord.

Hosanna in the highest.

The Canon of the Mass

TE IGITUR, cle-
mentissime Pa-
ter, per Jesum Chris-
tum Filium tuum, Do-
minum nostrum, sup-
plices rogamus ac
petimus, uti accepta
habeas, et benedicas
hæc ✠ dona, hæc ✠
munera, hæc ✠ sanc-
ta sacrificia illibata,
in primis, quæ tibi
offerimus pro Eccle-
sia tua sancta catho-
lica: quam pacificare,
custodire, adunare, et
regere digneris toto
orbe terrarum: una
cum famulo tuo Papa
nostro N., et Antis-
tite nostro N., et om-
nibus orthodoxis, at-
que catholicæ et
apostolicæ fidei cul-
toribus.

WHEREFORE,
we humbly
pray and beseech
Thee, most merciful
Father, through Je-
sus Christ Thy Son
our Lord, to receive
and to bless these ✠
gifts, these ✠ pres-
ents, these ✠ holy
unspotted sacrifices,
which we offer up to
Thee, in the first
place, for Thy holy
Catholic Church, that
it may please Thee to
grant her peace, to
guard, unite, and
guide her throughout
the world; as also for
Thy servant N., our
Pope, and N., our
Bishop, and for all
who are orthodox in
belief and who pro-
fess the Catholic and
apostolic faith.

Commemoration of the Living

MEMENTO, Do-
mine, famulo-
rum famularumque
tuarum, N. et N., et
omnium circumstan-

BE MINDFUL, O
Lord, of Thy
servants, N. and N.,
and of all here pres-
ent, whose faith and

tium, quorum tibi fides cognita est, et nota devotio, pro quibus tibi offerimus, vel qui tibi offerunt hoc sacrificium laudis, pro se suisque omnibus: pro redemptione animarum suarum, pro spe salutis, et incolumitatis suæ: tibique reddunt vota sua æterno Deo vivo et vero.

devotion are known to Thee, for whom we offer, or who offer up to Thee, this sacrifice of praise, for themselves, their families, and their friends, for the salvation of their souls and the health and welfare they hope for, and who now pay their vows to Thee, God eternal, living, and true.

COMMUNICANTES, et memoriam venerantes, in primis gloriosæ semper Virginis Mariæ, Genitricis Dei et Domini nostri Jesu Christi: sed et beatorum apostolorum ac martyrum tuorum, Petri et Pauli, Andreæ, Jacobi, Joannis, Thomæ, Jacobi, Philippi, Bartholomæi, Matthæi, Simonis et Thaddæi, Lini, Cleti, Clementis, Xysti, Cornelii, Cypriani, Laurentii, Chrysogoni, Joannis

HAVING communion with and venerating the memory, first, of the glorious Mary, ever a virgin, mother of Jesus Christ, our God and our Lord: likewise of Thy blessed apostles and martyrs, Peter and Paul, Andrew, James, John, Thomas, James, Philip, Bartholomew, Matthew, Simon and Thaddeus; of Linus, Cletus, Clement, Xystus, Cornelius, Cyprian, Lawrence, Chrysogonus, John

et Pauli, Cosmæ et Damiani, et omnium sanctorum tuorum; quorum meritus precibusque concedas, ut in omnibus protectionis tuæ muniamur auxilio. Per eumdem Christum Dominum nostrum. Amen.

and Paul, Cosmas and Damian, and of all Thy saints: for the sake of whose merits and prayers do Thou grant that in all things we may be defended by the help of Thy protection. Through the same Christ our Lord. Amen.

HANC igitur oblationem servitutis nostræ, sed et cunctæ familiæ tuæ, quæsumus, Domine, ut placatus accipias: diesque nostros in tua pace disponas, atque ab æterna damnatione nos eripi, et in electorum tuorum jubeas grege numerari. Per Christum Dominum nostrum. Amen.

WHEREFORE, we beseech Thee, O Lord, graciously to receive this oblation which we Thy servants, and with us Thy whole family, offer up to Thee: dispose our days in Thy peace; command that we be saved from eternal damnation and numbered among the flock of Thine elect. Through Christ our Lord. Amen.

QUAM oblationem tu, Deus, in omnibus, quæsumus bene☩dictam, adscrip☩tam, ra☩tam, rationabilem acceptabilemque facere

AND do Thou, O God, vouchsafe in all respects to bless, ☩ consecrate, ☩ and approve ☩ this our oblation, to perfect it and to ren-

digneris: ut nobis cor✠pus et san✠guis fiat dilectissimi Filii tui Domini nostri Jesu Christi.

der it well-pleasing to Thyself, so that it may become for us the body ✠ and blood ✠ of Thy most beloved Son, Jesus Christ our Lord.

QUI pridie quam pateretur, accepit panem in sanctas ac venerabiles manus suas, et elevatis oculis in cœlum ad te Deum Patrem suum omnipotentem, tibi gratias agens, bene✠dixit, fregit, deditque discipulis suis, dicens: Accipite, et manducate ex hoc omnes:

WHO, the day before He suffered, took bread into His holy and venerable hands and having lifted up His eyes to heaven to Thee, God, His almighty Father, giving thanks to Thee, blessed ✠ it, broke it, and gave it to His disciples, saying: Take ye, and eat ye all of this:

Hoc est enim Corpus meum.

For this is My Body.

SIMILI modo postquam cœnatum est, accipiens et hunc præclarum calicem in sanctas ac venerabiles manus suas: item tibi gratias agens bene✠dixit, deditque discipulis suis, dicens: Accipite, et bibite ex eo omnes:

IN LIKE manner after He had supped, taking also into His holy and venerable hands this goodly chalice, again giving thanks to Thee, He blessed it ✠ , and gave it to His disciples, saying: Take ye, and drink ye all of this:

Hic est enim Calix Sanguinis mei, novi et æterni testamenti: mysterium fidei, qui pro vobis et pro multis effundetur in remissionem peccatorum.

For this is the chalice of My blood, of the new and everlasting testament, the mystery of faith, which for you and for many shall be shed unto the remission of sins.

Hæc quotiescumque feceritis, in mei memoriam facietis.

As often as ye shall do these things, ye shall do them in memory of Me.

UNDE et memores, Domine, nos servi tui, sed et plebs tua sancta, ejusdem Christi Filii tui Domini nostri, tam beatæ passionis, necnon et ab inferis resurrectionis, sed et in cœlos gloriosæ ascensionis: offerimus præclaræ majestati tuæ de tuis donis ac datis, hostiam ✠ puram, hostiam ✠ sanctam, hostiam ✠ immaculatam, panem sanctum ✠ vitæ æternæ, et calicem ✠salutis perpetuæ.

WHEREFORE, O Lord, we Thy servants, as also Thy holy people, calling to mind the blessed passion of the same Christ Thy Son, our Lord, His resurrection from the grave, and His· glorious ascension into heaven, offer up to Thy most excellent majesty of Thine own gifts bestowed upon us, a victim ✠ which is pure, a victim ✠ which is holy, a victim ✠ which is stainless, the holy bread ✠ of life everlasting, and the chalice ✠ of eternal salvation.

SUPRA quæ propitio ac sereno vultu respicere digneris, et accepta habere, sicuti accepta habere dignatus es munera pueri tui justi Abel, et sacrificium Patriarchæ nostri Abrahæ: et quod tibi obtulit summus sacerdos tuus Melchisedech, sanctum sacrificium, immaculatam hostiam.

SUPPLICES te rogamus, omnipotens Deus, jube hæc perferri per manus sancti angeli tui in sublime altare tuum, in conspectu divinæ majestatis tuæ: ut quotquot, ex hac altaris participatione, sacrosanctum Filii tui cor ✠ pus et san ✠ guinem sumpserimus, omni benedictione cœlesti et gratia repleamur. Per eumdem Christum Dominum nostrum. Amen.

VOUCHSAFE to look upon them with a gracious and tranquil countenance, and to accept them, even as Thou wast pleased to accept the offerings of Thy just servant Abel, and the sacrifice of Abraham, our patriarch, and that which Melchisedech, Thy high priest, offered up to Thee, a holy sacrifice, a victim without blemish.

WE HUMBLY beseech Thee, almighty God, to command that these our offerings be borne by the hands of Thy holy angel to Thine altar on high in the presence of Thy Divine Majesty; that as many of us as shall receive the most sacred ✠ body and ✠ blood of Thy Son by partaking thereof from this altar may be filled with every heavenly blessing and grace: Through the same Christ our Lord. Amen.

Commemoration of the Dead

MEMENTO etiam, Domine, famulorum famularumque tuarum N. et N., qui nos præcesserunt cum signo fidei, et dormiunt in somno pacis.

BE MINDFUL also, O Lord, of Thy servants N. and N., who have gone before us with the sign of faith and who sleep the sleep of peace.

IPSIS, Domine, et omnibus in Christo quiescentibus, locum refrigerii, lucis et pacis, ut indulgeas, deprecamur. Per eumdem Christum Dominum nostrum. Amen.

TO THESE, O Lord, and to all who rest in Christ, grant, we beseech Thee, a place of refreshment, light, and peace. Through the same Christ our Lord. Amen.

NOBIS quoque peccatoribus famulis tuis, de multitudine miserationum tuarum sperantibus, partem aliquam, et societatem donare digneris, cum tuis sanctis apostolis et martyribus: cum Joanne, Stephano, Matthia, Barnaba, Ignatio, Alexandro, Marcellino, Petro, Felicitate, Perpetua, Agatha, Lucia, Agne-

TO US sinners, also, Thy servants, who put our trust in the multitude of Thy mercies, vouchsafe to grant some part and fellowship with Thy holy apostles and martyrs: with John, Stephen, Matthias, Barnabas, Ignatius, Alexander, Marcellinus, Peter, Felicitas, Perpetua, Agatha, Lucy, Agnes, Cecilia, Anastasia, and with

te, Cæcilia, Anastasia, et omnibus sanctis tuis: intra quorum nos consortium, non æstimator meriti, sed veniæ, quæsumus, largitor admitte. Per Christum Dominum nostrum.

all Thy saints. Into their company do Thou, we beseech Thee, admit us, not weighing our merits but freely pardoning our offenses. Through Christ our Lord.

PER quem hæc omnia, Domine, semper bona creas, sancti✠ficas, vivi✠ficas, bene✠dicis, et præstas nobis.

BY WHOM, O Lord, Thou dost always create, sanctify, ✠ quicken, ✠ bless, ✠ and bestow upon us all these good things.

PER ip✠sum, et cum ip✠so, et in ip✠so, est tibi Deo Patri ✠ omnipotenti, in unitate Spiritus ✠ Sancti, omnis honor et gloria.

THROUGH Him, ✠ and with Him, ✠ and in Him, ✠ is to Thee, God the Father✠almighty, in the unity of the Holy ✠ Ghost, all honor and glory.

P. Per omnia sæcula sæculorum.
R. Amen.

P. World without end.
R. Amen.

The Pater Noster

Oremus

PRÆCEPTIS salutaribus moniti, et divina institutione formati, audemus dicere:

Let us pray

ADMONISHED by salutary precepts, and following divine directions, we presume to say:

PATER noster, qui es in cœlis: sanctificetur nomen tuum: adveniat regnum tuum: fiat voluntas tua, sicut in cœlo, et in terra. Panem nostrum quotidianum da nobis hodie: et dimitte nobis debita nostra, sicut et nos dimittimus debitoribus nostris. Et ne nos inducas in tentationem.

R. Sed libera nos a malo.

P. Amen.

LIBERA nos, quæsumus, Domine, ab omnibus malis præteritis, præsentibus, et futuris: et intercedente beata et gloriosa semper. virgine Dei genitrice Maria, cum beatis apostolis tuis Petro et Paulo atque Andrea, et omnibus sanctis, ✠ da propitius pacem in diebus nostris: ut ope misericordiæ tuæ adjuti, et a peccato simus semper liberi, et ab omni perturba-

OUR Father, Who art in heaven, hallowed be Thy name; Thy kingdom come; Thy will be done on earth as it is in heaven; give us this day our daily bread; and forgive us our trespasses, as we forgive those who trespass against us; and lead us not into temptation.

R. But deliver us from evil.

P. Amen.

DELIVER us, we beseech Thee, O Lord, from all evils, past, present, and to come: and by the intercession of the blessed and glorious Mary, ever a virgin, Mother of God, and of Thy holy apostles Peter and Paul, of Andrew, and of all the saints, ✠ graciously grant peace in our days, that through the help of Thy bountiful mercy we may always be free from

tione securi. Per eumdem Dominum nostrum Jesum Christum Filium tuum, qui tecum vivit et regnat in unitate Spiritus Sancti Deus.

sin and secure from all disturbance. Through the same Jesus Christ, Thy Son, our Lord, Who liveth and reigneth with Thee in the unity of the Holy Ghost.

P. Per omnia sæcula sæculorum.

R. Amen.

P. Pax ✠ Domini sit ✠ semper vobis✠ cum.

R. Et cum spiritu tuo.

P. World without end.

R. Amen.

P. May the peace ✠ of the Lord ✠ be always with you.

R. And with thy spirit.

HÆC commixtio et consecratio corporis et sanguinis Domini nostri Jesu Christi fiat accipientibus nobis in vitam æternam. Amen.

MAY this commingling and consecrating of the body and blood of our Lord Jesus Christ avail us who receive it unto life everlasting. Amen.

The Agnus Dei

AGNUS Dei, qui tollis peccata mundi: dona eis requiem.

LAMB of God, Who takest away the sins of the world: Grant them rest.

Agnus Dei, qui tollis peccata mundi: dona eis requiem.

Lamb of God, Who takest away the sins of the world: Grant them rest.

Agnus Dei, qui tollis peccata mundi: dona eis requiem sempiternam.

Lamb of God, Who takest away the sins of the world; grant them rest for evermore.

DOMINE Jesu Christe, Fili Dei vivi, qui ex voluntate Patris, cooperante Spiritu Sancto, per mortem tuam mundum vivificasti: libera me per hoc sacrosanctum Corpus et Sanguinem tuum ab omnibus iniquitatibus meis, et universis malis: et fac me tuis semper inhærere mandatis, et a te nunquam separari permittas: qui cum eodem Deo Patre et Spiritu Sancto vivis et regnas Deus in sæcula sæculorum. Amen.

LORD Jesus Christ, Son of the living God, Who, according to the will of the Father through the co-operation of the Holy Ghost, hast by Thy death given life to the world; deliver me by this Thy most sacred body and blood from all my iniquities, and from every evil. Make me always cleave to Thy commandments and never suffer me to be separated from Thee, Who with the same God the Father and the Holy Ghost livest and reignest God, world without end. Amen.

PERCEPTIO corporis tui, Domine Jesu Christe, quod ego indignus sumere præsumo, non mihi proveniat in

LET not the partaking of Thy body, O Lord Jesus Christ, which I, all unworthy, presume to receive, turn to my

judicium et condemnationem: sed pro tua pietate prosit mihi ad tutamentum mentis et corporis, et ad medelam percipiendam. Qui vivis et regnas cum Deo Patre in unitate Spiritus Sancti Deus, per omnia sæcula sæculorum. Amen.

judgment and condemnation; but through Thy lovingkindness may it be to me a safeguard and remedy for soul and body; Who, with God the Father, in the unity of the Holy Ghost, livest and reignest, God, world without end. Amen.

At the Communion

PANEM cœlestem accipiam, et nomen Domini invocabo.

I WILL take the bread of heaven, and will call upon the name of the Lord.

DOMINE, non sum dignus, ut intres sub tectum meum: sed tantum dic verbo, et sanabitur anima mea.

LORD, I am not worthy that Thou shouldst enter under my roof; but only say the word, and my soul shall be healed.

CORPUS Domini nostri Jesu Christi custodiat animam meam in vitam æternam. Amen.

MAY the body of Our Lord Jesus Christ keep my soul unto life everlasting. Amen.

QUID retribuam Domino pro omnibus quæ retribuit mihi? Calicem

WHAT shall I render unto the Lord for all the things that He hath

salutaris accipiam, et nomen Domini invocabo. Laudans invocabo Dominum, et ab inimicis meis salvus ero.

rendered unto me? I will take the chalice of salvation and will call upon the name of the Lord. With high praises will I call upon the Lord, and I shall be saved from all mine enemies.

SANGUIS Domini nostri Jesu Christi custodiat animam meam in vitam æternam. Amen.

MAY the blood of Our Lord Jesus Christ keep my soul unto life everlasting. Amen.

QUOD ore sumpsimus, Domine, pura mente capiamus: et de munere temporali fiat nobis remedium sempiternum.

INTO a pure heart, O Lord, may we receive the heavenly food which has passed our lips; bestowed upon us in time, may it be the healing of our souls for eternity.

CORPUS tuum, Domine, quod sumpsi, et sanguis, quem potavi, adhæreat visceribus meis: et præsta, ut in me non remaneat scelerum macula, quem pura et sancta refecerunt sacramenta: Qui vivis et regnas in sæcula

MAY Thy body, O Lord, which I have received, and Thy blood, which I have drunk, cleave to mine inmost parts; and do Thou grant that no stain of sin remain in me, whom pure and holy mysteries have refreshed: Who livest and reign-

sæculorum. Amen.   est, world without end. Amen.

The Communion

LUX æterna luceat eis, Domine: Cum sanctis tuis in æternum, quia pius es.

MAY light eternal shine upon them, O Lord: With Thy saints forever, because Thou art merciful.

V. Requiem æternam dona eis, Domine, et lux perpetua luceat eis.

Eternal rest grant unto them, O Lord, and let perpetual light shine upon them.

Cum sanctis, etc.

With Thy saints, etc.

P. Dominus vobiscum.

P. The Lord be with you.

R. Et cum spiritu tuo.

R. And with thy spirit.

P. Oremus.

P. Let us pray.

The Postcommunion

PRÆSTA, quæsumus, omnipotens Deus, ut anima famuli tui N., quæ hodie de hoc sæculo migravit, his sacrificiis purgata, et a peccatis expedita, indulgentiam pariter et requiem capiat sempiternam. Per Dominum nostrum Jesum Christum, etc.

GRANT, we beseech Thee, O Almighty God, that the soul of Thy servant, N., which hath to-day departed this life, being purified by this sacrifice and rid of sins, may obtain alike pardon and everlasting rest. Through our Lord Jesus Christ, etc.

P. Dominus vobiscum.

R. Et cum spiritu tuo.

P. Requiescant in pace.

R. Amen.

P. The Lord be with you.

R. And with thy spirit.

P. May they rest in peace.

R. Amen.

PLACEAT tibi, Sancta Trinitas, obsequium servitutis meæ: et præsta ut sacrificium quod oculis tuæ majestatis indignus obtuli, tibi sit acceptabile, mihique, et omnibus, pro quibus illud obtulit, sit, te miserante, propitiabile. Per Christum Dominum nostrum. Amen.

MAY the lowly homage of my service be pleasing to Thee, O most holy Trinity: and do Thou grant that the sacrifice which I, all unworthy, have offered up in the sight of Thy majesty may be acceptable to Thee, and, because of Thy loving-kindness, may avail to atone to Thee for myself and for all those for whom I have offered it up. Through Christ our Lord. Amen.

P. Dominus vobiscum.

R. Et cum spiritu tuo.

P. Initium sancti Evangelii secundum Joannem.

R. Gloria tibi, Domine.

P. The Lord be with you.

R. And with thy spirit.

P. The beginning of the Gospel, according to St. John.

R. Glory be to Thee, O Lord.

The Last Gospel

IN PRINCIPIO erat Verbum, et Verbum erat apud Deum, et Deus erat Verbum. Hoc erat in principio apud Deum. Omnia per ipsum facta sunt, et sine ipso factum est nihil quod factum est. In ipso vita erat, et vita erat lux hominum, et lux in tenebris lucet, et tenebræ eam non comprehenderunt. Fuit homo missus a Deo, cui nomen erat Joannes. Hic venit in testimonium, ut testimonium perhiberet de lumine, ut omnes crederent per illum. Non erat ille lux, sed ut testimonium perhiberet de lumine. Erat lux vera, quæ illuminat omnem hominem venientem in hunc mundum. In mundo erat, et mundus per ipsum factus est, et mundus eum non cognovit. In propria venit, et sui eum

IN THE beginning was the Word, and the Word was with God, and the Word was God. The same was in the beginning with God. All things were made by Him, and without Him was made nothing that was made. In Him was life, and the life was the light of men: and the light shineth in darkness, and the darkness did not comprehend it. There was a man sent from God, whose name was John. This man came for a witness to give testimony of the light, that all men might believe through him. He was not the light, but was to give testimony of the light. That was the true light which enlighteneth every man that cometh into this world. He was in the world, and the world was made by

non receperunt. Quotquot autem receperunt eum, dedit eis potestatem filios Dei fieri, his qui credunt in nomine ejus, qui non ex sanguinibus, neque ex voluntate carnis, neque ex voluntate viri, sed ex Deo nati sunt. *Et Verbum caro factum est* et habitavit in nobis: et vidimus gloriam ejus, gloriam quasi unigeniti a Patre, plenum gratiæ et veritatis.

Him, and the world knew Him not. He came unto His own, and His own received Him not. But as many as received Him, to them He gave power to become the sons of God: to them that believe in His name: who are born, not of blood, nor of the will of the flesh, nor of the will of man, but of God. *And the Word was made flesh* and dwelt among us, and we saw His glory, the glory as of the only-begotten of the Father, full of grace and truth.

R. Deo gratias.

R. Thanks be to God.

The Absolution

(After Mass)

The priest says:

NON intres in judicium cum servo tuo, Domine, quia nullus apud te justificabitur homo, nisi per te omnium peccatorum ei tribua-

ENTER not into judgment with Thy servant, O Lord, for in Thy sight shall no man be justified, unless remission of all sins be accorded

tur remissio. Non ergo eum, quæsumus, tua judicialis sententia premat, quem tibi vera supplicatio fidei Christianæ commendat: sed gratia tua illi succurrente, mereatur evadere judicium ultionis, qui dum viveret, insignitus est signaculo sanctæ Trinitatis: Qui vivis et regnas in sæcula sæculorum.

him by Thee. We beseech Thee, therefore, that Thy judicial sentence weigh not heavily upon him [her] who is commended to Thee by the true supplication of the Christian faith; but, with the help of Thy grace, may he [she] be worthy to escape the sentence of vengeance, seeing that, while he [she] lived, he [she] was sealed with the seal of the Holy Trinity. Who livest and reignest world without end.

R. Amen.

R. Amen.

Then is sung or said the following:

LIBERA me, Domine, de morte æterna, in die illa tremenda: Quando cœli movendi sunt et terra: Dum veneris judicare sæculum per ignem.

DELIVER me, O Lord, from eternal death on that dreadful day: when the heavens and the earth shall be moved, and Thou shalt come to judge the world by fire.

V. Tremens factus sum ego, et timeo, dum discussio vene-

V. I am struck with fear and trembling when I reflect

rit, atque ventura ira. Quando cœli movendi sunt, et terra.

upon the judgment and the wrath to come. When the heavens and the earth shall be moved.

V. Dies illa, dies iræ, calamitatis et miseriæ, dies magna, et amara valde: Dum veneris judicare sæculum per ignem.

V. That day, a day of wrath, of wasting, and of misery, a dreadful and exceeding bitter day, when Thou shalt come to judge the world by fire.

V. Requiem æternam dona ei, Domine, et lux perpetua luceat ei.

V. Eternal rest grant unto him [her], O Lord; and let perpetual light shine upon him [her].

R. Libera me *usque ad V.* Tremens.
Kyrie eleison.

R. Deliver me, etc., *as far as V.* I am struck.
Lord, have mercy on us.

Christe eleison.

Christ, have mercy on us.

Kyrie eleison.

Lord, have mercy on us.

Pater noster (*secreto*).

Our Father (*inaudibly*).

During the Our Father the priest sprinkles the corpse with Holy Water and incenses it; then he says:

V. Et ne nos inducas in tentationem.

V. And lead us not into temptation.

R. Sed libera nos a malo.

R. But deliver us from evil.

V. A porta inferi.

R. Erue, Domine, animam ejus.

V. Requiescat in pace.

R. Amen.

V. Domine, exaudi orationem meam.

R. Et clamor meus ad te veniat.

V. Dominus vobiscum.

R. Et cum spiritu tuo.

V. From the gate of hell.

R. Deliver his [her] soul, O Lord.

V. May he [she] rest in peace.

R. Amen.

V. O Lord, hear my prayer.

R. And let my cry come unto Thee.

V. The Lord be with you.

R. And with thy spirit.

Oremus

DEUS, cui proprium est misereri semper et parcere: te supplices exoramus pro anima famuli tui N., quam hodie de hoc sæculo migrare jussisti: ut non tradas eam in manus inimici, neque obliviscaris in finem, sed jubeas eam a sanctis angelis suscipi, et ad patriam paradisi perduci: ut quia in te speravit et credidit, non pœnas inferni sustineat, sed gaudia æterna possideat. Per

Let us pray

O GOD, Whose property is always to have mercy and to spare, we humbly beseech Thee for the soul of Thy servant N., which Thou hast this day commanded to depart out of this world: that Thou deliver it not into the hands of the enemy, nor forget it unto the end; but command it to be received by Thy holy angels, and conducted into paradise, its true country;

Christum Dominum nostrum.

that, as in Thee it hath hoped and believed, it may not suffer the pains of hell, but may take possession of eternal joys. Through Christ our Lord.

R. Amen.

R. Amen.

After this, the body is borne to the grave. On the way the following prayer is said:

IN PARADISUM deducant te angeli: in tuo adventu suscipiant te martyres, et perducant te in civitatem sanctam Jerusalem. Chorus angelorum te suscipiat, et cum Lazaro quondam paupere æternam habeas requiem.

MAY the angels lead thee into paradise: may the martyrs receive thee at thy coming, and take thee to Jerusalem the holy city. May the choirs of the angels receive thee and mayest thou have rest everlasting with Lazarus once a beggar.

On reaching the grave, if it be not blessed, it is blessed by the priest as follows:

Oremus

Let us pray

DEUS, cujus miseratione animæ fidelium requiescunt, hunc tumulum benedicere dignare, eique angelum tuum sanctum deputa custo-

O GOD, through Whose tender mercy the souls of the faithful departed are at rest, vouchsafe to bless this grave, and assign thereto

dem: et quorum quarumque corpora hic sepeliuntur, animas eorum ab omnibus absolve vinculis delictorum, ut in te semper cum sanctis tuis sine fine lætentur. Per Christum Dominum nostrum.

R. Amen.

Thy holy angel as its keeper; and absolve from all the bonds of sin the souls of those whose bodies are here buried, that with Thy saints they may ever rejoice in Thee to all eternity. Through Christ our Lord.

R. Amen.

The corpse and grave are sprinkled with Holy Water and incensed by the priest, whereupon the body is deposited in the grave. The priest then says:

Ant. Ego sum.

Ant. I am.

Canticum Zachariæ
Luc. i. 68, 79

Canticle of Zachary
Luke i. 68, 79

BENEDICTUS Dominus Deus Israel,* quia visitavit, et fecit redemptionem plebis suæ.

BLESSED be the Lord God of Israel, because He hath visited, and wrought the redemption of His people:

Et erexit cornu salutis nobis,* in domo David pueri sui.

And hath raised up a horn of salvation to us, in the house of David His servant.

Sicut locutus est per os sanctorum,* qui a sæculo sunt, prophetarum ejus.

As He spoke by the mouth of His holy prophets, who are from the beginning.

Salutem ex inimicis nostris,* et de manu omnium qui oderunt nos.

Salvation from our enemies and from the hand of all who hate us.

Ad faciendam misericordiam cum patribus nostris:* et memorari testamenti sui sancti.

To show mercy to our fathers, and to remember His holy covenant:

Jusjurandum, quod juravit ad Abraham patrem nostrum,* daturum se nobis:

The oath, which He swore to Abraham our father, that He would grant unto us.

Ut sine timore de manu inimicorum nostrorum liberati,* serviamus illi.

That being delivered from the hand of our enemies, we may serve Him without fear.

In sanctitate et justitia coram ipso,* omnibus diebus nostris.

In holiness and justice before Him all our days.

Et tu puer, Propheta Altissimi vocaberis:* præibis enim ante faciem Domini parare vias ejus:

And thou, child, shalt be called the prophet of the Most High; for thou shalt go before the face of the Lord to prepare His ways.

Ad dandam scientiam salutis plebi ejus:* in remissionem peccatorum eorum.

To give knowledge of salvation to His people, unto the remission of their sins;

Per viscera miseri-

Through the bow-

cordiæ Dei nostri:* in quibus visitavit nos oriens ex alto:

els of the mercy of our Lord, in which the Dayspring from on high hath visited us.

Illuminare his, qui in tenebris et in umbra mortis sedent:* ad dirigendos pedes nostros in viam pacis.

To enlighten them that sit in darkness, and in the shadow of death; to direct our feet into the way of peace.

Requiem æternam dona ei, Domine.

Eternal rest grant unto him [her], O Lord.

Et lux perpetua luceat ei.

And let perpetual light shine upon him [her].

Ant. Ego sum resurrectio et vita; qui credit in me, etiam si mortuus fuerit, vivet; et omnis qui vivet, et credit in me, non morietur in æternum.

Ant. I am the resurrection and the life; he who believeth in Me, although he be dead, shall live: and every one who liveth and believeth in Me shall not die forever.

Kyrie eleison.

Lord, have mercy on us.

Christe eleison.

Christ, have mercy on us.

Kyrie eleison.

Lord, have mercy on us.

Pater noster (*secreto*).

Our Father (*inaudibly*).

The corpse is sprinkled with Holy Water by the priest.

V. Et ne nos inducas in tentationem.

R. Sed libera nos a malo.

V. A porta inferi.

R. Erue, Domine, animam ejus.

V. Requiescat in pace.

R. Amen.

V. Domine, exaudi orationem meam.

R. Et clamor meus ad te veniat.

V. Dominus vobiscum.

R. Et cum spiritu tuo.

V. And lead us not into temptation.

R. But deliver us from evil.

V. From the gate of hell.

R. Deliver his [her] soul, O Lord!

V. May he [she] rest in peace.

R. Amen.

V. O Lord, hear my prayer.

R. And let my cry come unto Thee.

V. The Lord be with you.

R. And with thy spirit.

Oremus

HAC, quæsumus Domine, hanc cum servo tuo defuncto [*vel* famula tua defuncta] misericordiam, ut factorum suorum in pœnis non recipiat vicem, qui [*vel* quæ] tuam in votis tenuit voluntatem; ut sicut hic eum [*vel* eam] vera fides junxit fidelium turmis,

Let us pray

GRANT, O Lord, we beseech Thee, this mercy unto Thy servant deceased, that, having in desire kept Thy will, he [she] may not suffer in requital of his [her] deeds: and as a true faith joined him [her] unto the company of Thy faithful here below,

ita illic eum [*vel* eam] tua miseratio societ angelicis choris. Per Christum Dominum nostrum.

R. Amen.

V. Requiem æternam dona ei, Domine.

R. Et lux perpetua luceat ei.

V. Requiescat in pace.

R. Amen.

V. Anima ejus, et animæ omnium fidelium defunctorum per misericordiam Dei requiescant in pace.

R. Amen.

so may Thy tender mercy give him [her] place above, among the angel choirs. Through Christ our Lord.

R. Amen.

V. Eternal rest grant unto him [her], O Lord!

R. And let perpetual light shine upon him [her].

V. May he [she] rest in peace.

R. Amen.

V. May his [her] soul and the souls of all the faithful departed, through the mercy of God, rest in peace.

R. Amen.

In returning from the grave the Antiphon Si iniquitates *and the Psalm* De profundis *(p. 226) are recited.*

Prayers at the Grave

Let us pray

O GOD, the Creator and Redeemer of all the faithful, hear our supplications and through Thine infinite love and mercy graciously grant to the soul of Thy servant departed the remission of all his [her] sins, by which he [she] may have deserved the severity of Thy divine justice and punishments in the world to come. Vouchsafe to him [her] grace and mercy before Thy divine tribunal, and let him [her] attain to everlasting rest and happiness through the infinite merits of Jesus Christ. Amen.

O God, great and omnipotent Judge of the living and the dead, before Whom we are all to appear after this short life, to render an account of our works, let our hearts, we pray Thee, be deeply moved at this sight of death, and while we consign the body of the deceased to the earth let us be mindful of our own frailty and mortality, that, walking always in Thy fear and in the ways of Thy commandments, we may after our departure from this world experience a merciful judgment and rejoice in everlasting happiness. Through Christ our Lord. Amen.

Let us pray

GRANT, O Lord, we beseech Thee, that whilst we lament the departure of our brother [sister], Thy servant, out of this life, we may bear in mind that we are most certainly to follow him [her]. Give us grace to make ready for that last hour by a devout and holy life, and protect us against a sudden and unprovided death. Teach us how to watch and pray, that when Thy summons comes, we may go forth to meet the Bridegroom and enter with Him into life everlasting. Through the same Christ our Lord. Amen.

Let us pray

ALMIGHTY and most merciful Father, Who knowest the weakness of our nature, bow down Thine ear in pity unto Thy servants, upon whom Thou hast laid the heavy burden of sorrow. Take away out of their hearts the spirit of rebellion and teach them to see Thy good and gracious purpose working in all the trials which Thou dost send upon them. Grant that they may not languish in fruitless and unavailing grief, nor sorrow as those who have no hope, but through their tears look meekly up to Thee, the God of all consolation. Through the same Christ our Lord. Amen.

Mass on the Third, Seventh, or Thirtieth Day after the Death of One of the Faithful

On the third, seventh, and thirtieth days after the death, or (if such be the custom) after the funeral of one of the faithful, the Mass is the same as on page 283, but with Collect, Secret, and Postcommunion as follows:

Collect

WE BESEECH Thee, O Lord, that Thou vouchsafe to grant to the soul of Thy servant, N., the third (*or* seventh *or* thirtieth) day of whose burial we commemorate, companionship with Thy saints and elect, and pour upon it the perennial dew of Thy mercy. Through Our Lord.

Secret

LOOK with favor, we beseech Thee, O Lord, upon the offerings we make for the soul of Thy servant, N., that, being purged by the heavenly remedies, it may repose in Thy love. Through Our Lord.

Postcommunion

RECEIVE, O Lord, our prayers for the soul of Thy servant, N., that whatever blemishes may have adhered to it from its contact with earth may be wiped away, by the mercy of Thy pardon. Through Our Lord.

Mass on the Anniversary Day of the Death of One or More of the Faithful

The Mass is said as on page 232, but the Collect, Epistle, Gospel, Secret, and Postcommunion are as below.

Should the anniversary be kept of one person only, the words of the prayers are put into the singular number.

Collect

O GOD, the Lord of mercies, grant to the souls of Thy servants and handmaids, the anniversary of whose burial we commemorate, an abode of refreshment, the beatitude of rest, and the brightness of light. Through Our Lord.

Epistle

2 Mach. xii. 43-46

IN THOSE days, the most valiant man Judas, making a gathering, sent twelve thousand drachms of silver to Jerusalem for sacrifice to be offered for the sins of the dead, thinking well and religiously concerning the resurrection (for if he had not hoped that they that were slain should rise again, it would have seemed superfluous and vain to pray for the dead); and because he considered that they who had fallen asleep with godliness, had great grace laid up for them. It is therefore a holy and wholesome thought to pray for the dead, that they may be loosed from sins.

Gospel

John vi. 37-40

AT THAT time, Jesus said to the multitudes of the Jews, All that the Father giveth Me shall come to Me; and him that cometh to Me I will not cast out: because I came down from heaven, not to do My own will, but the will of Him that sent Me. Now this is the will of the Father Who sent Me, that of all that He hath given Me, I should lose nothing, but should raise it up again in the last day; and this is the will of My Father that sent Me, that every one who seeth the Son, and believeth in Him, may have life everlasting; and I will raise him up in the last day.

Secret

BE PROPITIATED, O Lord, by our supplications for the souls of Thy servants and handmaids, whose anniversary is kept to-day, for whom we offer Thee the sacrifice of praise, that Thou vouchsafe to join them to the company of Thy saints. Through Our Lord.

Postcommunion

GRANT, we beseech Thee, O Lord, that the souls of Thy servants and handmaids, the anniversary of whose burial we commemorate, may be purged by this sacrifice and obtain alike forgiveness and everlasting rest. Through Our Lord.

The Mass of All Souls' Day

The Mass is said as on page 232, but the Collect Epistle, Gospel, Secret, and Postcommunion are as below.

Collect

O GOD, the Creator and Redeemer of all the faithful, grant to the souls of Thy servants and handmaids the remission of all their sins, that they may obtain by loving prayers the forgiveness which they have always desired. Through Our Lord.

Epistle

I Cor. xv. 51–57

BRETHREN, behold, I tell you a mystery: we shall all indeed rise again, but we shall not all be changed. In a moment, in the twinkling of an eye, at the last trumpet; for the trumpet shall sound, and the dead shall rise again incorruptible, and we shall be changed. For this corruptible must put on incorruption, and this mortal must put on immortality. And when this mortal hath put on immortality, then shall come to pass the saying that is written, Death is swallowed up in victory. O death, where is thy victory? O death, where is thy sting? Now the sting of death is sin: and the strength of sin is the law. But thanks be to God, Who hath given us the victory through Our Lord Jesus Christ.

Gospel

John v. 25–29

AT THAT time, Jesus said to the multitudes of the Jews, Amen, amen, I say unto you, that the hour cometh, and now is, when the dead shall hear the voice of the Son of God; and they that hear shall live. For as the Father hath life in Himself, so He hath given to the Son also to have life in Himself; and He hath given Him power to do judgment, because He is the Son of man. Wonder not at this, for the hour cometh wherein all that are in the graves shall hear the voice of the Son of God; and they that have done good things shall come forth unto the resurrection of life, but they that have done evil, unto the resurrection of judgment.

Secret

MERCIFULLY look down, we beseech Thee, O Lord, upon the sacrifice which we offer Thee for the souls of Thy servants and handmaids, that, to those on whom Thou didst confer the merit of Christian faith, Thou mayst also grant its reward. Through Our Lord.

Postcommunion

MAY the prayer of Thy suppliants profit the souls of Thy servants and handmaids, we beseech Thee, O Lord, that Thou mayst free them from all sins and make them sharers in Thy redemption. Who livest.

NOTE

Pope Benedict XV has granted priests permission to offer three Masses on All Souls' Day. One of these Masses the Celebrant may say according to his own intention; one must be offered for the faithful departed and the third for the intention of the Holy Father. The first Mass is that of All Souls' Day, page 283, the second, the Anniversary Mass, page 281, omitting in the prayers the few words referring to the anniversary only. In the third Mass the Epistle and Gospel are from the Common or Daily Mass of the Dead, page 286. The Prayer, Secret, and Postcommunion are modified so as to be general. In the prayer, " O God, the bestower of pardon," page 287, instead of "brethren, kindred, and benefactors," the words, " the souls of Thy servants and handmaids " are substituted; and so with the Secret and Postcommunion.

The Common or Daily Mass for the Dead

Any Mass whatever, whether festal, ferial, or votive, may be offered up for the repose of the soul or souls of one or more of the faithful departed. But it is not lawful to celebrate in black vestments, with the rite proper to Masses for the Dead on certain days of the year. In this Common or Daily Mass for the Dead (*Missa Quotidiana*), the number of prayers, with their corresponding Secrets and Postcommunions, may not be less than three; the first, that answering to the particular intention for which the Mass is offered up (for instance, for one or for several persons deceased, for a priest, for all buried in a graveyard, etc.), the second, either for all deceased brethren, relatives, and benefactors, or another at choice, and the last, that for all the faithful departed. The Sequence in low Masses of this kind may be recited or omitted at the choice of the celebrant. If the Mass be offered for the faithful departed *in general,* the prayers found in the *Common or Daily Mass for the Dead* are said.

It is of counsel, that, should the day on which it is desired to have a Mass said for the repose of the soul of a deceased person, happen to be one on which Masses for the dead are not permitted, the Mass of the occurring feast or feria be offered up for the intention, rather than that the benefit accruing to the suffering soul be delayed by waiting until a day supervene on which a Mass in black vestments may be said.

(The Mass is said as on page 232, but the Collects, Secrets, and Postcommunions are as mentioned above, and the Epistle and Gospel as given below.)

Collects
For Bishops or Priests Deceased

O GOD, Who, in the apostolic priesthood, didst cause Thy servants to be honored with pontifical (*or* sacerdotal) dignity, grant, we beseech Thee, that they may be joined in fellowship with Thine apostles for evermore. Through Our Lord.

For Deceased Brethren, Friends, and Benefactors

O GOD, the bestower of pardon and lover of man's salvation, we beseech Thy clemency, through the intercession of blessed Mary, ever a virgin, and all Thy saints, that the brethren, kindred, and benefactors of our congregation who have passed out of this world may together enjoy everlasting happiness.

For the Souls of All the Faithful Departed

O GOD, the creator and redeemer of all the faithful, grant to the souls of Thy servants and handmaids the remission of all their sins, that by devout prayers they may obtain the pardon which they ever desired. Who livest, etc.

Epistle

Apoc. xiv. 13

IN THOSE days I heard a voice from heaven, saying to me, Write, blessed are the dead, who die in the Lord. From henceforth now, saith the Spirit, that they may rest from their labors, for their works follow them.

Gospel

John vi. 51–55

AT THAT time, Jesus said to the multitudes of the Jews: I am the living bread, which came down from heaven. If any man eat of this bread he shall live for ever: and the bread that I will give is My flesh for the life of the world. The Jews therefore strove among themselves, saying, How can this man give us His flesh to eat? Then Jesus said to them, Amen, amen, I say unto you, Except you eat the flesh of the Son of man, and drink His blood, you shall not have life in you. He that eateth My flesh, and drinketh My blood, hath everlasting life: and I will raise him up in the last day.

Secrets

For Deceased Bishops or Priests

RECEIVE, we beseech Thee, O Lord, the sacrifices which we offer for the souls of Thy servants, bishops (*or* priests); that Thou mayst command those whom on earth Thou didst invest with the episcopal (*or* sacerdotal) dignity to be joined to the fellowship of Thy saints in the heavenly kingdom. Through.

For Deceased Brethren, Friends, and Benefactors

O GOD, Whose mercy is boundless, mercifully receive the prayers of our lowliness, and grant, through these sacraments of our salvation, to the souls of our brethren, kindred, and benefactors, to whom Thou didst grant the confession of Thy name, the remission of all sins.

For the Souls of All the Faithful Departed

MERCIFULLY look down, we beseech Thee, O Lord, upon the sacrifice which we offer Thee for the souls of Thy servants and handmaids, that, to those on whom Thou didst confer the gift of Christian faith, Thou mayst also grant its reward. Through.

Postcommunions

For Deceased Bishops or Priests

MAY Thy clemency, which we implore, O Lord, benefit the souls of Thy servants, bishops, (*or* priests), that, by Thy mercy they may attain to everlasting fellowship with Him in Whom they hoped and believed. Through.

For Deceased Brethren, Friends, and Benefactors

GRANT, we beseech Thee, O almighty and merciful God, that the souls of our brethren, kindred, and benefactors, for whom we have offered this sacrifice of praise to Thy majesty, being purified of all sins by the virtue of this sacrament, may, by Thy mercy, receive the beatitude of perpetual light.

For the Souls of All the Faithful Departed

MAY the prayer of Thy suppliants profit the souls of Thy servants and handmaids, we beseech Thee, O Lord, that Thou mayst free them from all sins and make them sharers in Thy redemption. Who livest.

Various Prayers for the Dead

See Note under the caption: "The Common or Daily Mass for the Dead," p. 286.

For a Deceased Pope

Prayer

O GOD, Who, in Thine ineffable providence, didst will that Thy servant, N., should be numbered among the high priests, grant, we beseech Thee, that he, who on earth held the place of Thine only-begotten Son, may be joined forevermore to the fellowship of Thy holy pontiffs. Through Our Lord.

Secret

RECEIVE, we beseech Thee, O Lord, the sacrifices, which we offer for the soul of Thy servant, N., supreme pontiff, that Thou mayst command him whom on earth Thou didst invest with the pontifical dignity to be joined to the fellowship of Thy saints in the heavenly kingdom.

Postcommunion

MAY Thy clemency, which we implore, O Lord, benefit the soul of Thy servant, N., supreme pontiff, that he may by Thy mercy attain to everlasting fellowship with Him in Whom he hoped and believed. Through Our Lord.

For a deceased cardinal the Prayer, Secret, and Postcommunion are those appointed, as follows, for a bishop, priest, or deacon, with mention inserted in these of his rank as a Prince of the Church.

For a Deceased Bishop

Prayer

O GOD, Who didst cause Thy servant, N., to be honored in the apostolic priesthood with the episcopal dignity, grant, we beseech Thee, that he may be joined to the fellowship of Thine apostles for evermore. Through.

Secret

RECEIVE, we beseech Thee, O Lord, the sacrifice which we offer for the soul of Thy servant, the pontiff, N., that Thou mayst command him, whom on earth Thou didst invest with the episcopal dignity, to be joined to the fellowship of Thy saints in the heavenly kingdom.   Through Our Lord.

Postcommunion

MAY Thy clemency, which we implore, O Lord, benefit the soul of Thy servant, the bishop, N., that, by Thy mercy, he may attain to everlasting fellowship with Him in Whom he hoped and believed. Through Our Lord.

Or the following:

Prayer

GRANT us, O Lord, that Thou give to be a companion of Thy saints the soul of Thy servant, N., bishop, whom Thou hast taken out of the toilsome struggle of this world. Through Our Lord.

Secret

GRANT us, we beseech Thee, O Lord, that this oblation may benefit the soul of Thy servant, N., bishop, as by its offering Thou hast granted the sins of the whole world to be forgiven. Through Our Lord.

Postcommunion

PURIFIED by this sacrifice, we beseech Thee, O almighty God, may the soul of Thy servant, N., bishop, be worthy to be pardoned and enter into everlasting rest. Through Our Lord.

For a Priest Deceased

Prayer

O GOD, Who didst cause Thy servant, N., to be honored in the apostolic priesthood with the sacerdotal dignity, grant, we beseech Thee, that he may be joined to the fellowship of Thine apostles for evermore. Through Our Lord.

Secret

RECEIVE, we beseech Thee, O Lord, the sacrifice which we offer for the soul of Thy servant, N., that Thou mayst command him, whom on earth Thou didst invest with the sacerdotal dignity, to be joined to the fellowship of Thy saints in the heavenly kingdom. Through Our Lord.

Postcommunion

MAY Thy clemency, which we implore, O Lord, benefit the soul of Thy servant, N., priest, that he may attain to everlasting fellowship with Him in Whom he hoped and believed. Through Our Lord.

Or the following:

Prayer

GRANT, we beseech Thee, O Lord, that the soul of Thy servant, N., the priest, whom, while he dwelt in this world, Thou didst adorn with sacred gifts, may evermore rejoice in the glory of heaven. Through Our Lord.

Secret

RECEIVE, we beseech Thee, O Lord, the sacrifice we offer for the soul of Thy servant, N., that, as Thou didst grant him the dignity of the priesthood, Thou wilt also grant him its reward. Through Our Lord.

Postcommunion

GRANT, we beseech Thee, O almighty God, that Thou command the soul of Thy servant, N., the priest, to be a sharer of

everlasting beatitude in the congregation of
the just.   Through Our Lord.

For a Man, Other than a Priest, Deceased

Prayer

INCLINE Thine ear, O Lord, to our
prayers, with which we supplicate Thy
mercy that Thou set the soul of Thy servant,
which Thou hast commanded to pass from
this world, in a region of peace and light,
and order that it be of the fellowship of the
saints.   Through Our Lord.

Secret

CONSENT, we beseech Thee, O Lord,
that the soul of Thy servant may be
benefited by this oblation, by the offering of
which Thou hast granted the sins of the
whole world to be forgiven.   Through.

Postcommunion

ABSOLVE, we beseech Thee, O Lord,
the soul of Thy servant from every
bond of sin, that, in the glory of the resurrection, he may rise to a new and better life
with Thy saints and elect.   Through Our
Lord.

For a Woman Deceased

Prayer

WE BESEECH Thee, O Lord, that of
Thy loving-kindness Thou have mercy on the soul of Thy handmaid, free her
from the defilements of this mortal life and

number her for evermore among the saved. Through Our Lord.

Secret

BY THESE sacrifices, without which no one hath ever been free of offence, may the soul of Thy handmaid be rid of all sins, we beseech Thee, O Lord; that by these offices of pious propitiation it may obtain everlasting mercy. Through.

Postcommunion

MAY the soul of Thy handmaid, we beseech Thee, O Lord, partake of eternal light, as it hath obtained the sacrament of Thine everlasting mercy. Through Our Lord.

For the Father and Mother of the Celebrating Priest
Prayer

O GOD, Who hast commanded us to honor our father and mother, in Thy clemency have mercy upon the souls of my father and mother, and pardon their sins; and make me to see them in the joy of the eternal brightness. Through Our Lord.

Secret

RECEIVE, O Lord, the sacrifice which I offer Thee for the souls of my father and mother, and grant them everlasting joy in the land of the living; and make me to share with them in the happiness of the saints. Through Our Lord.

Postcommunion

MAY the partaking of the heavenly sacrament, we beseech Thee, O Lord, obtain rest and light everlasting for the souls of my father and mother; and may Thy eternal grace crown me with them. Through Our Lord.

Should the Mass be offered up by a priest for his father only, or for his mother only, the above prayers are worded in the singular number. When the Holy Sacrifice is offered up for the fathers and mothers of others besides the celebrant, in place of " my father and mother " is said " our fathers and mothers."

For Deceased Brethren, Friends, and Benefactors

The Prayer, O God, the bestower of pardon (see " Common or Daily Mass for the Dead,' p. 287), Secret, and Postcommunion are said with the proper variations.

For All Who Are Buried in a Cemetery or Graveyard

Prayer

O GOD, by Whose mercy the souls of the faithful find rest, mercifully grant pardon of sins to Thy servants and handmaids, and to all who, here and elsewhere, repose in Christ, that, being freed from all guilt, they may rejoice with Thee for evermore. Through the same Our Lord.

Secret

GRACIOUSLY receive, O Lord, the sacrifice offered for the souls of Thy servants and handmaids, and of all Catholics who sleep in Christ, whether in this place or elsewhere, that, being delivered from the bonds of grim death by this most excellent sacrifice, they may be found worthy of life everlasting. Through the same Our Lord.

Postcommunion

O GOD, the light of faithful souls, give ear to our supplications, and grant to Thy servants and handmaids, whose bodies, here and elsewhere, repose in Christ, an abode of refreshment, the blessedness of rest, and the brightness of light. Through the same Our Lord.

For More than One Person Deceased

Prayer

O GOD, Whose property is ever to pity and to spare, have mercy on the souls of thy servants and handmaids, and forgive them all their sins, that, being loosed from the bonds of mortality, they may be found worthy to enter into life. Through Our Lord.

Secret

CONSENT, we beseech Thee, O Lord, that this oblation benefit the souls of Thy servants and handmaids, as Thou hast granted that by the offering of it the sins of all the world should be forgiven. Through Our Lord.

Postcommunion

O GOD, Who alone art competent to administer healing remedies after death, grant, we beseech Thee, that the souls of Thy servants and handmaids, rid of earthly contagion, may be numbered among those whom Thou hast redeemed. Who livest.

For More than One Person Deceased. Other Prayers

Prayer

GRANT, we beseech Thee, O Lord, everlasting mercy to the souls of Thy servants and handmaids, that the faith and hope which they placed in Thee may avail them for eternity. Through Our Lord.

Secret

LOOK with favor upon these gifts, we beseech Thee, O Lord, and may that which we offer with supplication to the praise of Thy name avail for the pardon of the departed. Through Our Lord.

Postcommunion

WE POUR forth, O Lord, our prayers and supplications for the souls of Thy servants and handmaids, beseeching that Thou mercifully forgive whatever faults they have committed in their earthly careers, and set them in the blissful abode of Thy redeemed. Through Our Lord.

Devotions for Confession

Before Confession

Reflect that this confession may be the last of your life. Therefore, prepare yourself for it as if you were lying sick upon your death-bed, and already at the brink of the grave. Ask God to give you the grace to make a good examination of conscience, the light to see your sins clearly, and the strength to make a sincere confession and to amend your life.

Prayer

MOST merciful God, Father in heaven, relying on Thy goodness and mercy, I come to Thee with filial confidence to confess my sins and to implore Thy forgiveness. Thou wilt not despise a contrite and humble heart. Bless me and receive me again into Thy favor; I acknowledge that I have been most ungrateful to Thee, but I sincerely repent and detest the wrong I have done, and I desire henceforth to walk in the way of perfection, in accordance with Thy holy will.

O Jesus, my Saviour, my good Shepherd, I have strayed far from the path that Thou hast marked out for me; I did not follow in Thy footsteps; I wandered into forbidden places. Repentant and sorrowful, I beg to be admitted again into the fold of Thy faithful followers. I want to confess my sins with perfect sincerity, as if I were at the

209

point of death. My Jesus, I look to Thee with confidence for the grace to examine my conscience well.

O Holy Spirit, come in Thy mercy; enlighten my mind and strengthen my will that I may know my sins, humbly confess them, and sincerely amend my life.

Mary, my mother, immaculate spouse of the Holy Ghost, refuge of sinners, assist me by thy intercession.

Holy angels and saints of God, pray for me. Amen.

Examination of Conscience

BEGIN by examining yourself on your last confession: Whether a grievous sin was forgotten through want of proper examination, or concealed or disguised through shame. Whether you confessed without a true sorrow and a firm purpose of amendment. Whether you have repaired evil done to your neighbor. Whether the penance was performed without voluntary distractions. Whether you have neglected your confessor's counsel, and fallen at once into habitual sin.

Then examine yourself on the ten commandments, the commandments of the Church, the seven capital sins, the duties of your state of life, and your ruling passion. Calmly recall the different occasions of sin which have fallen in your way, or to which your state and condition in life expose you, the places you have frequented, the persons with whom you have associated. Do not neglect to consider the circumstances which alter the grievousness of the sin, nor the various ways in which we become accessory to the sins of others.

Preliminary Examination

WHEN did you make your last confession? Did you take sufficient pains to awaken contrition?

Did you omit to confess a mortal sin either intentionally or through forgetfulness?

Did you intentionally neglect to say the penance which was imposed on you, or were you so careless as to forget it?

Have you carried out the resolutions you made at your last confession or have you paid no heed at all to them?

Examination on the Ten Commandments of God

I. HAVE you doubted in matters of faith? Murmured against God at your adversity or at the prosperity of others? Despaired of His mercy?

Have you believed in fortune-tellers or consulted them?

Have you gone to places of worship belonging to other denominations?

Have you recommended yourself daily to God? Neglected your morning or night prayers? Omitted religious duties or practices through motives of human respect?

Have you read books, papers, and periodicals of anti-Catholic or atheistic tendency? Made use of superstitious practices? Spoken with levity or irreverence of priests, Religious, or sacred objects?

II. Have you taken the name of God in vain? Profaned anything relating to religion?

Have you sworn falsely, rashly, or in slight and trivial matters? Cursed yourself or others, or any creature? Angered others so as to make them swear, or blaspheme God?

III. Have you kept holy the Lord's Day, and all other days commanded to be kept holy? Bought or sold things not of necessity on that day? Done or commanded some servile work not of necessity? Missed Mass or been wilfully distracted during Mass? Talked, gazed, or laughed in the church?

IV. Have you honored your parents, superiors, and masters, according to your just duty? Deceived them? Disobeyed them?

Have you failed in due reverence to aged persons?

V. Have you procured, desired, or hastened the death of any one? Borne hatred? Oppressed any one? Desired revenge? Not forgiven injuries? Refused to speak to others? Used provoking language? Injured others? Caused enmity between others?

VI and IX. Have you been in lewd company? Read immodest books? Been guilty of unchaste songs, discourses, words, or actions? Wilfully entertained impure thoughts or desires?

VII. Have you been guilty of stealing, or of deceit in buying, or selling, in regard to wares, prices, weights, or measures? Have you wilfully damaged another man's goods or negligently spoiled them?

VIII. Have you borne false witness? Called injurious names? Disclosed another's sins? Flattered others? Judged rashly?

X. Have you coveted unjustly anything that belongs to another?

Examination on the Precepts of the Church

HAVE you gone to confession at least once a year? Received holy communion during Eastertime?

Have you violated the fasts of the Church, or eaten flesh-meat on prohibited days?

Have you sinned against any other Commandment of the Church?

Examine yourself also in regard to the seven capital sins and the nine ways of being accessory to another's sin.

After the Examination

HAVING discovered the sins of which you have been guilty, together with their number, enormity, or such circumstances as may change their nature, you should endeavor to excite in yourself a *heartfelt sorrow* for having committed them, and a sincere detestation of them. This being the most essential of all the dispositions requisite for a good confession, with what humility, fervor, and perseverance should you not importune Him who holds the hearts of men in His hands to grant it to you!

An Act of Contrition

Recite very attentively one of the following acts of contrition:

I

O MY God, I am heartily sorry for having offended Thee, and I detest all my sins, because I dread the loss of heaven and the pains of hell, but most of all because they displease Thee, my God, Who art all-good and deserving of all my love. I firmly resolve, with the help of Thy grace, to confess my sins, to do penance, and to amend my life.

II

O MY God, I am truly sorry that I have sinned, because Thou art infinitely good and sin displeases Thee. I purpose, with the help of Thy grace, never more to offend Thee, and to avoid the occasions of sin.

III

O MY God, I am heartily sorry for having offended Thee; and I detest my sins above every other evil, because they displease Thee, my God, Who for Thy infinite goodness art so deserving of all my love; and I firmly resolve, by Thy holy grace, never more to offend Thee, and to amend my life.

An Act of Charity

O MY God, I love Thee with my whole heart and soul, and above all things, because Thou art infinitely good and perfect, and most worthy of all my love; and, for Thy sake, I love my neighbor as myself. Mercifully grant, O my God, that, having loved Thee on earth, I may love and enjoy Thee forever in heaven.

Approach the confessional with the same recollectedness and reverence as would fill your heart if Christ Our Lord were seated there in person ready to hear your confession. The priest is really the representative of Christ.

When you kneel down, say: " Bless me, Father, for I have sinned." Then tell when you made your last confession and begin the avowal of your sins. Confess all your sins with a contrite and humble heart, and conclude thus:

For these and all the sins of my past life, especially my sins of (*naming some grievous sin*), I am heartily sorry, beg pardon of God, and absolution of you, my Father.

Listen then with humility and docility to the instruction of your confessor.

While the priest pronounces the words of absolution, endeavor to excite an act of perfect contrition.

Thanksgiving after Confession

ETERNAL Father! I thank Thee for Thy goodness and mercy. Thou hast had compassion on me, although in my folly I had wandered far away from Thee and offended Thee most grievously. With fatherly love Thou hast received me anew after so many relapses into sin and forgiven me my offences through the holy sacrament of Penance. Blessed forever, O my God, be Thy loving-kindness, Thy infinite mercy! Never again will I grieve Thee by ingratitude, by disobedience to Thy holy will. All that I am, and all that I have, shall be consecrated to Thy service and Thy glory.

Ejaculations

ALL for Thee, most sacred Heart of Jesus!

Indulgence: 300 days, each time.—Pius X, Nov. 26, 1908.

Sacred Heart of Jesus, I trust in Thee.

Indulgence: 300 days, each time.—Pius X, June 27, 1906.

Jesus, my God, I love Thee above all things.

Indulgence: 50 days, each time, Pius IX, May 7, 1854.

Sweet Heart of Mary, be my salvation.

Indulgence: 300 days, each time.—Pius IX, Sept. 30, 1852.

Mary, our hope, have pity on us!

Indulgence: 300 days, each time.—Pius X, Jan. 8, 1906.

Devotions for Holy Communion

Before receiving holy communion, direct your intention; that is, offer to God your Mass and communion for the glory of His holy name, in thanksgiving for benefits received, in reparation for your sins and in humble supplication that you may obtain new graces and blessings, above all the gift of final perseverance. Offer to God also some special intention, *e.g.*, the conversion of a friend, the welfare of your family, the relief of the souls in Purgatory. Pray, also, according to the Holy Father's intention.

The Pope's intention always includes the following objects:

The progress of the Faith and triumph of the Church.

Peace and union among Christian princes and rulers.

The conversion of sinners.

The uprooting of heresy.

Resolve to struggle earnestly against your ruling passion and pray that the spirit of Christ may dominate all your actions.

Before Communion

Direct your intention [1]

O MOST high and mighty God, I, an unworthy sinner, desire to receive the

[1] From The Paradise of the Christian Soul.

sacrament of the most holy body and blood of Thy Son, for the praise and glory of Thy supreme majesty; in memory of the most holy life, passion, and death of Jesus Christ my Saviour; in thanksgiving for all Thy gifts and blessings bestowed upon me, an unworthy sinner, and on Thy whole Church; for the propitiation of my numberless sins; for the salvation of myself and my relations, N., N., and for the repose of the departed, N., N. Truly, O Lord, in Thee alone is all that can satisfy my heart's desire. For besides Thee what have I in heaven, or what do I desire upon earth? Wilt Thou not Thyself be our reward exceeding great?

Acts of Faith, Adoration, Hope, Charity, and Contrition

JESUS, I believe in Thee, because Thou art Truth itself.

JESUS, my God, I adore Thee here present in the Sacrament of Thy love.

JESUS, I hope in Thee, because Thou art merciful, and faithful to Thy promises.

JESUS, I love Thee, because Thou art all good, and worthy of all my love.

JESUS, my God, I am truly sorry for having sinned, because Thou art infinitely good and sin displeases Thee. I firmly resolve by the help of Thy grace never to offend Thee again.

Prayer

BEHOLD, my most loving Jesus, to what an excess Thy boundless love has carried Thee. Of Thine own flesh and precious blood Thou hast made ready for me a divine banquet in order to give me all Thyself. What was it that impelled Thee to this transport of love? It was Thy Heart, Thy loving Heart. O adorable Heart of my Jesus! burning furnace of divine Love! within Thy most sacred wound receive Thou my soul; that in that school of charity I may learn to requite the love of that God Who has given me such wondrous proofs of His love. Amen.

Indulgence: 100 days, once a day.—Pius VII, Feb. 9, 1818.

O JESUS, sweetest Love, come Thou to me;
Come down in all Thy beauty unto me;
Thou Who didst die for longing love of me;
And never, never more depart from me.
Free me, O beauteous God, from all but Thee;
Sever the chain that holds me back from Thee;
Call me, O tender Love, I cry to Thee;
Thou art my all! O bind me close to Thee.
                                        —Shapcote.

COME, my Jesus, come!

LORD, I am not worthy that Thou shouldst enter under my roof; but only say the word, and my soul shall be healed.

MAY the body of Our Lord Jesus Christ keep my soul unto life everlasting. Amen.

After Communion

Acts of Adoration, Thanksgiving, Reparation, and Prayer

WELCOME, dearest Jesus, welcome to my heart! With most holy Mary, with the angels and the saints, *I adore* Thee, my Lord and my God. To Thee be praise and glory now and forevermore.

With Magdalen I kiss Thy sacred feet. With John, the beloved disciple, I rest upon Thy Sacred Heart. I love Thee and desire to love Thee more and more. Speak to me and tell me what Thou wishest me to do. I am Thy servant, ready to follow Thee and willing to make any sacrifice for love of Thee. Establish Thy kingdom firmly in my heart; crush out its self-love and pride. I give *thanks* to Thee, O Lord, for condescending to come to me in the Sacrament of Thy love—to me, a sinner, to me, so wayward and unfaithful.

MARY, my queen, my mother, and all ye angels and saints of heaven, thank the Lord for me; praise Him for His goodness; bless Him for His mercy.

MY GOD! I am truly *sorry* for having offended Thee because Thou art infinitely good and worthy of all my love. Oh, how often and how grievously I have sinned against Thee! Have mercy on me, and according to the multitude of Thy tender mercies, blot out my iniquity. My loving Jesus, out of the grateful love I bear Thee, and to make *reparation* for my unfaithfulness to grace, I give Thee my heart, and I consecrate myself wholly to Thee; and with Thy help I purpose never to sin again. I will do all things to Thy greater glory. I will, indeed, seek to please Thee perfectly in thought, word, and deed; and I will honor Thee especially in the Holy Eucharist. My watchword shall be:

" *All for Thee, most Sacred Heart of Jesus!*"

I AM resolved to overcome my predominant passion and to resist every evil inclination of my heart. For love of Thee, my Lord and my God, I will also be kind to others in thought, word, and deed.

Now, my good Jesus, I *pray* Thee to bless me; keep me in Thy love; grant me the grace of final perseverance. Help me to become a saint.

Safeguarded by Thee in soul and in body, may I never swerve from the right road, but surely reach Thy kingdom, where—not in dim mysteries, as in this dark world of ours, but—face to face we shall look upon Thee. There wilt Thou satisfy me with Thyself and fill me with such sweetness that I shall neither hunger nor thirst forevermore: Who

with God the Father and the Holy Ghost
livest and reignest world without end. Amen.

Suscipe

MAKE, O Lord, and receive all my liberty,
my memory, my understanding, and
my whole will. Thou hast given me all that
I am, and all that I possess. I surrender it
all to Thee, that Thou mayst dispose of it
according to Thy will. Give me only Thy
love and Thy grace; with these I will be
rich enough, and will have no more to
desire.—St. Ignatius Loyola.

Indulgence: 300 days, once a day.—Leo XIII, May 26, 1883.

The Anima Christi

SOUL of Christ, sanctify me.
Body of Christ, save me.
Blood of Christ, inebriate me.
Water from the side of Christ, wash me.
Passion of Christ, strengthen me.
O good Jesus, hear me.
Within Thy wounds hide me.
Permit me not to be separated from Thee.
From the malignant enemy defend me.
In the hour of my death call me.
And bid me come to Thee,
That, with Thy saints, I may praise Thee
For ever and ever. Amen.

Indulgences: 300 days, each time. Seven years, if said after communion.—Pius IX, Jan. 9, 1854.

Prayer for the Church and the Supreme Pontiff;
for Friends, Relatives, and Benefactors; and for
the Holy Souls in Purgatory

O MOST Sacred Heart of Jesus, pour
down Thy blessings abundantly upon
Thy Church; upon the Supreme Pontiff, and
upon all the clergy; give perseverance to the
just; convert sinners; enlighten unbelievers; bless our parents, friends, and benefactors; help the dying; free the souls in
Purgatory; and extend over all hearts the
sweet empire of Thy love. Amen.

*Indulgence: 300 days, once a day.—Pius X, June 16,
1906.*

Ejaculation

DIVINE Heart of Jesus, convert sinners,
save the dying, deliver the Holy Souls
from Purgatory!

*Indulgence: 300 days, each time.—Pius X, Nov. 6,
1906.*

✠ Sacrum Convivium

Ant. O SACRED banquet, in which Christ
is received, the memory of His
passion is renewed, the mind is filled with
grace, and a pledge of future glory is given
to us.

V. Thou gavest them bread from heaven.

R. And therein was sweetness of every
kind.

Let us pray

O GOD, Who, in this wonderful sacrament, hast left us a memorial of Thy passion: grant us, we beseech Thee, so to venerate the sacred mysteries of Thy body and blood that we may ever feel within us the fruit of Thy redemption.

Prayer before a Representation of Jesus Crucified

LOOK down upon me, good and gentle Jesus, while before Thy face I humbly kneel, and with burning soul pray and beseech Thee 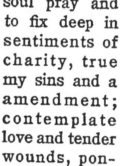 to fix deep in my heart lively sentiments of faith, hope, and charity, true contrition for my sins and a firm purpose of amendment; and while I contemplate with great love and tender pity Thy five wounds, pondering over them within me, and calling to mind the words which David, Thy prophet, said of Thee, my Jesus: " They have pierced My hands and My feet; they have numbered all My bones." (Ps. xxi. 17, 18.)

A plenary indulgence, applicable to the souls in Purgatory, may be gained by the faithful who, after having confessed their sins with sorrow and received holy communion, shall devoutly recite this prayer before an image or picture of Christ crucified, and shall pray for the intentions of the Holy Father.—Pius IX, July 31, 1858.

Our Father, Hail Mary, Glory, five times, for the intentions of the Pope.

Prayer [1]

JESUS, my Master, I am not my own. I have been bought at a great price by Thee! I desire not henceforth to live to myself, but to Thee, Who hast died for me. My life and my actions I dedicate to Thee, and whatever I do in word or work I sincerely desire and firmly resolve to do all in Thy name. My Jesus! this is all I can say. Do Thou in Thy mercy give me strength and wisdom to accomplish what I have resolved in Thy presence this day. Jesus, my God! Thou hast told me in Thine unerring word to cast all my care upon Thee, because Thou hast care of me! I do so; I cast all my sorrows, my solicitudes, and my uneasiness upon Thee. On *my part*, I will employ myself in promoting Thine honor and glory, by doing everything in Thy name. I know that on *Thine*, Thou wilt take into Thy hands all that concerns me. I will attend to Thee; Thou wilt take care of me. Divine Jesus! Sweet Saviour of my soul, let this contract be inviolable and eternal between us—"I to my Beloved, and my Beloved to me." Amen.

[1] Rev. Robert Haly, S.J., in A Gleaner's Sheaf.

Another Form of Devotions for Holy Communion

Before Communion

An Act of Faith and Adoration

MY LORD Jesus Christ, I believe that Thou art truly present in the Blessed Sacrament. I believe that in holy communion I shall receive Thy sacred body and Thy precious blood. My faith in Thy real presence in the Holy Eucharist is firmly founded on Thy word, O eternal Truth. My Saviour and my God, with the angels who surround Thy altar-throne, I bow down in humble adoration before Thy majesty.

An Act of Hope

JESUS, my God, Who in this wonderful sacrament hast left us a memorial of Thy passion and a pledge of future glory, I hope in Thee because Thou art infinitely good, almighty, and faithful to Thy promises. Through the merits of Thy precious blood I hope to obtain the pardon of my sins, the grace of final perseverance, and the everlasting happiness of heaven.

" In the shadow of Thy wings will I hope, until iniquity pass away." (Ps. lvi. 2.)

" Let Thy mercy come upon me, O Lord; Thy salvation, according to Thy word." (Ps. cxviii. 41.)

313

An Act of Love and Desire

O MY Jesus, I love Thee because Thou art infinitely good. Thou knowest well that I love Thee, but I do not love Thee enough. Oh, make me to love Thee more! O Love which burnest always and never failest, my God, Thou Who art charity itself, come, and kindle in my heart that divine fire which consumes the saints and transforms them into Thee. Eucharistic Heart of my Jesus, Whose blood is the life of my soul, may it be no longer I that live, but do Thou alone live in me.

An Act of Contrition

MY LORD and my God, I detest all the sins of my life. I am truly sorry that I have offended Thee, because Thou art infinitely good. I firmly resolve, by the help of Thy grace, never to offend Thee again, and carefully to avoid the occasions of sin. " Have mercy on me, O God, according to Thy great mercy." (Ps. l. 3.) " A contrite and humble heart, O God, Thou dost not despise." (Ps. li. 19.)

An Act of Humility

"O LORD of glory, O God of infinite sanctity, who am I that Thou shouldst deign to come to me!" "The heavens are not pure in Thy sight," and wilt Thou dwell in my heart? "Lord, I am not worthy that Thou shouldst enter under

my roof." The consciousness of my unworthiness would prompt me to exclaim,
"Depart from me, O Lord, for I am a
sinner," but Thy pressing invitation to approach Thy holy table encourages me, and
dispels all my fears. "Here I am, for Thou
didst call me." Come, then, O Jesus, take
possession of a heart that wishes to belong to
Thee. "Create in me a clean heart, O God,
and renew a right spirit within me." (Ps. l.
12.) "Have mercy on me, O God, and
according to the multitude of Thy tender
mercies blot out my iniquity." (Ps. l. 3.)

Domine Non Sum Dignus

LORD, I am not worthy that Thou
shouldst enter under my roof; but
only say the word, and my soul shall be
healed.

MAY the body of Our Lord Jesus Christ
keep my soul unto life everlasting.
Amen.

After Communion

Welcome

Acts of Faith, Adoration, Hope, Love, Consecration, Reparation, and Thanksgiving

"NOW, therefore, your King is here,
Whom you have chosen and desired." (I Kings xii.)

JESUS! Jesus! Jesus!
Thou hast come to me in the Sacrament

of Thy love. Thou hast been pleased to make my poor heart Thy sanctuary.

Welcome, Jesus, welcome! Thou art the God of my heart, and the God that is my portion forever. I praise Thee and bless Thee for Thy goodness and mercy. "Let all Thy works, O Lord, praise Thee; and let Thy saints bless Thee." (Ps. cxliv. 10.)

Faith and Adoration

RECEIVE, O Lord, my most profound homage in union with that of the angels and the saints. I bow down before Thee, and with all the powers of my soul I adore Thee. Thou art Christ, the Son of the living God.

"I see not with mine eyes Thy wounds,
as Thomas saw,
Yet own Thee for my God with equal love
and awe;
Oh, grant me, that my faith may ever
firmer be,
That all my hope and love may still repose
in Thee." —*Annus Sanctus.*

JESUS, light of the world, I believe in Thee, because Thou art truth itself, but do Thou increase and invigorate my faith that it may be productive of great things to Thy glory. Grant that I may do all things to please Thee.

" *Quid hoc ad æternitatem?* " All day long, in every varying circumstance, may my watchword be: " *How does this look in the light of eternity?* "

" THOU Who of old didst love Thy hand
   to lay
On the dull, vacant eyes that craved for
 light,
Behold I come to Thee, and, crying, pray:
O Christ, O Son of David, give me sight!

" A faith scarce clouded by the mists of
   earth,
A faith that pierceth heaven I ask of
 Thee,
Faith to prize all things by their lasting
 worth:
Thou canst, Thou wilt—O Lord, that I
 may see! "—*Before the Most Holy,*
    by Mother Mary Loyola.

" ' SHOW, O Lord, Thy ways to me, and
 teach me Thy paths.' (Ps. xxiv. 4.)
No one knows better than I how blind and
weak I am, but I wish to know, I wish to see,
what Thou desirest of me, and I will try
with all my heart, regardless of all obstacles, to accomplish it."—*Ibid.*

May the holy faith which ever illumines
my mind shine forth in all my actions before
the world to the glory of Thy name.

Hope

JESUS, I hope in Thee, I put all my trust
 in Thee, because Thou art full of compassion and mercy. " Thou art my Father;
my God, and the support of my salvation."
(Ps. lxxxviii. 27.)

 " To Thee, O Lord, have I lifted up my

soul: In Thee, O God, I put my trust."
(Ps. xxiv. 1, 2.)

Strengthen my hope, O Lord, and vouchsafe in Thy mercy that, fighting and conquering self on earth, I may one day rejoice triumphantly with Thee in heaven.

"O JESUS, lying here concealed before mine eye,
I pray Thou grant me that for which I ceaseless sigh,
To see the vision clear of Thine unveiled face,
Blest with the glories bright that fill Thy dwelling-place."
—*Annus Sanctus.*

Love

JESUS, I love Thee, because Thou art infinitely good. I love Thee because Thou hast redeemed me by Thy precious blood; I love Thee and thank Thee because Thou hast given Thyself to me in the Sacrament of Thy love.

Oh, grant that I may love Thee ever more and more. Thou art the Lamb of God, the Lamb without spot, that takest away the sins of the world. Take away from me whatever is hurtful to me and displeasing to Thee, and give me what Thou knowest to be pleasing to Thee and profitable to me.

May the sweet flame of Thy love consume my soul, so that I may die to the world for love of Thee, Who hast vouchsafed to die upon the cross for love of me.

MY GOD, my only good, Thou art all mine: Grant that I may be all Thine.

Consecration

MY LOVING Jesus, out of the grateful love I bear Thee, and to make reparation for my unfaithfulness to grace, I give Thee my heart, and I consecrate myself wholly to Thee; and with Thy help I purpose never to sin again. Dear Lord, I could never vie with Thee in generosity, but I love Thee, deign to accept my poor heart, and, though it is worth nothing, yet it may become something by Thy grace. Since it loves Thee, do Thou make it good and take it into Thy custody.

Prayer

O LORD Jesus, do Thou henceforth alone live within me. May the tongue whereon Thou hast rested never move to utter words other than such as would proceed from Thy meek and humble Heart. May the thoughts of my heart be in unison with Thine. May that mind which is in Thee be likewise in me. May I be consumed with the same desires; may I be one heart, one soul with Thee, O Jesus, Whom I bear within me. And let this union of my heart with Thine shed its influence over my whole life and conduct at all times and in all events, that so I may be able to draw other hearts to love Thee, and to devote themselves to Thy interests. This is the desire, O my

Jesus, with which Thou dost inspire me—
that Thy sweet name may be hallowed, that
Thy kingdom may come, and extend, and
triumph over all hearts and nations, and
that Thy will, which is ever one with Thy
Father's, may be perfectly accomplished.
Amen, Amen.

—The Voice of the Sacred Heart.

Oblation [1]

O SOVEREIGN and true leader, O Christ,
my king, I kneel before Thee here like
a vassal in the old feudal times to take my
oath of fealty. I place my joined hands
within Thy wounded hands and promise
Thee inviolable loyalty. I dedicate to Thee
all the powers of my soul, all the senses of
my body, all the affections of my heart.

MAKE, O Lord, all my liberty. Receive
my memory, my understanding, and
my whole will. All that I am, all that I have,
Thou hast given me, and I restore it all to
Thee, to be disposed of according to Thy
good pleasure. Give me only Thy love and
Thy grace; with these I am rich enough, and
I desire nothing more.

Thanksgiving

" I WILL extol Thee, O God, my king, and
I will bless Thy name forever; yea,
for ever and ever." (Ps. cxliv. 1). O ye
angels, archangels, thrones and domina-

[1] Oblation and Thanksgiving, adapted from Confession and
Communion, by Mother Mary Loyola.

tions, principalities and powers, virtues of heaven, cherubim and seraphim, adore our God for me; thank Him, and love Him with me. Patriarchs and prophets, apostles, all ye martyrs of Christ, holy confessors, virgins of the Lord, and all ye saints, adore Him, thank Him, love Him with me.

MOTHER of God, adore thy Son for me, thank Him, and love Him, for me.

Oh, give thanks to the Lord because He is good, because His mercy endureth forever.

Eternal Father, look upon the face of Thy Christ. Through Him and with Him and in Him be to Thee in the unity of the Holy Spirit all honor and glory.

" To the King of ages, immortal, invisible, the only God, be honor and glory for ever and ever. Amen." (I Tim. i. 17.)

Prayer of St. Thomas Aquinas

I GIVE thanks to Thee, O Lord, most holy, Father almighty, eternal God, that Thou hast vouchsafed, for no merit of mine own, but out of Thy pure mercy, to appease the hunger of my soul with the precious body and blood of Thy Son, Our Lord Jesus Christ.

Humbly I implore Thee, let not this holy communion be to me an increase of guilt unto my punishment, but an availing plea unto pardon and salvation. Let it be to me the armor of faith and the shield of good will. May it root out from my heart all vice; may it utterly subdue my evil passions and all my unruly desires. May it perfect me in charity and patience, in humility and obedience, and in all other virtues. May it be my sure defence against the snares laid for me by my enemies, visible and invisible. May it restrain and quiet all my evil impulses and make me ever cleave to Thee, Who art the one true God. May I owe to it a happy ending of my life. And do thou, O heavenly Father, vouchsafe one day to call me, a sinner, to that ineffable banquet, where Thou together with Thy Son and the Holy Ghost, art to Thy saints true and unfailing light, fulness of content, joy forevermore, gladness without alloy, consummate and everlasting happiness. Through the same Christ Our Lord. Amen.

Offerings, Thanksgiving and Petitions of St. Gertrude

O MOST holy Father, behold I, Thy most unworthy servant, trusting only in Thine ineffable compassion, have received Thy beloved Son, Our Lord Jesus Christ, and even now hold Him in my heart as my own possession, most intimately united with me. Wherefore, receiving this Thy Son into my arms, even as did holy Simeon, I offer Him to Thee with all that love and that fulness of intention wherewith He offered Himself to Thee for Thine everlasting glory, while lying in the manger, and when

He was hanging upon the cross. Look, O compassionate Father, on this offering, which I, Thine unworthy servant, make to Thee, my living and true God, to Thine everlasting praise and glory, for Thine infinite rejoicing and delight.

I offer to Thee the same, Thy Son, for myself, and for all those for whom I am accustomed or bound to pray, in thanksgiving for all the benefits Thou hast bestowed on us, and in reparation for all our negligence regarding the practice of virtues and the performance of good works. I offer Him to Thee to obtain Thy grace and Thy mercy, that we may be preserved and delivered from all evil and sin, succored in every necessity of body or of soul, and brought forth through a happy death into everlasting joys. Finally, I offer Him to Thee for the remission of all my sins, and in satisfaction for that huge debt which I cannot pay Thee, seeing that it far exceeds even ten thousand talents; humbly casting myself at Thy feet, O most merciful Father, I acknowledge and plead my utter poverty, in union with the bitterness of the passion of Thy most sinless Son, in Whom Thou hast declared Thyself well pleased; and in and through Him I make Thee full reparation and satisfaction for my sins, offering Thee all His sorrows, griefs, and tears, and all that expiation which He made upon the cross for the sins of the whole world.

Remember, also, O Lord, Thy servants who have gone before us with the sign of faith, and sleep the sleep of peace: for all and each of whom (and especially for N.) I offer Thee that saving victim Whom I have now received, the body and blood of Thy beloved Son; beseeching Thee, that through His infinite dignity and worth, and through the merits of all saints, Thou wouldst grant them pardon of all their sins, and merciful release from all their pains. Amen.

Anima Christi, Sanctifica Me

SOUL of Christ, be my sanctification.
Body of Christ, be my salvation.
Blood of Christ, fill all my veins.
Water of Christ's side, wash out my stains.
Passion of Christ, my comfort be.
O good Jesu, listen to me.
In Thy wounds I fain would hide,
Ne'er to be parted from Thy side.
Guard me should the foe assail me.
Call me when my life shall fail me.
Bid me come to Thee above,
With Thy saints to sing Thy love
World without end.   Amen.
      —Cardinal Newman's translation.

Indulgences: 300 days, each time. Seven years, if said after communion.—Pius IX, Jan. 9, 1854.

Prayer to Jesus in the Sacrament of the Altar

DEAR Jesus, present in the Sacrament of the Altar, be forever thanked and praised. Love, worthy of all celestial and terrestrial love, Who, out of infinite love for me, ungrateful sinner, didst assume our human nature, didst shed Thy most precious blood in the cruel scourging, and didst expire on a shameful cross for our eternal welfare! Now, illumined with lively faith, with the outpouring of my whole soul and the fervor of my heart, I humbly beseech Thee, through the infinite merits of Thy painful sufferings, give me strength and courage to destroy every evil passion which sways my heart, to bless Thee in my greatest afflictions, to glorify Thee by the exact fulfilment of all my duties, supremely to hate all sin, and thus to become a saint.

Indulgence: 100 days, once a day.—Pius IX, Jan. 1, 1866.

Ejaculations

EUCHARISTIC Heart of Jesus, have mercy on us!

Indulgence: 300 days, each time.—Pius X, Dec. 26, 1907.

DIVINE Heart of Jesus, convert sinners, save the dying, set free the Holy Souls in Purgatory.

Indulgence: 300 days, each time.—Pius X, Nov. 6, 1906.

Prayer to the Sacred Heart of Jesus

O MOST Sacred Heart of Jesus, pour down Thy blessings abundantly upon Thy Church, upon the Supreme Pontiff, and upon all the clergy; give perseverance to the just, convert sinners, enlighten unbelievers, bless

our parents, friends, and benefactors, help
the dying, free the souls in Purgatory, and
extend over all hearts the sweet empire of
Thy love. Amen.

Indulgence: 300 days, once a day.—Pius X, June 16,
1906.

Thanksgiving and Petitions

MY DEAR Lord Jesus, it is not in my
power to show my gratitude to Thee
in any way that is worthy of Thee or in pro-
portion to Thy goodness in deigning to come
to me, Thy poor creature, but I do thank
Thee with all my heart, and with grateful
affection I offer Thee my will, my liberty,
myself—all that I am and all that I have.
From this day forward I will be no longer
my own, but Thine, entirely Thine.

I love Thee, O adorable Saviour, and because I love Thee I am resolved to keep Thy
holy law in the midst of my heart; because
I love Thee I am inconsolable at the sight of
so many offences committed against Thee,
and burn with a desire of atoning for them
in future. Come, adversity, dangers, trou-
bles—come, hunger, persecutions, and the
sword—I defy and despise you all. Which
of you shall be able to separate me from the
love of God, which is in Christ Jesus? Be
Thou alone, dear Jesus, my defence and my
only fear. I dread not a life of tribulations,
provided my tribulations be endured for
Thee; I fear not even death itself, provided

I die in Thee and for Thee. To live or to die is my gain, if, living and dying, I give glory to Thee, and persevere in Thy holy grace.

Since, dear Jesus, Thou hast visited my soul to heal its infirmities, deliver me, I beseech Thee, from my evil habits, which Thou knowest well. Eradicate and expel them from my heart, and in their place sow the fruitful seeds of virtue. I seek not the goods of this earth, honors, pleasures, or riches; I ask only through the merits of Thy passion a great sorrow for my sins. Give me light by which I may be enabled to discover the vanity of the world and to see that Thou deservest to be loved with my whole heart and with my whole strength. Detach me from all earthly affections and bind me to Thy holy love so that I may will only what Thou willest. Give me patience and resignation in infirmity, in poverty, and in all things which are contrary to my self-love. Give me mildness toward those who insult and despise me. Let not any earthly object make me waver in my resolutions or render me faithless to Thy holy love. Complete the work Thou hast begun in me by daily sanctifying me more and more. Place a guard upon my lips, so that they may never utter any words which savor of detraction, indecency, anger, pride, or falsehood. Preserve my eyes from vain and dangerous curiosity, and grant that they may henceforth weep bitterly over the offences which are committed against Thy supreme majesty. Bless my heart, which Thou hast chosen for Thy habitation, and make it always the seat of Thy grace. Never, O Lord, let me be separated from Thee! Give me the grace to be ever mindful of Thy benefits, ever to appreciate Thy maxims, ever to imitate Thy example, to live with Thee, to die for Thee, and to reign eternally with Thee in Thy holy love.

(Here pause a little, and ask for some particular grace for yourself and for your neighbors. Offer your petitions to our dear Lord with perfect resignation to His holy will; rest assured that He will give and do what is best for you; fail not to repeat again and again the petitions which He Himself has put upon our lips: "Hallowed be Thy name; Thy kingdom come; Thy will be done on earth as it is in heaven." Pray for the Pope's intention, which always includes the following objects: i. The progress of the Faith and triumph of the Church. ii. Peace and union among Christian princes and rulers. iii. The conversion of sinners. iv. The uprooting of heresy.

Be mindful, also of the poor souls in Purgatory.)

O MOST holy Mary, my mother and my hope, obtain for me the graces which I desire; obtain for me the grace of loving thee sincerely, and of recommending myself to thee in all my necessities.

—*Anima Divota.*

Indulgenced Prayer to be Said after Holy Communion

HOW full of delight is the sweetness of Thy heavenly bread! How admirable is the tranquillity and how complete the peace of those who receive Thee, after detesting and sincerely confessing their sins. Be Thou blessed a thousand times, my Jesus! When I was in sin, I was unhappy. Now not only do I find my soul tranquil, but I seem to enjoy a very foretaste of the peace of paradise. How true it is that our hearts are made for Thee, my beloved Lord, and that they rejoice only when they repose in Thee. I, then, render Thee thanks, and firmly purpose ever to fly sin and its occasions, to fix my abode in Thy divine Heart, and thence to look for help to love Thee until death. Amen.

Indulgence: 300 days if said after communion.—Leo XIII, June 2, 1896.

Prayer for Perseverance

GOOD Jesus, what strength Thou hast imparted to my soul in this sacred banquet! But, oh, how much I need it. Keep me in Thy love; keep me in Thy grace to the end of my life. The road I have to traverse is so difficult, that without Thee I should fear to venture upon it. In a short time I shall return to my daily occupations; I shall continue my life of yesterday; I shall be exposed to the same temptations, I shall find myself with my usual faults. But Jesus, Thou Who didst help the saints, Thou hast come to me. Stay, oh stay with me, and do Thou by Thy grace help me to preserve in all my words and actions modesty, meekness, and humility. Help me to make Thy presence within me visible to all: let others see in me the sweetness of Thy charity and kindness.

Ejaculations

JESUS meek and humble of Heart, make my heart like unto Thine!

Indulgence: 300 days, each time.—Pius X, Sept. 15, 1905.

Sweet Heart of Jesus, be my love!

Indulgence: 300 days, once a day.—Leo XIII, May 21, 1892.

Sweet Heart of Mary, be my salvation!

Indulgence: 300 days, each time.—Pius IX, Sept. 20, 1852.

A Plenary Indulgence at the Hour of Death

By a decree of the Sacred Congregation of Indulgences of March 9, 1904, His Holiness, Pope Pius X granted a plenary indulgence at the moment of death to all the faithful who, on any day they may choose, shall receive the sacraments of Penance and Holy Eucharist and make the following act with sincere love toward God.

O LORD my God, I now at this moment readily and willingly accept at Thy hand whatever kind of death it may please Thee to send me, with all its pains, penalties, and sorrows.

Or the following

MY LORD God, even now resignedly and willingly, I accept at Thy hand, with all its anxieties, pains, and sufferings, whatever kind of death it shall please Thee to be mine.

Thanksgiving to the Holy Trinity [1]

ETERNAL Father, I thank Thee for the gift that Thou hast given me. It is Thy beloved Son, in Whom Thou art well pleased. In Him and by Him give me strength to keep all my good resolutions.

Eternal Son, I thank Thee for the gift that Thou hast given me. It is Thyself Who didst die for me. Make me, dear Jesus, wiser with Thy heavenly wisdom, and show me clearly all the things I should do for God.

Eternal Spirit, I thank Thee for the gift that Thou hast given me. It is Jesus, Whose soul Thou didst sanctify with Thy holiest treasures. Make me, dear Spirit, more loving, that I may cling more closely to God.

O ever-blessed Trinity, three Persons and one God, help me to live according to this gift of gifts which I have received at the altar of Jesus.

[1] From The Bread of Life, by Father Rawes.

Indulgenced Prayer to Jesus Crucified [1]

LOOK down upon me, good and gentle Jesus, while before Thy face I humbly kneel, and with burning soul pray and beseech Thee 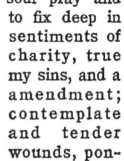 to fix deep in my heart lively sentiments of faith, hope, and charity, true contrition for my sins, and a firm purpose of amendment; and while I contemplate with great love and tender pity Thy five wounds, pondering over them within me, and calling to mind the words which David Thy prophet said of Thee, my Jesus: " They have pierced My hands and My feet; they have numbered all My bones." (Ps. xxi. 17, 18.)

Our Father, Hail Mary, Glory, five times, for the intentions of the Pope.

" The Raccolta " gives the following version of the prayer " En Ego ":

O GOOD and sweetest Jesus, before Thy face I humbly kneel, and with the greatest fervor of spirit I pray and beseech Thee to vouchsafe to fix deep in my heart lively sentiments of faith, hope, and charity, true contrition for my sins, and a most firm purpose of amendment; whilst I contemplate with great sorrow and affection Thy five

[1] A plenary indulgence, applicable to the souls in Purgatory, may be gained by the faithful who, after having confessed their sins with sorrow and received holy communion, shall devoutly recite this prayer before an image or picture of Christ crucified, and shall pray for the intentions of the Holy Father.—Pius IX, July 31, 1858.

wounds, and ponder them over in my mind, having before my eyes the words which, long ago, David the prophet spoke in Thy own person concerning Thee, my Jesus: " They have pierced My hands and My feet; they have numbered all My bones." (Ps. xxi. 17, 18.)

Our Father, Hail Mary, Glory, five times, for the intentions of the Pope.

Benediction of the Blessed Sacrament

Prayers at Benediction

I

O JESUS, Who art about to give Thy benediction to me, and to all who are here present, I humbly beseech Thee that it may impart to each and all of us the special graces we need. Yet more than this I ask. Let Thy blessing go forth far and wide. Let it be felt in the souls of the afflicted who cannot come here to receive it at Thy feet. Let the weak and tempted feel its power wherever they may be. Let poor sinners feel its influence, arousing them to come to Thee. Grant to me, O Lord, and to all here present, a strong personal love of Thee, a lively horror of sin, a higher esteem of grace, great zeal for Thy honor and glory, for the interest of Thy Sacred Heart, for our own sanctification, and for the salvation of souls. Amen.

JESUS! dear Pastor of the flock,
We crowd in love about Thy feet;
Our voices yearn to praise Thee, Lord,
And joyfully Thy presence greet.
Sweet Sacrament, we Thee adore,
Oh! make us love Thee more and more.

II

O DIVINE Redeemer, Who in Thy infinite goodness hast been pleased to leave us Thy precious body and blood in the blessed Eucharist, we adore Thee with the most profound respect, and return Thee our most humble thanks for all the favors Thou hast bestowed upon us, especially for the institution of this most holy sacrament. As Thou art the source of every blessing, we entreat Thee to pour down Thy benediction this day upon us and upon our relatives, friends, and benefactors; upon our Supreme Pontiff, our bishops, and our priests; and upon all those for whom we offer our prayers, and, that nothing may interrupt the course of Thy blessing, take from our hearts whatever is displeasing to Thee. Pardon our sins, O my God, which, for the love of Thee, we sincerely detest; purify our hearts, sanctify our souls, and bestow a blessing on us like that which Thou didst grant to Thy disciples at Thy ascension into heaven; grant us a blessing that may change us, consecrate us, unite us perfectly to Thee, fill us with Thy spirit, and be to us in this life a foretaste of those blessings which Thou hast prepared for Thy elect in Thy heavenly kingdom. Amen.

MY LORD and my God! Jesus, my God, I adore Thee here present in the sacrament of Thy love.

Blessed and praised every moment be the most holy and divine sacrament.

Versicle and Responses for the Dead

V. ETERNAL rest give unto them, O Lord.

R. And let perpetual light shine upon them.

V. May they rest in peace.

R. Amen.

O Salutaris Hostia

O SALUTARIS Hostia,
Quæ cœli pandis ostium.
Bella premunt hostilia;
Da robur, fer auxilium.
Uni trinoque Domino,
Sit sempiterna gloria:

Qui vitam sine termino,

O SAVING Victim opening wide
The gate of heav'n to man below!
Our foes press on from every side;
Thine aid supply, Thy strength bestow.
To Thy great name be endless praise,
Immortal Godhead, One in Three;
Oh, grant us endless length of days,

Nobis donet in patria. Amen.	In our true native land with Thee. Amen.

Tantum Ergo Sacramentum

TANTUM ergo sacramentum, Veneremur cernui;	DOWN in adoration falling, Lo the sacred host we hail!
Et antiquum documentum Novo cedat ritui;	Lo o'er ancient forms departing, Newer rites of grace prevail;
Præstet fides supplementum Sensuum defectui.	Faith for all defects supplying Where the feeble senses fail.
Genitori, Genitoque,	To the everlasting Father,
Laus et jubilatio;	And the Son Who reigns on high,
Salus, honor, virtus quoque Sit et benedictio:	With the Holy Ghost proceeding Forth from each eternally,
Procedenti ab utroque Compar sit laudatio. Amen.	Be salvation, honor, blessing, Might, and endless majesty. Amen.
V. Panem de cœlo præstitisti eis.	V. Thou didst give them bread from heaven.
R. Omne delectamentum in se habentem.	R. Containing in itself all sweetness.

Prayer

DEUS, qui nobis sub sacramento mirabili, passionis tuæ memoriam reliquisti: tribue, quæsumus, ita nos corporis et sanguinis tui sacra mysteria venerari, ut redemptionis tuæ fructum in nobis jugiter sentiamus. Qui vivis et regnas in sæcula sæculorum. Amen.

O GOD, Who in this wonderful sacrament hast left us a memorial of Thy passion; grant us, we beseech Thee, so to venerate the sacred mysteries of Thy body and blood, that we may ever feel within us the fruit of Thy redemption. Who livest, etc. Amen.

The celebrant blesses the people, silently making over them the sign of the cross with the monstrance in which the sacred host is enshrined.

Adoremus in æternum

ADOREMUS in æternum Sanctissimum Sacramentum.

LET us adore forever the Most Holy Sacrament.

Laudate Dominum

LAUDATE Dominum omnes gentes; laudate eum omnes populi.

Quoniam confirmata est super nos misericordia ejus: et

PRAISE the Lord, all ye nations: praise Him, all ye people.

Because His mercy is confirmed upon us: and the truth of the

veritas Domini manet in æternum.	Lord remaineth forever.
Gloria Patri, et Filio, et Spiritui Sancto.	Glory be to the Father, and to the Son, and to the Holy Ghost.
Sicut erat in principio, et nunc, et semper, et in sæcula sæculorum. Amen.	As it was in the beginning, is now, and ever shall be, world without end. Amen.
Adoremus in æternum Sanctissimum Sacramentum.	Let us adore forever the Most Holy Sacrament.

An Act of Reparation for Profane Language

BLESSED be God.

Blessed be His holy name.

Blessed be Jesus Christ, true God and true man.

Blessed be the name of Jesus.

Blessed be His most sacred Heart.

Blessed be Jesus in the most holy Sacrament of the Altar.

Blessed be the great Mother of God, Mary most holy.

Blessed be her holy and immaculate conception.

Blessed be the name of Mary, virgin and mother.

Blessed be St. Joseph, her most chaste spouse.

Blessed be God in His angels and in His saints.

Indulgence: two years, when said publicly after Mass or Benediction.—Leo XIII, Feb. 2, 1897.

The Stations of the Cross

Note.—The pious exercise of the Stations of the Cross is a continued meditation on the passion of Our Lord. To it innumerable indulgences have been annexed by the Sovereign Pontiffs, even the same as those of the Via Crucis in Jerusalem, or other places of the Holy Land, whence it appears how profitable this exercise must be to the Holy Souls. We read in the life of the Venerable Mary of Antigua that a nun of her convent, having died, appeared to her, and said: " Why is it that you do not offer for me and for the other souls the Stations of the Cross?" The servant of God remained in suspense at these words, when she heard Our Lord say to her: " The exercise of the Way of the Cross is so profitable to the souls in Purgatory that this soul has come to ask it of you in the name of all. The Via Crucis is a suffrage of great importance for these souls. By offering it for them you will have them as so many protectors, who will pray for you and defend your cause before My justice. Tell your sisters to rejoice in this treasure and the precious capital they have in it, that they may profit by it."
—*Forget-me-nots from Many Gardens.*

Preparatory Prayer

O GOOD and merciful Jesus, with a contrite heart and penitent spirit I purpose now to perform this devotion in honor of Thy bitter passion and death. I adore Thee most humbly as my Lord and my God. I thank Thee most heartily, my divine Saviour, for the infinite love wherewith Thou didst make the painful journey to Calvary for me, a wretched sinner, and didst die upon the cross for my salvation. I am truly sorry for all my sins, because by them I have offended Thee, Who art infinitely good. I detest them and I am resolved to amend my life. Grant that I may gain all the indulgences which are attached to this devotion, and since Thou hast promised to draw all things to Thyself, draw my heart and my love to Thee, that I may live and die in union with Thee. Amen.

First Station

Jesus Is Condemned to Death

V. We adore Thee, O Christ, and praise Thee:

R. Because by Thy holy cross Thou hast redeemed the world!

Meditation

JESUS, most innocent and perfectly sinless, was condemned to death, and, moreover, to the most ignominious death of the cross. To remain a friend of Cæsar, Pilate delivered Him into the hands of His enemies. A fearful crime—to condemn Innocence to death, and to offend God in order not to displease men!

Prayer

O INNOCENT Jesus, having sinned, I am guilty of eternal death; but that I might live Thou dost willingly accept the unjust sentence of death. For whom, then, shall I henceforth live, if not for Thee, my Lord?

Should I desire to please men, I could not be Thy servant. Let me, therefore, rather displease men and all the world than not please Thee, O my Jesus.

Our Father, etc.; Hail Mary, etc.

V. Lord Jesus, crucified:

R. Have mercy on us!

Versicles and Responses for the Dead

V. REQUIEM æternam dona eis, Domine.

R. Et lux perpetua luceat eis.

V. Requiescant in pace.

R. Amen.

V. ETERNAL rest grant unto them, O Lord.

R. And let perpetual light shine upon them.

V. May they rest in peace.

R. Amen.

Indulgence: 300 days, each time, applicable only to the dead.—Pius X, Feb. 13, 1908.

N.B.—Repeat these Versicles and Responses for the Dead at the end of each Station.

Second Station

Jesus Carries His Cross

V. We adore Thee, O Christ, and praise Thee:

R. Because by Thy holy cross Thou hast redeemed the world!

Meditation

WHEN our divine Saviour beheld the cross, He stretched out His bleeding arms toward it with eager desire, lovingly embraced it, tenderly kissed it, and, placing it on His bruised shoulders, joyfully carried it, although He was worn and weary unto death.

Prayer

O MY Jesus, I cannot be Thy friend and follower if I refuse to carry the cross. O dearly beloved cross! I embrace thee, I kiss thee, I joyfully accept thee from the hands of my God. Far be it from me to glory in anything, save in the cross of my Redeemer. By it the world shall be crucified to me and I to the world, that I may be Thine, O Jesus, forever.

Our Father, etc.; Hail Mary, etc.

V. Lord Jesus, crucified:

R. Have mercy on us!

Third Station

Jesus Falls the First Time

V. We adore Thee, O Christ, and praise Thee:

R. Because by Thy holy cross Thou hast redeemed the world!

Meditation

OUR dear Saviour carrying the cross was so weakened by its heavy weight as to fall exhausted to the ground. Our sins and misdeeds were the heavy burden which oppressed Him; the cross was to Him light and sweet, but our sins were galling and insupportable.

Prayer

O MY Jesus, Thou didst bear my burden and the heavy weight of my sins. Should I, then, not bear in union with Thee my easy burden of suffering, and accept the sweet yoke of Thy commandments? Thy yoke is sweet and Thy burden is light: I therefore willingly accept it, I will take up my cross and follow Thee.

Our Father, etc.; Hail Mary, etc.

V. Lord Jesus, crucified:

R. Have mercy on us!

Fourth Station

Jesus Meets His Afflicted Mother

V. We adore Thee, O Christ, and praise Thee:

R. Because by Thy holy cross Thou hast redeemed the world!

Meditation

HOW painful and sad it must have been for Mary, the sorrowful Mother, to behold her beloved Son laden with the burden of the cross! What unspeakable pangs her most tender heart experienced! How earnestly did she desire to die in place of Jesus, or at least with Him! Implore this sorrowful Mother to assist you graciously in the hour of your death.

Prayer

O JESUS, O Mary, I am the cause of the great and manifold pains which pierce your loving Hearts. O that my heart also would experience at least some of your sufferings! Mother of sorrows! Pray for me that I may be truly sorry for my sins, bear my sufferings patiently in union with thee and merit to enjoy thy assistance in the hour of my death.

Our Father, etc.; Hail Mary, etc.

V. Lord Jesus, crucified:

R. Have mercy on us!

Fifth Station

Simon of Cyrene Helps Jesus to Carry the Cross

V. We adore Thee, O Christ, and praise Thee:

R. Because by Thy holy cross Thou hast redeemed the world!

Meditation

SIMON of Cyrene was compelled to assist Jesus in carrying His cross, and Jesus accepted his assistance. How willingly would He also permit you to carry the cross. He calls, but you hear Him not; He invites you, but you decline His invitation. What a reproach it is to bear the cross reluctantly!

Prayer

O JESUS, whosoever does not take up his cross and follow Thee is not worthy of Thee. Behold, I will accompany Thee on the way of the cross; I will carry my cross cheerfully; I will walk in Thy blood-stained footsteps, and follow Thee, that I may be with Thee in life eternal.

Our Father, etc.; Hail Mary, etc.

V. Lord Jesus, crucified:

R. Have mercy on us!

Sixth Station

Veronica Wipes the Face of Jesus

V. We adore Thee, O Christ, and praise Thee:

R. Because by Thy holy cross Thou hast redeemed the world!

Meditation

VERONICA, impelled by devotion and compassion, wipes the disfigured face of Jesus with her veil. And Jesus imprints on it His holy countenance: a great recompense for so small a service. What return do you make to your Saviour for His great and manifold benefits?

Prayer

MOST merciful Jesus, what return shall I make for all the benefits Thou hast bestowed upon me? Behold I consecrate myself entirely to Thy service. I offer and consecrate to Thee my heart: imprint on it Thy sacred image, never again to be effaced by sin.

Our Father, etc.; Hail Mary, etc.

V. Lord Jesus, crucified:

R. Have mercy on us!

Seventh Station

Jesus Falls the Second Time

V. We adore Thee, O Christ, and praise Thee:

R. Because by Thy holy cross Thou hast redeemed the world!

Meditation

THE suffering Jesus, under the weight of His cross, again falls to the ground; but the cruel executioners do not permit Him to rest a moment. Pushing and striking Him, they urge Him onward. It is the frequent repetition of our sins which oppresses Jesus. Knowing and realizing this, how can I continue to sin?

Prayer

O JESUS, Son of David, have mercy on me! Extend to me Thy gracious hand and support me, that I may never fall again into my old sins. From this very moment I will earnestly strive to reform my life and to avoid every sin. Help of the weak,

strengthen me by Thy grace, without which
I can do nothing, that I may carry out
faithfully my good resolution.

Our Father, etc.; Hail Mary, etc.

V. Lord Jesus, crucified:

R. Have mercy on us!

Eighth Station

The Daughters of Jerusalem Weep over Jesus

V. We adore Thee, O Christ, and praise
Thee:

R. Because by Thy holy cross Thou hast
redeemed the world!

Meditation

THESE devoted women, moved by compassion, weep over the suffering Saviour. But He turns to them saying: " *Weep
not for Me Who am innocent, but weep for
yourselves and for your children.*" Weep
thou also, for there is nothing more pleasing
to Our Lord, and nothing more profitable for
thyself, than tears that are shed in contrition for sin.

Prayer

O JESUS, Who will give to my eyes a
fountain of tears, that day and night I
may weep for my sins. I beseech Thee,
through Thy bitter tears, to move my heart
to compassion and repentance, so that I may

weep all my days over Thy sufferings and still more over their cause, my sins.

Our Father, etc.; Hail Mary, etc.

V. Lord Jesus, crucified:

R. Have mercy on us!

Ninth Station

Jesus Falls the Third Time

V. We adore Thee, O Christ, and praise Thee:

R. Because by Thy holy cross Thou hast redeemed the world!

Meditation

JESUS, arriving exhausted at the foot of Calvary, falls the third time to the ground. His love for us, however, remains strong and fervent.

What a fearfully oppressive burden our sins must be to cause Jesus to fall so often! Had He, however, not taken them upon Himself, they would have plunged us into the abyss of hell.

Prayer

MOST merciful Jesus, I return Thee infinite thanks for not permitting me to continue in sin and to fall, as I have so often deserved, into the depths of hell. Enkindle in me an earnest desire of amendment; let me never again relapse, but vouchsafe me

the grace to persevere in penance to the
end of my life.

Our Father, etc.; Hail Mary, etc.

V. Lord Jesus, crucified:

R. Have mercy on us!

Tenth Station

Jesus Is Stripped of His Garments

V. We adore Thee, O Christ, and praise
Thee:

R. Because by Thy holy cross Thou hast
redeemed the world!

Meditation

WHEN Our Saviour had arrived on
Calvary, He was cruelly despoiled of
His garments. How painful must this have
been, because they adhered to His wounded
and torn body and with them parts of His
bloody skin were removed. All the wounds
of Jesus are renewed. Jesus is despoiled
of His garments that He might die possessed
of nothing; how happy shall I also die after
casting off my evil self with all its sinful
inclinations!

Prayer

HELP me, Jesus, to conquer myself and
to be renewed according to Thy will
and desire. I will not count the cost, but
will struggle bravely to cast off my evil pro-
pensities; despoiled of things temporal, of

my own will, I desire to die, that I may live to Thee forever more.

Our Father, etc.; Hail Mary, etc.

V. Lord Jesus, crucified:

R. Have mercy on us!

Eleventh Station

Jesus Is Nailed to the Cross

V. We adore Thee, O Christ, and praise Thee:

R. Because by Thy holy cross Thou hast redeemed the world!

Meditation

JESUS, after He had been stripped of His garments, was violently thrown upon the cross, to which His hands and His feet were nailed most cruelly. In this excruciating pain He remained silent, and perfectly resigned to the will of His heavenly Father. He suffered patiently, because He suffered for me. How do I act in sufferings and in trouble? How fretful and impatient, how full of complaints I am!

Prayer

O JESUS, meek and gentle Lamb of God, I renounce forever my impatience. Crucify, O Lord, my flesh and its concupiscences. Punish me, afflict me in this life, as Thou willest, only spare me in eternity. I commit my destiny to Thee, resigning myself to Thy holy will: Not my will but Thine be done!

Our Father, etc.; Hail Mary, etc.

V. Lord Jesus, crucified:

R. Have mercy on us!

Twelfth Station

Jesus Dies on the Cross

V. We adore Thee, O Christ, and praise Thee:

R. Because by Thy holy cross Thou hast redeemed the world!

Meditation

BEHOLD Jesus crucified! Behold His wounds, received for love of you! His whole appearance betokens love! His head is bent to kiss you, His arms are extended to embrace you, His Heart is open to receive you. O superabundance of love! Jesus, the Son of God, dies upon the cross that man may live and be delivered from everlasting death.

Prayer

O MOST amiable Jesus, if I cannot sacrifice my life for love of Thee, I will at least endeavor to die to the world. How must I regard the world and its vanities, when I behold Thee hanging on the cross, covered with wounds? O Jesus! receive me into Thy wounded Heart! I belong entirely to Thee; for Thee alone do I desire to live and to die.

Our Father, etc.; Hail Mary, etc.

V. Lord Jesus, crucified:

R. Have mercy on us!

Thirteenth Station

Jesus Is Taken Down from the Cross

V. We adore Thee, O Christ, and praise Thee:

R. Because by Thy holy cross Thou hast redeemed the world!

Meditation

JESUS did not descend from the cross, but remained on it until He died. And when taken down from it, He, in death as in life, rested on the bosom of His blessed Mother. Persevere in your resolutions of reform and do not part from the cross: he who persevereth to the end shall be saved. Consider, moreover, how pure the heart should be that receives the body and blood of Christ in the adorable Sacrament of the Altar.

Prayer

O LORD Jesus, Thy lifeless body, mangled and lacerated, found a worthy resting-place on the bosom of Thy virgin Mother. Have I not often compelled Thee to dwell in my heart despite its unworthiness to receive Thee? Create in me a new heart, that I may worthily receive Thy most sacred body in holy communion, and that Thou mayest remain in me and I in Thee, for all eternity.

Our Father, etc.; Hail Mary, etc.

V. Lord Jesus, crucified:

R. Have mercy on us!

Fourteenth Station

Jesus Is Laid in the Sepulchre

V. We adore Thee, O Christ, and praise Thee:

R. Because by Thy holy cross Thou hast redeemed the world!

Meditation

THE body of Jesus is interred in a stranger's sepulcher. He Who in this world had not whereupon to rest His head would not even have a grave of His own, because He was not of this world. You who are so attached to the world, henceforth despise it, that you may not perish with it.

Prayer

O JESUS, Thou hast set me apart from the world: what, then, shall I seek therein? Thou hast created me for heaven; what, then, have I to do with the world? Depart from me, deceitful world, with thy vanities! Henceforth I will follow the way of the cross traced out for me by my Redeemer, and journey onward to my heavenly home, my eternal dwelling-place.

Our Father, etc.; Hail Mary, etc.

V. Lord Jesus, crucified:

R. Have mercy on us!

Conclusion

ALMIGHTY and eternal God, Who hast given to the human race Thy beloved Son as an example of humility, obedience, and patience, to precede us on the way of the cross, the way that leadeth to life, graciously grant that we, inflamed by His infinite love, may take upon us the sweet yoke of His Gospel together with the mortification of the cross, following Him as His true disciples, so that we may one day gloriously rise with Him and joyfully hear the final sentence: " *Come, ye blessed of My Father, possess you the kingdom prepared for you from the foundation of the world.*" (Matt. xxv. 34.)

Litanies

Litany of the Holy Name of Jesus

LORD, have mercy on us.
Christ, have mercy on us.
Lord, have mercy on us.
Jesus, hear us.
Jesus, graciously hear us.
God the Father of heaven,[1]
God the Son, Redeemer of the world,
God, the Holy Ghost,
Holy Trinity, one God,

[1] Have mercy on us.

Jesus, Son of the living God,[1]
Jesus, splendor of the Father,
Jesus, brightness of eternal light,
Jesus, king of glory,
Jesus, sun of justice,
Jesus, son of the Virgin Mary,
Jesus, most amiable,
Jesus, most admirable,
Jesus, mighty God,
Jesus, father of the world to come,
Jesus, angel of great counsel,
Jesus, most powerful,
Jesus, most patient,
Jesus, most obedient,
Jesus, meek and humble of heart,
Jesus, lover of chastity,
Jesus, lover of us,
Jesus, God of peace,
Jesus, author of life,
Jesus, model of virtues,
Jesus, zealous for souls,
Jesus, our God,
Jesus, our refuge,
Jesus, father of the poor,
Jesus, treasure of the faithful,·
Jesus, good shepherd,
Jesus, true light,
Jesus, eternal wisdom,
Jesus, infinite goodness,
Jesus, our way and our life,
Jesus, joy of angels,
Jesus, king of patriarchs,

[1] Have mercy on us.

Jesus, master of apostles,[1]
Jesus, teacher of evangelists,
Jesus, strength of martyrs,
Jesus, light of confessors,
Jesus, purity of virgins,
Jesus, crown of all saints,
Be merciful, spare us, O Jesus.
Be merciful, graciously hear us, O Jesus.
From all evil,[2]
From all sin,
From Thy wrath,
From the snares of the devil,
From the spirit of fornication,
From everlasting death,
From the neglect of Thy inspirations,
Through the mystery of Thy holy incarnation,
Through Thy nativity,
Through Thine infancy,
Through Thy most divine life,
Through Thy labors,
Through Thine agony and passion,
Through Thy cross and dereliction,
Through Thy sufferings,
Through Thy death and burial,
Through Thy resurrection,
Through Thine ascension,
[Through the most holy institution of Thy
    Eucharist,] [3]
Through Thy joys,
Through Thy glory,

[1] Have mercy on us.   [2] Jesus, deliver us.
[3] Where authorized by the Bishop, the following invocation
may be added here: " Through the most holy institution of
Thy Eucharist." Congr. of Rites, Feb. 8, 1905.

Lamb of God, Who takest away the sins of the world, spare us, O Jesus.

Lamb of God, Who takest away the sins of the world, graciously hear us, O Jesus.

Lamb of God, Who takest away the sins of the world, have mercy on us, O Jesus.

Jesus, hear us.

Jesus, graciously hear us.

Let us pray

O LORD Jesus Christ, Who hast said: Ask, and ye shall receive; seek, and ye shall find; knock, and it shall be opened unto you; mercifully attend to our supplications, and grant us the gift of Thy divine charity, that we may ever love Thee with our whole hearts, and never desist from Thy praise.

GIVE us, O Lord, a perpetual fear and love of Thy holy name, for Thou never ceasest to direct and govern by Thy grace those whom Thou instructest in the solidity of Thy love; Who livest and reignest world without end. Amen.

Indulgence: 300 days, once a day.—Leo XIII, Jan. 16, 1886.

Litany of the Sacred Heart of Jesus

LORD, have mercy on us.
Christ, have mercy on us.

Lord, have mercy on us.

Christ, hear us.

Christ, graciously hear us.

God the Father of heaven,[1]
God the Son, Redeemer of the world,
God the Holy Ghost,
Holy Trinity, one God,
Heart of Jesus, Son of the Eternal Father,
Heart of Jesus, formed in the womb of the Virgin Mother by the Holy Ghost,
Heart of Jesus, united substantially with the Word of God,
Heart of Jesus, of infinite majesty,
Heart of Jesus, holy temple of God,
Heart of Jesus, tabernacle of the Most High,
Heart of Jesus, house of God and gate of heaven,
Heart of Jesus, glowing furnace of charity,
Heart of Jesus, vessel of justice and love,
Heart of Jesus, full of goodness and love,
Heart of Jesus, abyss of all virtues,
Heart of Jesus, most worthy of all praise,
Heart of Jesus, king and center of all hearts,
Heart of Jesus, in which are all the treasures of wisdom and knowledge,
Heart of Jesus, in which dwelleth all the fulness of the divinity,
Heart of Jesus, in which the Father is well pleased,
Heart of Jesus, of whose fulness we have all received,
Heart of Jesus, desire of the eternal hills,
Heart of Jesus, patient and rich in mercy,
Heart of Jesus, rich to all who invoke Thee,
Heart of Jesus, fount of life and holiness,

[1] Have mercy on us.

Heart of Jesus, propitiation for our sins,[1]
Heart of Jesus, saturated with revilings,
Heart of Jesus, crushed for our iniquities,
Heart of Jesus, made obedient unto death,
Heart of Jesus, pierced with a lance,
Heart of Jesus, source of all consolation,
Heart of Jesus, our life and resurrection,
Heart of Jesus, our peace and reconciliation,
Heart of Jesus, victim for our sins,
Heart of Jesus, salvation of those who hope
in Thee,
Heart of Jesus, hope of those who die in
Thee,
Heart of Jesus, delight of all saints,
Lamb of God, Who takest away the sins of
the world, spare us, O Lord.
Lamb of God, Who takest away the sins of
the world, graciously hear us, O Lord.
Lamb of God, Who takest away the sins of
the world, have mercy on us.
V. Jesus, meek and humble of heart,
R. Make our heart like unto Thine.

Let us pray

ALMIGHTY and everlasting God, graciously regard the Heart of Thy wellbeloved Son and the acts of praise and satisfaction which He renders Thee on behalf of us sinners, and through their merit, grant pardon to us who implore Thy mercy, in the name of Thy Son Jesus Christ, Who liveth

[1] Have mercy on us.

and reigneth with Thee in the unity of the
Holy Spirit, world without end.   Amen.

*Indulgence: 300 days, once a day.—Leo XIII, April 2,
1899.*

Litany of the Blessed Virgin Mary

*Indulgences: i. 300 days, every time.   ii. Plenary, to
all who say it daily, on the Immaculate Conception,
the Nativity, the Annunciation, the Purification, and
the Assumption.—Pius VII, Sept. 30, 1817.*

LORD, have mercy on us.
   Christ, have mercy on us.
Lord, have mercy on us.
Christ, hear us.
Christ, graciously hear us.
God the Father of heaven,[1]
God the Son, Redeemer of the world,
God the Holy Ghost,
Holy Trinity, one God,
Holy Mary,[2]
Holy Mother of God,
Holy Virgin of virgins,
Mother of Christ,
Mother of divine grace,
Mother most pure,
Mother most chaste,
Mother inviolate,
Mother undefiled,
Mother most amiable,
Mother most admirable,
Mother of good counsel,
Mother of our Creator,

[1] Have mercy on us.   [2] Pray for us.

Mother of our Saviour,[1]
Virgin most prudent,
Virgin most venerable,
Virgin most renowned,
Virgin most powerful,
Virgin most merciful,
Virgin most faithful,
Mirror of justice,
Seat of wisdom,
Cause of our joy,
Spiritual vessel,
Vessel of honor,
Singular vessel of devotion,
Mystical rose,
Tower of David,
Tower of ivory,
House of gold,
Ark of the covenant,
Gate of heaven,
Morning star,
Health of the sick,
Refuge of sinners,
Comforter of the afflicted,
Help of Christians,
Queen of angels,
Queen of patriarchs,
Queen of prophets,
Queen of apostles,
Queen of martyrs,
Queen of confessors,
Queen of virgins,
Queen of all saints,

[1] Pray for us.

Queen conceived without original sin,[1]
Queen of the most holy Rosary,
Queen of peace,
Lamb of God, Who takest away the sins of
the world, spare us, O Lord.
Lamb of God, Who takest away the sins of
the world, graciously hear us, O Lord.
Lamb of God, Who takest away the sins of
the world, have mercy on us.
V. Pray for us, O holy Mother of God.
R. That we may be made worthy of the
promises of Christ.

Let us pray

GRANT us, Thy servants, we beseech
Thee, O Lord God, to enjoy continual
health of soul and body; and by the glorious
intercession of Blessed Mary, ever a virgin,
to be delivered from present sorrow, and to
attain everlasting joy. Through Christ our
Lord. Amen.

*In Advent and at Christmas time, in lieu of
the above Prayer there may be said the following:*

In Advent

O GOD, Who wast pleased to will that at
the message of an angel Thy Word
should take flesh in the womb of the blessed
Virgin Mary; grant that we, Thy suppliants,
who believe her to be truly the Mother of
God, may be helped by her intercession with
Thee. Through the same Christ our Lord.

[1] Pray for us.

From Christmas Day to the Feast of the Purification
(Feb. 2)

O GOD, Who, by the fruitful virginity of blessed Mary, hast assured to mankind the blessings of eternal life; grant, we beseech Thee, that we may ever experience the intercession in our behalf of her, through whom we have been found worthy to receive the author of life, Our Lord Jesus Christ, Thy Son.

Or the versicle and prayer may be varied according to the season of the ecclesiastical year.

In Advent

V. The angel of the Lord declared unto Mary.

R. And she conceived by the Holy Ghost.

Let us pray

POUR forth, we beseech Thee, O Lord, Thy grace into our hearts; that we to whom the incarnation of Christ Thy Son was made known by the message of an angel, may by His passion and cross be brought to the glory of His resurrection. Through the same Christ our Lord.

From Christmas Day to the Purification

V. After childbirth thou didst remain a most pure virgin.

R. O Mother of God, intercede for us.

Prayer, O God, Who by the fruitful virginity, etc.

From the Purification to Easter

V. Make me worthy to praise thee, O holy Virgin.

R. Give me strength against thine enemies.

Let us pray

VOUCHSAFE unto us, O merciful God, a defence in our weakness; and grant that the prayers of the most holy Mother of God, whom we commemorate, may make us to rise out of our evil life. Through the same Christ our Lord.

In Paschal-time

V. Rejoice and be glad, O Virgin Mary. Alleluia.

R. For the Lord hath truly risen. Alleluia.

Let us pray

O GOD, Who didst vouchsafe to give joy to the world through the resurrection of Thy Son, Our Lord Jesus Christ; grant, we beseech Thee, that, through His Mother, the Virgin Mary, we may obtain the joys of everlasting life. Through the same Christ our Lord.

From Pentecost to Advent

V. Pray for us, O holy Mother of God.

R. That we may be made worthy of the promises of Christ.

Let us pray

ALMIGHTY and everlasting God, Who by the cooperation of the Holy Ghost didst in body and in soul prepare Mary, the glorious virgin mother, to be a befitting dwelling-place of Thy Son; grant that we who rejoicingly commemorate her may, by her loving intercession, be safeguarded from all the evils that threaten us and from that death which is eternal. Through the same Christ our Lord. *R.* Amen.

Litany of St. Joseph

LORD, have mercy on us.
     Christ, have mercy on us.
Lord, have mercy on us.
Christ, hear us.
Christ, graciously hear us.
God the Father of heaven,[1]
God the Son, Redeemer of the world,
God the Holy Ghost,
Holy Trinity, one God,
Holy Mary,[2]
St. Joseph,
Renowned offspring of David,
Light of patriarchs,
Spouse of the Mother of God,
Chaste guardian of the Virgin,
Foster-father of the Son of God,
Diligent protector of Christ,

---

[1] Have mercy on us.   [2] Pray for us.

Head of the Holy Family,[1]
Joseph most just,
Joseph most chaste,
Joseph most prudent,
Joseph most strong,
Joseph most obedient,
Joseph most faithful,
Mirror of patience,
Lover of poverty,
Model of artisans,
Glory of home life,
Guardian of virgins,
Pillar of families,
Solace of the wretched,
Hope of the sick,
Patron of the dying,
Terror of demons,
Protector of Holy Church,
Lamb of God, Who takest away the sins of
the world, spare us, O Lord.
Lamb of God, Who takest away the sins of
the world, graciously hear us, O Lord.
Lamb of God, Who takest away the sins of
the world, have mercy on us.

V. He made him the lord of His house-
hold.

R. And prince over all His possessions.

Let us pray

O GOD, Who in Thy ineffable providence
didst vouchsafe to choose blessed
Joseph to be the spouse of Thy most holy

[1] Pray for us.

Mother; grant, we beseech Thee, that we may have for our advocate in heaven him whom we venerate as our protector on earth: Who livest and reignest world without end. Amen.

Indulgence: 300 days, once a day, also applicable to the souls in Purgatory.—Pius X, March 18, 1909.

The Litany of the Saints for the Faithful Departed

LORD, have mercy on us.
　　Christ, have mercy on us.
Lord, have mercy on us.
Christ, hear us.
Christ, graciously hear us.
God the Father of heaven,[1]
God the Son, Redeemer of the world,
God the Holy Ghost,
Holy Trinity, one God,
Holy Mary,[2]
Holy Mother of God,
Holy Virgin of virgins,
St. Michael,
All ye holy angels and archangels,
St. John Baptist,
St. Joseph,
All ye holy patriarchs and prophets,
St. Peter,
St. Paul,
St. John,
All ye holy apostles and evangelists,
St. Stephen,

[1] Have mercy on the Holy Souls.　　[2] Pray for them.

St. Laurence,[1]
All ye holy martyrs,
St. Gregory,
All ye holy bishops and confessors,
All ye holy monks and hermits,
St. Mary Magdalen,
St. Barbara,
St. Catherine,
St. Teresa,
All ye holy virgins and widows,
All ye saints of God,
Be merciful, Spare them, O Lord.
Be merciful, Deliver them, O Lord.
From all evil,[2]
From all punishment,
From Thy wrath,
From Thy severe justice,
From the power of evil spirits,
From the gnawing worm of conscience,
From their long yearning,
From cruel flames,
From horrible darkness,
From weeping and wailing,
From their dreadful captivity,
Through the mystery of Thy holy incarnation,
Through Thy holy nativity,
Through Thy flight into Egypt,
Through Thy holy name,
Through Thy baptism and rigorous fasting,
Through Thy profound humiliations,
Through Thy extreme poverty,

---

[1] Pray for them.   [2] Deliver them, O Lord.

Through Thy perfect obedience,[1]
Through Thy admirable meekness and patience,
Through Thy infinite love,
Through Thy bitter passion,
Through Thy anguish in the garden,
Through Thy bloody sweat,
Through the ignominy of the false accusation against Thee,
Through Thy cruel scourging,
Through Thy painful crowning with thorns,
Through Thy laborious carrying of the cross,
Through the awful agony of Thy crucifixion,
Through Thy bitter death,
Through Thy holy wounds,
Through Thy most precious blood,
Through Thy glorious resurrection,
Through Thy admirable ascension,
Through the sending of the Holy Ghost,
Through the merits and intercession of Thy holy Mother,
Through the merits and intercession of all Thy saints,
We sinners beseech Thee, hear us,
That Thou wouldst spare the souls departed,[2]
That Thou wouldst pardon all their transgressions,
That Thou wouldst hear their prayers and supplications,
That Thou wouldst deliver them from their sufferings,

[1] Deliver them, O Lord.   [2] We beseech Thee, hear us.

That by the blood of the new and eternal covenant Thou wouldst release them from their cruel imprisonment,[1]

That Thou wouldst make them partakers of the good works and merits of all Christendom,

That Thou wouldst ever hear our prayer for them and their own prayer in our behalf,

That through Thy holy angels Thou wouldst console them,

That through the holy Archangel Michael Thou wouldst lead them unto the holy light,

That Thou wouldst soon favor them with Thy beatific vision,

That Thou wouldst render eternal blessings to the souls of our departed parents, relatives, friends, and benefactors,

That Thou wouldst grant eternal rest to all the faithful departed,

That Thou wouldst vouchsafe graciously to hear us,

Lamb of God, Who takest away the sins of the world, grant unto them eternal rest.

Lamb of God, Who takest away the sins of the world, grant unto them eternal rest.

Lamb of God, Who takest away the sins of the world, grant unto them eternal rest.

Christ, hear us.

Christ, graciously hear us.

Lord, have mercy on us.

Christ, have mercy on us.

[1] We beseech Thee, hear us.

Lord, have mercy on us.

V. O Lord, hear my prayer.

R. And let my cry come unto Thee.

Let us pray

O GOD, Whose property is always to have mercy and to spare, we humbly beseech Thee for the souls of Thy servants, N., N., whom Thou hast commanded to depart out of this world, that Thou deliver them not into the hands of their enemy, nor forget them unto the end, but command them to be received by Thy holy angels and conducted into paradise, their true country; that, as in Thee they have hoped and believed, they may not suffer the pains of hell, but may take possession of eternal joys. Through Our Lord Jesus Christ.

V. Eternal rest give unto them, O Lord.

R. And let perpetual light shine upon them.

V. May they rest in peace.

R. Amen.

Grades of the Passion of Our Lord Jesus Christ

JESU dulcissime, in horto mœstus: Patrem orans: et in agonia positus; sanguineum sudorem ef-

MOST sweet Jesus, sorrowful in the Garden praying to the Father, in agony, and covered

fundens: Miserere nobis.

Miserere nostri, Domine, miserere nostri.

JESU dulcissime, osculo traditoris in manus impiorum traditus: et tanquam latro captus, et ligatus: et a discipulis derelictus: Miserere nobis.

Miserere nostri, Domine, miserere nostri.

JESU dulcissime, ab iniquo Judæorum concilio reus mortis acclamatus: ad Pilatum tanquam malefactor ductus: et ab iniquo Herode spretus, et delusus: Miserere nobis.

Miserere nostri, Domine, miserere nostri.

JESU dulcissime, vestibus denudatus, et ad columnam dirissimis verberibus

with a sweat of blood. Have mercy on us.

Have mercy on us, O Lord, have mercy on us.

MOST sweet Jesus, kissed by the traitor, delivered into the hands of the wicked, taken and bound as a robber, and forsaken by Thy disciples. Have mercy on us.

Have mercy on us, O Lord, have mercy on us.

MOST sweet Jesus, found guilty of death by the iniquitous Council of the Jews, led to Pilate as a malefactor, by the impious Herod despised and mocked. Have mercy on us.

Have mercy on us, O Lord, have mercy on us.

MOST sweet Jesus, stripped of Thy garments and most cruelly scourged

flagellatus: Miserere nobis.

at the pillar. Have mercy on us.

Miserere nostri, Domine, miserere nostri.

Have mercy on us, O Lord, have mercy on us.

JESU dulcissime, spinis coronatus: colaphis cæsus: arundine percussus: facie velatus: veste purpurea circumdatus: multipliciter derisus: et opprobriis saturatus: Miserere nobis.

MOST sweet Jesus, crowned with thorns, hit with blows, struck with a reed, clothed with purple in derision, in many ways mocked and saturated with opprobrium. Have mercy on us.

Miserere nostri, Domine, miserere nostri.

Have mercy on us, O Lord, have mercy on us.

JESU dulcissime, latroni Barabbæ postpositus: a Judæis reprobatus: et ad mortem crucis injuste condemnatus: Miserere nobis.

MOST sweet Jesus, Who wast esteemed inferior to Barabbas, refuted by the Jews, unjustly condemned to death. Have mercy on us.

Miserere nostri, Domine, miserere nostri.

Have mercy on us, O Lord, have mercy on us.

JESU dulcissime, ligno crucis oneratus: et ad locum supplicii, tanquam ovis ad occisionem, ductus: Miserere

MOST sweet Jesus, weighed down by the wood of the cross, and as a sheep to be slaughtered led to the place

nobis.

of execution. Have mercy on us.

Miserere nostri, Domine, miserere nostri.

Have mercy on us, O Lord, have mercy on us.

JESU dulcissime, inter latrones deputatus: blasphematus, et derisus: felle et aceto potatus: et horribilibus tormentis ab hora sexta usque ad horam nonam in ligno cruciatus: Miserere nobis.

MOST sweet Jesus, Who wast numbered among thieves, blasphemed and derided, given gall and vinegar to drink, and from the sixth to the ninth hour in horrible torments crucified upon the cross. Have mercy on us.

Miserere nostri, Domine, miserere nostri.

Have mercy on us, O Lord, have mercy on us.

JESU dulcissime, in patibulo crucis mortuus: et coram tua Sancta Matre lancea perforatus: simul sanguinem et aquam emittens: Miserere nobis.

MOST sweet Jesus, Who didst die on the cross, and wast pierced by the lance in the presence of Thy holy Mother, issuing blood and water from Thy side, have mercy on us.

Miserere nostri, Domine, miserere nostri.

Have mercy on us, O Lord, have mercy on us.

JESU dulcissime, de cruce deposi-

MOST sweet Jesus, Who, when

tus, et lacrymis mœstissimæ Matris tuæ perfusus: Miserere nobis.

Miserere nostri, Domine, miserere nostri.

JESU dulcissime, plagis circumdatus: quinque vulneribus signatus: aromatibus conditus et in sepulcro repositus: Miserere nobis.

Miserere nostri, Domine, miserere nostri.

taken down from the cross, wast covered with the tears of Thy most holy Mother. Have mercy on us. Have mercy on us, O Lord, have mercy on us.

MOST sweet Jesus, covered with bruises, and marked with five wounds, anointed with spices, and laid in the tomb. Have mercy on us. Have mercy on us, O Lord, have mercy on us.

Indulgence of 9 years at each Grade; plenary once a day for the Passionists and the members of the Confraternity of the Passion.—Rescript of the S. Penitentiary, April 5, 1918.

Prayer of St. Alphonsus Liguori for a Visit to the Blessed Sacrament

LORD Jesus Christ, Who, through the love which Thou bearest to men, dost remain with them day and night in this sacrament, full of mercy and of love, expecting, inviting, and receiving all who come to visit Thee, I believe that Thou art present in the Sacrament of the Altar. From the abyss of my nothingness I adore Thee, and

I thank Thee for all the favors which Thou hast bestowed upon me, particularly for having given me Thyself in this sacrament, for having given me for my advocate Thy most holy Mother, Mary, and for having called me to visit Thee in this church.

I this day salute Thy most loving Heart, and I wish to salute it for three ends: first, in thanksgiving for this great gift; secondly, in compensation for all the injuries Thou hast received from Thy enemies in this sacrament; thirdly, I wish by this visit to adore Thee in all places in which Thou art least honored and most abandoned in the Holy Sacrament. My Jesus, I love Thee with my whole heart. I am sorry for having hitherto offended Thy infinite goodness. I purpose, with the assistance of Thy grace, never more to offend Thee; and, at this moment, miserable as I am, I consecrate my whole being to Thee. I give Thee my entire will, all my affections and desires, and all that I have. From this day forward, do what Thou wilt with me, and with whatever belongs to me. I ask and desire only Thy holy love, the gift of final perseverance, and the perfect accomplishment of Thy will. I recommend to Thee the souls in Purgatory, particularly those who were most devoted to the Blessed Sacrament and to most holy Mary; and I also recommend to Thee all poor sinners. Finally, my dear Saviour, I unite all my affections with the affections of

Thy most loving Heart; and, thus united, I offer them to Thy eternal Father, and I entreat Him, in Thy name, and for Thy sake, to accept them.—*The New Raccolta.*

Indulgence: 300 days, every time, when said before the Blessed Sacrament.—Pius IX, Sept. 7, 1854.

Ejaculations

O JESUS in the Blessed Sacrament, have mercy on us.

Indulgence: 300 days, every time.—Pius X, May 20, 1911.

MAY the Heart of Jesus in the Most Blessed Sacrament be praised, adored, and loved with grateful affection, at every moment, in all the tabernacles of the world, even to the end of time. Amen.

Indulgence: 100 days, once a day.—Pius IX, Feb. 29, 1868.

Prayer for the Church and the Supreme Pontiff; for Relatives, Friends, and Benefactors; for the Holy Souls in Purgatory, etc.

O MOST Sacred Heart of Jesus, pour down Thy blessings abundantly upon Thy Church, upon the Supreme Pontiff and upon all the clergy; give perseverance to the just, convert sinners, enlighten unbelievers, bless our parents, friends, and benefactors, help the dying, free the souls in Purgatory, and extend over all hearts the sweet empire of Thy love. Amen.

Indulgence: 300 days, once a day.—Pius X, June 16, 1906.

Short Act of Consecration and Reparation to be Made before a Representation of the Sacred Heart

MY LOVING Jesus, out of the grateful love I bear Thee, and to make reparation for my unfaithfulness to grace, I, N., give Thee my heart, and I consecrate myself wholly to Thee; and with Thy help I purpose never to sin again.

Indulgence: 100 days, once a day.—Pius IX, June 18, 1876.

Ejaculation of the Sacred Heart

ALL for Thee, most Sacred Heart of Jesus!

Indulgence: 300 days, every time.—Pius X, Nov. 26, 1908.

Prayer of St. Alphonsus Liguori to the Blessed Virgin Mary

MOST holy and immaculate Virgin! O my Mother! thou who art the Mother of my Lord, the Queen of the world, the advocate, hope, and refuge of sinners! I, the most wretched among them, now come to thee. I worship thee, great Queen, and give thee thanks for the many favors thou hast bestowed on me in the past; most of all do I thank thee for having saved me from hell, which I had so often deserved. I love thee, Lady most worthy of all love, and, by the love which I bear thee, I promise ever in the future to serve thee, and to do what

in me lies to win others to thy love. In thee
I put all my trust, all my hope of salvation.
Receive me as thy servant, and cover me
with the mantle of thy protection, thou who
art the Mother of mercy! And since thou
hast so much power with God, deliver me
from all temptations, or at least obtain for
me the grace ever to overcome them. From
thee I ask a true love of Jesus Christ, and
the grace of a happy death. O my Mother!
by thy love for God I beseech thee to be at
all times my helper, but above all at the last
moment of my life. Leave me not until
thou seest me safe in heaven, there for endless ages to bless thee and sing thy praises.
Amen.

*Indulgences: 300 days, every time, if said before a
representation of Our Lady; plenary indulgence once a
month, on the usual conditions.—Pius IX, Sept. 7, 1854.*

The Mysteries of the Holy Rosary

The Rosary is one of the most efficacious means
at our command to aid the Holy Souls.

The Fruit of Each Mystery

Joyful Mysteries

1. Annunciation . . Humility.
2. Visitation . . . Fraternal charity.
3. Nativity . . . . Spirit of poverty.
4. Presentation . . Obedience; purity.

5. Jesus with the
    Doctors . . . Love of Jesus and
                  devotedness to the
                  duties of our state
                  of life.

Sorrowful Mysteries

1. Agony . . . . Fervor in prayer.
2. Scourging . . . Penance, and espe-
                  cially mortifica-
                  tion of the senses.
3. Crowning with
    Thorns . . . Moral courage.
4. Carriage of the
    Cross . . . . Patience.
5. Crucifixion . . . Self-sacrifice for God
                  and for our neigh-
                  bor; forgiveness of
                  injuries.

Glorious Mysteries

1. Resurrection . . Faith.
2. Ascension . . . Hope.
3. Descent of the
    Holy Ghost . . Love and zeal for
                  souls.
4. Assumption . . Filial devotion to
                  Mary.
5. Coronation of the
    Blessed Virgin
    Mary . . . . Perseverance.

Petition for the Holy Souls in Purgatory

O MY God, I recommend to Thy clemency the Holy Souls in Purgatory, and especially those to whom I am most indebted by the bond of charity or of justice; and chiefly I implore Thee in behalf of those who, during their life, were most devout to the Blessed Sacrament; and those who have most loved the Blessed Virgin. For this I offer Thee, my good Jesus, Thy wounds, Thy agony, Thy death, and all the merits of Thy most bitter passion. These Holy Souls love Thee and desire most ardently to be united with Thee. Hear, then, dear Lord, and grant this my prayer in their behalf, which I present to Thee in the words of Thy holy Church:

"REQUIEM æternam dona eis, Domine.

R. Et lux perpetua luceat eis.

V. Requiescant in pace.

R. Amen."

"ETERNAL rest give unto them, O Lord.

R. And let perpetual light shine upon them.

V. May they rest in peace.

R. Amen."

(*Versicles and Responses Indulgenced.*)

An Hour of Prayer for the Souls Departed [1]

Hour of Adoration before the Blessed Sacrament in Behalf of the Souls in Purgatory

V. O LORD! open Thou my lips.
R. And my mouth shall show forth Thy praise.

Come unto my help, O God! O Lord, make haste to help me! Glory be to the Father and to the Son and to the Holy Ghost; as it was in the beginning, is now, and ever shall be, world without end. Amen.

Adoration

THE King, unto whom all live, I will adore with deepest veneration in the Most Holy Sacrament.

To the First-born of them that sleep, the Prince of the kings of the earth, Who has loved and has cleansed us from sin in His blood, I will render praise and thanks with fervent heart.

To Jesus Christ in the most holy mystery of life, to the Judge of the living and the dead, Who possesses the keys of death and hell, will I offer my highest adoration, honor,

[1] From Help for the Poor Souls in Purgatory, by Joseph Ackermann, edited by Rev. F. B. Luebbermann.

and love. With all the angels and saints I will joyfully intone the eternal chant: Holy, holy, holy, Lord God of hosts: Heaven and earth are full of Thy majesty, splendor, and glory.

Glory be to the Father and to the Son and to the Holy Ghost; as it was in the beginning, is now, and ever shall be, world without end. Amen.

Aspiration

LORD Jesus, I believe Thou art the Son of the living God, come into this world. Thou art the resurrection and the life; he that believeth in Thee, although he be dead, shall live. Thou in the tenderness of Thy mercy didst take compassion on the dead Lazarus and his sorrowing sisters Martha and Mary; Thou didst hear their confident prayer, " Call Lazarus, four days dead, from the grave and restore him to life." Loving Saviour, grant that my prayer in this hour may obtain mercy at Thy throne of grace for the departed, who, on account of their sins and weaknesses, are condemned to sit in the prison of Thy justice and in the shadow of death, and cannot yet behold Thy divine countenance! Hear my sighs and loose their bands, that they may be received unto the freedom of Thy children.

Christ Jesus, Thou hast offered Thyself to Thy heavenly Father as hostage for the debt of sin which the entire world owed.

Thou hast affixed to the cross the handwriting that was against us, and blotted it out in Thy precious blood. Grant in Thy mercy that the infinite value of Thy satisfaction be applied to the suffering souls in Purgatory; that what is impossible to them of their own power they may obtain through Thy holy passion and death. Jesus, Who art rich in Thy mercy and in the inexhaustible treasure of Thy merits, render the last farthing for these poor suffering souls, that they may be released from their place of pain and sing eternal praise to Thy infinite goodness in heaven.

Behold, divine Saviour! in Thy holy presence, before the great mystery of the altar, I spend this present hour, to obtain from Thee the release of these suffering souls. Remember these captives, for whom I offer to divine Justice Thy sufferings, Thy wounds, Thy blood, Thy death, and Thy merciful heart. Jesus, accept Thy sufferings in lieu of their penance and pain; let the oil of mercy pour forth from Thy sacred wounds upon them; let Thy blood extinguish their flames through Thy death and receive them into the joys of eternal life. Let Thy merciful heart take compassion upon those for whom it was wounded on the cross.

Contrition and Reparation

O JESUS, almighty and yet infinitely merciful God! Thy throne is from all eternity in heaven. The seraphim and all angels and all the heavens praise and glorify Thee forever. Yet Thou deignest to be truly and really present among us in Thy holy sacrament. Greatest wonder! incomprehensible mystery! unbounded love! Jesus, King of heaven and earth, Whom I adore as really present, though invisible in the visible host; to Thee be infinite honor, unbounded love, and unending thanks.

Yet, alas! what insult, malice, and ingratitude art Thou made to undergo from lukewarm and indifferent souls! What numberless offenses and insults have been offered Thee from the beginning in this most adorable mystery by the very sinners for whose salvation and consolation Thy love instituted it! I am sadly affected by the thought that even a large number of the souls in Purgatory perhaps suffer great torments for such contempt and offence against Thee. O highest Majesty, subjected to so great indignity out of love for us, I kneel before Thee to make reparation for myself, for all men; and in particular, in this hour devoted to the souls departed, do I make reparation for these suffering souls. O good and merciful God, I implore mercy and forgiveness for us all. Deign to accept my humble petition, my contrition and reparation, which I offer to Thee in the name of Thy holy Church, and especially for the Church Suffering.

The Five Sorrowful Mysteries of the Holy Rosary, Said before the Blessed Sacrament for the Souls Departed

Preparatory Prayer

MOST loving Jesus, present in the most adorable Sacrament of the Altar, in this devotion of the holy Rosary, earnestly contemplating the mysteries of Thy bitter passion, I implore Thy boundless mercy, through the intercession of Thy Virgin Mother, for the consolation of the souls departed. Assist me, O Lord, with Thy grace; and thou, Mary, ocean of grace, be my powerful intercessor.

Prayer before the First Decade

JESUS, my Saviour, I adore Thee in the Blessed Sacrament, mindful of Thy bitter passion and mortal agony on Mount Olivet. Let Thy precious blood, which Thou didst sweat so profusely, refresh and ransom the suffering souls; let it descend upon them to cleanse them and ease their sufferings. O Lord, I pray Thee, come to the assistance of Thy servants whom Thou hast redeemed by Thy precious blood.

Heavenly Father, God of mercy, look down upon Thy creatures, and through the blood of Thy Son pardon their sins.

Prayer before the Second Decade

JESUS, my Saviour, I adore Thee in the Blessed Sacrament, mindful of Thy bitter passion and Thy cruel scourging. Innocent Jesus, how severe a penance didst Thou practice for the sins of the souls in Purgatory! Grant them the fruit of Thy sufferings, Thy wounds, Thy precious blood, Thy satisfaction, unto their deliverance and entrance into the joys of heaven.

O Lord, I pray Thee, come to the assistance of Thy servants, whom Thou hast redeemed by Thy precious blood.

Only-begotten Son of God, loving Redeemer of the world, look down upon the souls Thou hast loved, and grant them perfect pardon, for which I offer up to Thy goodness the cruel torture of Thy scourging.

Prayer before the Third Decade

JESUS, my Saviour, I adore Thee in the Blessed Sacrament, mindful of Thy bitter passion and Thy painful crowning with thorns. Thou King of penitents, how cruel was the suffering which that ignominious crown inflicted upon Thee! Let the souls in Purgatory reap the advantage of this suffering, who, being visited by great torments, desire to behold Thy holy countenance. Show Thyself unto them, O King of glory, Who wouldst be for them a King of sorrow. O Lord, I pray Thee, come to the assistance of Thy servants whom Thou hast redeemed by Thy precious blood.

Holy Ghost, comforter of the afflicted, look down upon the souls Thou hast sanctified and preserved in Thy grace unto the end; grant them in their flames the refreshing dew of Thy mercy, and after their labor let them enter into eternal rest.

Prayer before the Fourth Decade

JESUS, my Saviour, I adore Thee in the Most Holy Sacrament, mindful of Thy bitter passion and Thy laborious carrying of the cross. Most patient Jesus, Thou hast borne the sins of the whole world upon Thy shoulders. O terrible burden! Among these sins were also those of the suffering souls. Grant them the merits of Thy suffering, that, loosed from the bands of their sins, they may attain to the freedom of the children of God. O Lord, I pray Thee, come to the assistance of Thy servants whom Thou hast redeemed by Thy precious blood.

Mary, Mother of grace and of holy hope, look down upon the suffering souls in Purgatory.. Turn thine eyes of tender mercy toward them, and through Thy powerful intercession show unto them Thy glorified Son Jesus. Who died for them on the cross.

Prayer before the Fifth Decade

JESUS, my Saviour, I adore Thee in the Most Holy Sacrament, mindful of Thy bitter passion and Thy most painful crucifixion. Divine Redeemer of the world, elevated on the cross, Thou hast by Thy death accomplished the work of the Redemption. Draw from the fiery prison unto Thee the souls whose debt Thou hast paid; grant them the blessings of Thy Redemption, that they may praise Thee forever in heaven. O Lord, I pray Thee, come to the assistance of Thy servants whom Thou hast redeemed by Thy precious blood.

All ye saints of God and elect of heaven, all ye holy guardian angels of the suffering souls, have mercy on these your future co-heirs of heaven. Offer up to the all-merciful God your merits and satisfactions, that they may no longer remain excluded from your blessed companionship. O all ye angels and saints, obtain for them grace and mercy!

Offering of the Rosary

O MARY, Mother of God, most glorious and wonderful! We offer up to thee these sorrowful mysteries, above all for the honor and praise of thy dearest Son, Jesus; for ourselves and all the members of the confraternity, for the living and the dead, and for the necessities of all Christendom. Amen.

If time will permit, say now the Litany of the Saints for the Faithful Departed, p. 370 (The Editor).

Concluding Prayer of the Hour of Adoration

JESUS CHRIST, my God and Saviour! Thy Most Holy Sacrament is a perpetual effect of Thy goodness. What may we not hope from Thee! Thou art infinitely rich, and there is no end to Thy mercy. Thou hast bidden me to practice charity toward my neighbor, that I myself may obtain mercy. I have in this hour poured forth before the throne of Thy grace my humble prayer for the poor suffering souls. O most benign Saviour, grant that my prayer may receive power and efficacy from the infinite merits of Thy bitter passion for the consolation and release of these Thy beloved Souls.

I conclude my devotion, earnestly commending to Thee my parents, relatives, benefactors, friends, and enemies; grant to myself and all the faithful Thy omnipotent grace, that, under the guidance of Thy loving providence, we may lead a good and virtuous life, and in death have no reason to fear Thy justice in the unspeakable sufferings of Purgatory, but immediately enter, through Thy merits and Thy mercy, into life everlasting. Show Thy infinite mercy unto the souls of the faithful departed. Hear their prayer and their desire to be delivered from their sufferings. Admit them unto eternal rest, that they may praise and glorify Thee in heaven in union with all the saints forever. Amen.

*

Prayer in honor of the Seben Sorrows of Mary for the Faithful Departed

1. HAIL Mary, most humble handmaid of the Blessed Trinity! Remember the sufferings thou didst endure in soul and body when thy beloved Son shed His precious blood for us on the eighth day after His birth. Through these thy sufferings we beseech thee, intercede with God for us sinners and for the souls in Purgatory, that they may be delivered from all their sufferings.

Our Father, Hail Mary.

2. Hail Mary, chosen from all eternity most holy daughter of God the Father! Remember the sufferings thou didst endure in soul and body when thou wast warned to take flight before the wrath of Herod, and to go with thy divine Son, an exile from thy country, into the land of Egypt. Through these thy sufferings we beseech thee, intercede with God for us sinners and for the souls in Purgatory, that they may be delivered from all their sufferings.

Our Father, Hail Mary.

3. Hail Mary, most worthy Mother of Jesus Christ, the Son of God! Remember the sufferings thou didst endure in soul and body when thou didst seek thy lost divine Son for three days. Through these thy sufferings we beseech thee, intercede with

God for us and for the souls in Purgatory, that they may be delivered from all their sufferings.

Our Father, Hail Mary.

4. Hail Mary, most beloved Spouse of the Holy Ghost! Remember the sufferings thou didst endure in soul and body when thy divine Son took leave of thee and foretold to thee that He must suffer death on the cross for the sins of the world. Through these thy sufferings we beseech thee, intercede with God for us sinners and for the souls in Purgatory, that they may be delivered from all their sufferings.

Our Father, Hail Mary.

5. Hail Mary, most beautiful Queen of the holy angels! Remember the sufferings thou didst endure in soul and body when thou didst hear that thy divine Son was condemned to death at the demand of the wicked Jews, and when thou didst behold Him carrying His cross upon His wounded sacred shoulders to the place of crucifixion. Through these thy sufferings we beseech thee, intercede with God for us sinners and for the souls in Purgatory, that they may be delivered from all their sufferings.

Our Father, Hail Mary.

6. Hail Mary, glorious Queen of the patriarchs! Remember the sufferings thou didst endure in soul and body when thy divine Son was nailed to the cross, and when thou didst behold Him hanging upon

the cross in unspeakable pain until He gave up His soul. Through these thy sufferings we beseech thee, intercede with God for us sinners and for the souls in Purgatory, that they may be delivered from all their sufferings.

Our Father, Hail Mary.

7. Hail Mary, Mother of the Messias foretold by the prophets and most anxiously awaited! Remember the sufferings thou didst endure in soul and body when thy divine Son was taken from the cross, laid on thy virginal bosom, and finally deposited in the tomb. Through these thy sufferings we beseech thee, intercede with God for us and for the souls in Purgatory, that they may be delivered from all their sufferings. Amen.

Our Father. Hail Mary.

Prayer in honor of the Seven Joys of Mary for the faithful Departed

1. HAIL Mary, tried counsellor of the apostles! Remember the joy thou didst experience in soul and body when the archangel Gabriel saluted thee and announced to thee the incarnation of thy divine Son. Through this thy joy we beseech thee, intercede with God for us sinners and for the souls in Purgatory, that they may be delivered and attain to the eternal joy of heaven. Amen.

Our Father, Hail Mary.

2. Hail Mary, truthful instructress of the

evangelists! Remember the joy thou didst experience in soul and body when, without violation of thy holy virginity, thou gavest birth at Bethlehem to thy divine Son. Through this thy joy we beseech thee, intercede with God for us sinners and for the souls in Purgatory, that they may be delivered and attain to the eternal joy of heaven. Amen. Our Father, Hail Mary.

3. Hail Mary, strong comfortress of the martyrs! Remember the joy thou didst experience in soul and body when the three holy kings made their worthy offerings to thy divine Son and adored Him as their true God. Through this thy joy we beseech thee, intercede with God for us sinners and for the souls in Purgatory, that they may be delivered and attain to the eternal joy of heaven. Amen.

Our Father, Hail Mary.

4. Hail Mary, wise preceptress of doctors and confessors! Remember the joy thou didst experience in soul and body when, after three days, thou didst find thy Son again in the temple. Through this thy joy we beseech thee, intercede with God for us sinners and for the souls in Purgatory, that they may be delivered and attain to the eternal joy of heaven. Amen.

Our Father, Hail Mary.

5. Hail Mary, most beautiful ornament of all holy women and virgins! Remember the joy thou didst experience in soul and

body when, on Easter-day, thy divine Son appeared to thee after His glorious resurrection and with filial love greeted and consoled thee. Through this thy joy we beseech thee, intercede with God for us sinners and for the souls in Purgatory, that they may be delivered and attain to the eternal joy of heaven. Amen.

Our Father, Hail Mary.

6. Hail Mary, shining crown of all the saints of God! Remember the joy thou didst experience in soul and body when thy divine Son of His own power ascended gloriously into heaven in the presence of His beloved disciples. Through this thy joy we beseech thee, intercede with God for us sinners and for the souls in Purgatory, that they may be delivered and attain to the eternal joy of heaven. Amen.

Our Father, Hail Mary.

7. Hail Mary, most willing helper and consoler of the living and the dead! Remember the joy thou didst experience in soul and body when thy divine Son invited thee to the bliss of heaven, and after Thy holy death introduced thy glorious soul and body into heaven, and placed thee above all the choirs of angels. Through this thy joy we beseech thee, intercede with God for us sinners and for the souls in Purgatory, that they may be delivered and attain to the eternal joys of heaven. Amen.

Our Father, Hail Mary.

𝔊𝔥𝔢 "𝔒𝔲𝔯 𝔉𝔞𝔱𝔥𝔢𝔯" 𝔣𝔬𝔯 𝔱𝔥𝔢 𝔉𝔞𝔦𝔱𝔥𝔣𝔲𝔩 𝔇𝔢𝔭𝔞𝔯𝔱𝔢𝔡

When St. Mechtilde one day offered up holy communion for the Holy Souls, Christ appeared to her, saying: " Say an ' Our Father ' for them." She was inspired to pray as follows. After this prayer she beheld a large number of souls ascending to heaven. (Bk. 5, ch. 21.)

OUR *Father Who art in heaven,* I pray Thee pardon the souls in Purgatory for not showing proper love and honor to Thee, their most adorable loving Father, Who hadst adopted them out of pure love as Thy children. Pardon them for expelling Thee from their hearts, wherein Thou wouldst always dwell. In atonement for this offence I offer up the love and honor which thy beloved Son always showed Thee on earth, and the abundant satisfaction He rendered for their sins.

Hallowed be Thy Name. I pray Thee, most loving Father, pardon the souls in Purgatory for not having always properly remembered and honored Thy holy name. Pardon them for having frequently even taken in vain Thy holy name and for having shown themselves unworthy of the Christian name by an evil life. In atonement for these sins I offer up the most perfect sanctity with which Thy divine Son ever exalted Thy holy name and honored it in all His works. Amen.

Thy kingdom come. I pray Thee, most

loving Father, pardon the souls in Purgatory for not having zealously desired and sought Thee and Thy kingdom, in which alone there is true peace and eternal glory. In atonement for this neglect and sloth in their good work, I offer up the most holy desire of Thy divine Son, to make them coheirs of His kingdom. Amen.

Thy will be done on earth as it is in heaven. I pray Thee, most loving Father, pardon the souls in Purgatory, especially the souls of religious, for having preferred their own will to Thine; for not loving Thy will, but following and doing their own. In atonement for this disobedience I offer up the union of the sweetest heart of Thy divine Son with Thy holy will, and that most ready submission by which He was obedient to Thee, even unto the death on the cross. Amen.

Give us this day our daily bread! I pray Thee, most loving Father! pardon the souls in Purgatory for not having received the most holy Sacrament of the Altar with perfect desire, or with proper love and devotion; also for having in many cases even rendered themselves entirely unworthy of this heavenly food, and never received it. In atonement for these sins I offer up the great sanctity and devotion of Thy Son, and the ardent desire with which He bequeathed to us this most precious treasure. Amen.

Forgive us our trespasses as we forgive

those who trespass against us. I pray Thee, most loving Father! grant pardon to the souls in Purgatory for all the sins they may have committed against the chief virtues, especially if they would not love their enemy and forgive those who had offended them. In atonement for these sins I offer up the loving prayer which Thy Son made on the cross for His enemies. Amen.

Lead us not into temptation. I pray Thee, most loving Father! grant pardon to the souls in Purgatory for not having resisted their evil inclinations and habits, and consenting to the suggestions of the devil and the flesh. In atonement for all these sins I offer up the glorious victory which Thy Son gained over the world and the devil, as likewise His most holy life and conduct, with all His labors, trials, fatigues, and His most bitter suffering and death. Amen.

But deliver us from evil, and from all punishment, through the merits of Thy beloved Son, and bring us to the kingdom of Thy glory, which is Thyself. Amen.

The "Hail Mary," Adapted for the Souls in Purgatory

HAIL MARY! Behold, most merciful Mother! thy poor and sorrowful children who suffer so grievously in the flames of Purgatory. We beseech thee for the sake of the great joy which the angelic salutation caused thee, have compassion on them, and send them thy holy angel to bring them also joyful greeting, and to announce to them release from their sufferings.

Full of grace! Obtain for them grace, mercy, and remission of the great punishment they now endure.

The Lord is with thee! He will deny thee nothing, but will hear thy prayer and mercifully come to the assistance of these poor souls.

Blessed art thou amongst women! ay, among all creatures in the whole world! Bless and render happy with thy intercession the poor imprisoned souls, and deliver them from their bonds.

And blessed is the fruit of thy womb, Jesus, Who is the Saviour and Redeemer of the whole world, born without pain of thee, a virgin! O merciful Jesus, blessed fruit of her inviolate virginity! have mercy on the souls departed! O merciful Mother, hasten to their assistance!

Holy Mary, Mother of God! Thou wonderful Virgin Mother, *pray for us sinners* and for the souls in Purgatory *now* and forever, *and at the hour of our death;* and as thou didst assist the souls departed in their last agony, so assist them now in their grievous suffering and imprisonment, that delivered by thy motherly intercession they may pass from present suffering to everlasting joy, from their anguish and torment to everlasting rest and glory, and rejoice with thee and the whole heavenly host through all eternity. Amen.

Conditions for Gaining Indulgences [1]

General Conditions Required for All Indulgences

I. The state of grace.

II. Intention of gaining the Indulgences: a general intention is sufficient. [2]

III. Accuracy and devotion in fulfilling the specified conditions.

Special Conditions Usually Required for Plenary, And Sometimes for Partial, Indulgences

I. *Confession.*

1. If confession is prescribed for an indulgence attached to a particular day, it may be made within the eight days immediately before or after that day.

2. To gain indulgences attached to pious exercises of a triduum, a week, etc., confession (and communion) may be made within the octave following the completion of the triduum, etc.

3. The faithful who are accustomed, unless lawfully impeded, to confess at least twice in the month, or who daily, or almost daily (though they omit holy communion a day or two in the week) receive holy communion in the state of grace and with the

---

[1] From Help for the Holy Souls, by Rev. Thomas McDonald, C.C.

[2] Editor's Note: It should be renewed from time to time, say every morning. (*The Raccolta.*)

404

right intention, may gain all occurring indulgences, without actual
confession otherwise necessary, except Jubilee indulgences.

II. *Communion.*
   1. May be made on the day before the
      day to which the indulgence is at-
      tached, or on the day itself or within
      the eight days immediately follow-
      ing.
   2. See 2 and 3 above.
III. *Visit* to a church or a public oratory,
      where required, may be made from
      noon the day before, till midnight of
      the day to which the indulgence is
      attached.
IV. *Prayer.*—*Vocal* prayer for the Pope's
      intentions.
      —*New Code*, Cans. 931, 923, 934.

Indulgenced Prayers [1]

Instructions

The Raccolta

1. Unless otherwise stated, e.g., " once
a day," a partial indulgence may be gained
any number of times in succession. This is
indicated by the letters T. Q.

2. To gain a " Plenary, once (or twice,
etc.) a month," the prayer or act must be

[1] The following indulgenced prayers are taken from The
Raccolta, by Ambrose St. John of the Oratory of St. Philip
Neri.

repeated daily for a month; and the communion may be made, unless otherwise declared, on any day of the month, or within eight days after. Note: Confession, if required as a condition, may be made within eight days before or eight days after the appointed day. Communion, if required, may be made on the Vigil, or within eight days after. In case of devotions spreading over several days, confession and communion may be made within eight days after the completion of the devotions. Confession made habitually twice a month, or daily communion, releases from all obligation of actual confession, except in cases of Jubilees or similar extraordinary indulgences (Can. 931). Cf. p. xii, 9 and 430 N. R.

3. The Roman numerals, I, II, III, IV, placed after an indulgence, indicate the special conditions, viz., I, CONFESSION; II, COMMUNION; III, VISIT to a church or public chapel; IV, PRAYER according to the Pope's intention.

4. The references at the foot of the page correspond with the indulgences; and the dates are those of rescripts of the Congregation of Indulgences, unless otherwise noted.

5. The Our Fathers, Hail Marys, and Glories prescribed for an indulgence are indicated throughout by the Latin *Pater Noster, Ave Maria,* and *Gloria Patria,* or in

short, *Pater, Ave,* and *Gloria.* They can of course be said in English, and this applies to similar references in Latin to familiar prayers, antiphons, etc.

N. B.—A general intention of gaining all Indulgences is sufficient. It should be renewed from time to time, say, every morning.

Indulgenced Prayers for the Faithful Departed

1.   The De Profundis

i. 100 days, to all the faithful, every time that, at the sound of the bell at nightfall, they say devotedly on their knees the Psalm De profundis or Pater, Ave and Requiem æternam.

ii. Plenary, once a year, if said daily, I, II, IV.

N.B.—In places where no bell is rung, these Indulgences may be gained by reciting the above at nightfall.

iii. 50 days, three times a day to all who say the De profundis with V. and R. Requiem æternam.

See Instructions, p. 405.

Psalmus cxxix

DE PROFUNDIS clamavi ad te, Domine: * Domine, exaudi vocem meam.

Fiant aures tuæ intendentes * in vocem deprecationis meæ.

Si iniquitates observaveris, Domine: * Domine, quis sustinebit?

Psalm cxxix

OUT of the depths I have cried unto Thee, O Lord: Lord, hear my voice.

Let Thine ears be attentive : to the voice of my supplication.

If Thou, O Lord, shalt mark our iniquities: O Lord, who can abide it?

[1] Clement XII, Br. Aug. 11, 1736; Pius VI, Prop. March 18, 1781; Pius IX, July 18, 1877; Leo XIII, Feb. 3, 1888.

Quia apud te pro-
pitiatio est: * et prop-
ter legem tuam susti-
nui te, Domine.

For with Thee
there is mercy: and
by reason of Thy law
I have waited on
Thee, O Lord.

Sustinuit anima
mea in verbo ejus: *
speravit anima mea
in Domino.

My soul hath
waited on His word:
my soul hath hoped
in the Lord.

A custodia matu-
tina usque ad noc-
tem * speret Israel in
Domino.

From the morning
watch even unto
night: let Israel hope
in the Lord.

Quia apud Domi-
num misericordia, *
et copiosa apud eum
redemptio.

For with the Lord
there is mercy: and
with Him is plente-
ous redemption.

Et ipse redimet
Israel * ex omnibus
iniquitatibus ejus.

And He shall re-
deem Israel: from
all his iniquities.

V. Requiem æter-
nam * dona eis, Do-
mine.

V. Eternal rest
give to them, O Lord.

R. Et lux perpetua
luceat eis.

R. And let perpet-
ual light shine upon
them.

2.   Holy Week

*Seven Years and Seven Quarantines, on Holy Thurs-
day, Good Friday, and Holy Saturday.*

See Instructions, p. 405.

*To those who, on Thursday, Friday, and Saturday in
Holy Week make one hour's mental or vocal prayer, or
who assist at the functions and services of Holy Week
by way of suffrage for the Holy Souls, seeing that on
these days they are deprived of the benefit of holy
Mass.*

[2] Benedict XIV, April 10, 1745; April 3, 1751.

3. 🕮 Pater and Ave Five Times, Etc.

i. 300 days, once a day, to all who, devoutly meditating on the passion, shall say for the departed the Pater and Ave five times with the following versicle or ejaculation, etc.

ii. Plenary, once a month, I, II, IV.

See Instructions, p. 405.

WE ERGO quæsumus, tuis famulis subveni, quos pretioso sanguine redemisti.

WE THERE-fore beseech Thee, help Thy servants, whom Thou hast redeemed with Thy precious blood.

Ejaculation

ETERNAL Father, by the precious blood of Jesus, mercy!

Eternal rest give unto them, O Lord, and let perpetual light shine upon them.

4. 🕮 Prayers

100 days, once a day, IV.

See Instructions, p. 405.

For Sunday

O LORD God Almighty, I pray Thee, by the precious blood which Thy divine Son Jesus shed in the Garden, deliver the souls in Purgatory, and especially that soul amongst them all which is most destitute of spiritual aid; and vouchsafe to bring it to Thy glory, there to praise and bless Thee forever. Amen.

Pater, Ave, De Profundis. (See p. 407.)

3 Pius VII, Br. Feb. 6, 1817.
4 Leo XII, Nov. 18, 1826.

For Monday

O LORD God Almighty, I pray Thee, by the precious blood which Thy divine Son Jesus shed in His cruel scourging, deliver the souls in Purgatory, and that soul especially amongst them all which is nearest to its entrance into Thy glory; that so it may forthwith begin to praise and bless Thee forever. Amen.

Pater, Ave, De Profundis.

For Tuesday

O LORD God Almighty, I pray Thee, by the precious blood which Thy divine Son Jesus shed in His bitter crowning with thorns, deliver the souls in Purgatory, and in particular that one amongst them all which would be the last to depart out of those pains, that it may not tarry so long a time before it come to praise Thee in Thy glory and bless Thee forever. Amen.

Pater, Ave, De Profundis.

For Wednesday

O LORD God Almighty, I pray Thee, by the precious blood which Thy divine Son Jesus shed in the streets of Jerusalem, when He carried the cross upon His sacred shoulders, deliver the souls in Purgatory, and especially that soul which is richest in merits before Thee; that so, in that throne of glory which awaits it, it may magnify Thee and bless Thee forever. Amen.

Pater, Ave, De Profundis.

For Thursday

O LORD God Almighty, I pray Thee, by the precious body and blood of Thy divine Son Jesus, which He gave with His own hands upon the eve of His passion to His beloved apostles to be their meat and drink, and which He left to His whole Church to be a perpetual sacrifice and the life-giving food of His own faithful people, deliver the souls in Purgatory, and especially that one which was most devoted to this mystery of infinite love, that it may with the same thy divine Son, and with thy Holy Spirit, ever praise Thee for Thy love therein in eternal glory. Amen.

Pater, Ave, De Profundis.

For Friday

O LORD God Almighty, I pray Thee, by the precious blood which Thy divine Son shed on this day upon the wood of the cross, especially from His most sacred hands and feet, deliver the souls in Purgatory, and in particular that soul for which I am most bound to pray; that no neglect of mine may hinder it from praising Thee in Thy glory and blessing Thee forever. Amen.

Pater, Ave, De Profundis.

For Saturday

O LORD God Almighty, I beseech Thee, by the precious blood which gushed forth from the side of Thy divine Son Jesus,

in the sight of, and to the extreme pain of
His most holy Mother, deliver the souls in
Purgatory, and especially that one amongst
them all which was the most devout to her;
that it may soon attain unto Thy glory, there
to praise Thee in her, and her in Thee, world
without end. Amen.

Pater, Ave, De Profundis.

5. Prayers for Nine or Seven Days

i. 300 days, each day.
ii. Plenary, during the period,'I, II, IV.
See Instructions, p. 405.
*Any form of prayers for the Holy Souls, sanctioned
by competent ecclesiastical authority, may be used.*

6. League of Perpetual Suffrage

*200 days, once a day, to all who say thrice daily the
versicle below.*
See Instructions, p. 405.

REQUIEM æternam dona eis
Domine, et lux perpetua luceat eis. Requiescant in pace.
Amen.

ETERNAL rest give unto them,
O Lord, and let perpetual light shine upon them. May they
rest in peace. Amen.

7. Month of November

i. Seven years and seven quarantines, each day.
ii. Plenary, once during the month. I, II, III, IV.
See Instructions, p. 405.
*Any daily devotions for the Holy Souls, public or
private, will suffice.*

⁵ Pius IX, Res. Jan. 5, 1840; Bps. Jan. 28, 1850; Nov. 26,
1876.
⁶ Leo XIII, Aug. 19, 1880.
⁷ Leo XIII, Jan. 17, 1888.

8. 𝔇𝔢𝔟𝔬𝔱𝔦𝔬𝔫 𝔱𝔬 𝔱𝔥𝔢 𝔉𝔦𝔳𝔢 𝔚𝔬𝔲𝔫𝔡𝔰

200 days, once a day.

See Instructions, p. 405.

GO BEFORE our actions, we beseech Thee, O Lord, with Thy inspiration, and follow after them with Thy help, that every prayer and work of ours may begin from Thee and through Thee be likewise ended. Through Christ our Lord. Amen.

Eternal rest give unto them, O Lord, and let perpetual light shine upon them.

I. WE OFFER unto Thee, O eternal Father, Father of mercies, for those souls so dear to Thee in Purgatory, the most precious blood shed on Calvary from the wound in the left foot of Jesus Thy Son, our Saviour, and the sorrow of Mary His most loving Mother in beholding it.

Pater, Ave, Requiem æternam.

II. We offer unto Thee, O eternal Father, Father of mercies, for those souls so dear to Thee in Purgatory, the most precious blood shed on Calvary from the wound in the right foot of Jesus, Thy Son, our Saviour, and the sorrow of Mary His most loving Mother in beholding it.

Pater, Ave, Requiem æternam.

III. We offer unto Thee, O eternal Father, Father of mercies, for those souls so dear to Thee in Purgatory, the most precious blood shed on Calvary from the wound in the left

8 Leo XIII, Sept. 15, 1888.

hand of Jesus Thy Son, our Saviour, and the sorrow of Mary His most loving Mother in beholding it.

Pater, Ave, Requiem æternam.

IV. We offer unto Thee, O eternal Father, Father of mercies, for those souls so dear to Thee in Purgatory, the most precious blood shed on Calvary from the wound in the right hand of Jesus Thy Son, our Saviour, and the sorrow of Mary His most loving Mother in beholding it.

Pater, Ave, Requiem æternam.

V. We offer unto Thee, O eternal Father, Father of mercies, for those souls so dear to Thee in Purgatory, the most precious blood and water flowing on Calvary from the pierced side of Jesus Thy Son, our Saviour, and the sorrow of Mary His most loving Mother in beholding it.

Pater, Ave, Requiem æternam.

Let us pray

AND now to give greater value to our feeble prayers, turning to Thee, most loving Jesus, we humbly pray Thee Thyself to offer to the eternal Father, the sacred wounds of Thy feet, hands and side, together with Thy most precious blood, and Thy agony and death; and do thou also, Mary, Virgin of sorrows, present, together with the most sorrowful passion of Thy well-beloved Son, the sighs, tears and all the sorrows suffered by thee through His sufferings, so that through their merits the souls who suffer in the most ardent flames of Purgatory may obtain refreshment, and, freed from this prison of torment, may be clothed with glory in heaven, there to sing the mercies of God forever.   Amen.

Absolve, O Lord, the souls of all the faithful departed from every bond of sin, so that by Thy aid they may deserve to escape the judgment of wrath, and come to the enjoyment of beatitude in eternal light.

V. Eternal rest give unto them, O Lord.

R. And let perpetual light shine upon them.

V. From the gate of hell.

R. Deliver their souls, O Lord.

V. May they rest in peace.

R. Amen.

V. O Lord, hear my prayer.

R. And let my cry come unto Thee.

V. The Lord be with you.

R. And with thy spirit.

Let us pray

O GOD, the Creator and Redeemer of all the faithful, grant to the souls of Thy servants departed the remission of all their sins, that through pious supplications they may obtain the pardon they have always desired.   Who livest and reignest world without end.   Amen.

Eternal rest, etc.

9. 𝔓rapers
100 days, once a day.
See Instructions, p. 405.

(M)Y JESUS, by that copious sweat of blood with which Thou didst bedew the ground in the Garden, have mercy on the souls of my nearest relations who are suffering in Purgatory.

Pater, Ave, Requiem æternam.

My Jesus, by that cruel scourging which Thou didst suffer, bound to the column, have pity on the souls of my other relations and friends who are suffering in Purgatory.

Pater, Ave, Requiem æternam.

My Jesus, by that crown of sharpest thorns which pierced Thy sacred temples, have mercy on that soul which is most neglected and least prayed for, and on that soul which is furthest from being released from the pains of Purgatory.

Pater, Ave, Requiem æternam.

My Jesus, by those sorrowful steps which Thou didst take with the cross on Thy shoulders, have mercy on that soul which is nearest to its departure from Purgatory; and by the pains which Thou didst suffer together with Thy most holy Mother Mary, when Thou didst meet her on the road to Calvary, deliver from the pains of Purgatory those souls who were devout to this beloved Mother.

Pater, Ave, Requiem æternam.

My Jesus, by Thy most holy body

⁹ Leo XIII, Dec. 14, 1880.

stretched on the cross, by Thy most holy hands and feet pierced with hard nails, by Thy most cruel death, and by Thy most holy side laid open with a lance, have pity and mercy on those poor souls; free them from the awful pains they suffer, call and admit them to thy most sweet embrace in paradise.

Pater, Ave, Requiem æternam.

O Holy Souls, tormented in most cruel pains, as one truly devoted to you, I promise. never to forget you, and continually to pray to the Most High for your release. I beseech you to respond to this offering which I make to you, and obtain for me from God, with Whom you are so powerful on behalf of the living, that I may be freed from all dangers of soul and body; I beg both for myself and for my relations and benefactors, friends, and enemies, pardon for our sins, and the grace of perseverance in good, whereby we may save our souls. Set us free from all misfortunes, miseries, sicknesses, trials, and labors. Obtain for us peace of heart; assist us in all our actions; succor us promptly in all our spiritual and temporal needs; console and defend us in our dangers. Pray for the Supreme Pontiff, for the exaltation of Holy Church, for peace between nations, for Christian princes, and for tranquillity among peoples; and obtain that we may one day all rejoice together in paradise. Amen.

418PRAYERS

10. 𝔓rayer for the 𝔇ead

50 days, T. Q. Applicable only to the dead.
See Instructions, p. 405.

V. Requiem æter-
nam dona eis, Do-
mine.
R. Et lux perpetua
luceat eis.

V. Eternal rest
give unto them, O
Lord.
R. And let perpet-
ual light shine upon
them.

11. 𝔙ersicles and 𝔚esponses for the 𝔇ead

300 days, T. Q. Applicable only to the dead.
See Instructions, p. 405.

V. Requiem æter-
nam dona eis, Do-
mine.
R. Et lux perpetua
luceat eis.

V. Eternal rest
give unto them, O
Lord.
R. And let perpet-
ual light shine upon
them.

V. Requiescant in
pace.
R. Amen.

V. May they rest
in peace.
R. Amen.

12. 𝔓rayer for 𝔊hildren in 𝔓urgatory

i. 100 days, once a day, for children who say this prayer.
ii. Plenary, on All Saints' Day, to those who recite it daily for at least half the year, I, II, III, IV.
N.B.—Bishops can authorize confessors to commute the communion in case of children who have not made their first communion.
See Instructions, p. 405.

SWEET Saviour Jesus, Who during Thy
life didst show such great love for
children; we who as children share with

[10] Leo XIII, Br., March 22, 1902.
[11] Pius X, Feb. 13, 1908.
[12] Leo XIII, May 15, 1886.

them Thy blessing, beseech Thee to open the gate of heaven to our companions who are lamenting in the place of sorrow and penance. Grant also their protection to us, to our relations, and to our common Father, the Supreme Pontiff.

Holy Virgin, good Mother, pray for us and for the children who suffer. Ave Maria.

13. All Souls' Day, Nov. 2—The Holy Souls

Plenary. Toties Quoties, I, II, IV.
See Instructions, p. 405.

Each visit to a church or public chapel, made on Nov. 2, for the purpose of praying for the Holy Souls.

N. B.—These indulgences are applicable only to the Holy Souls.

Indulgenced Ejaculations and Short Prayers [1]

1.   The Sign of the Cross

Indulgences: i. 50 days, T. Q.[2] ii. 100 days, if made with Holy Water, T. Q.

N. B.—The words must in either case be said: In the name of the Father, and of the Son, and of the Holy Ghost.

The Holy Trinity

2. OMNIPOTENCE of the Father, help my frailty, and rescue me from the depths of misery.

Wisdom of the Son, direct all my thoughts, words, and actions.

[13] Pius X, Off. June 25, 1914.
[1] Compiled from The Raccolta.
[2] Unless otherwise stated, e.g., once a day, a partial indulgence may be gained any number of times in succession. This is indicated by the letters: T. Q. (toties quoties).
       —The Raccolta

Love of the Holy Spirit, be the source of all
the operations of my soul, so that they may
be entirely conformed to the divine will.

Indulgence: 200 days, once a day.

The Angelic Trisagion

3. **S**ANCTUS, **H**OLY, Holy,
Sanctus, Holy, Lord God
Sanctus, Dominus of Hosts, earth is full
Deus exercituum: of Thy glory. Glory
plena est terra gloria be to the Father,
tua. Gloria Patri, Glory be to the Son,
Gloria Filio, Gloria Glory be to the Holy
Spiritui Sancto. Ghost.

*Indulgences: i. 100 days, once a day. ii. 100 days,
three times a day, on Sundays and during the Octave
of Trinity Sunday.*

Almighty God

4. **E**TERNAL Father, we offer Thee the
blood, passion, and death of Jesus
Christ, and the sorrows of the most holy
Mary and St. Joseph, in payment for our
sins, in suffrage for the Holy Souls in Purgatory, for the wants of our holy Mother
the Church, and for the conversion of
sinners. Amen.

Indulgence: 100 days, once a day.

5. O Lord Almighty, Who permittest evil
to draw good therefrom, hear our humble
prayers, and grant that we remain faithful
to Thee unto death. Grant us also, through
the intercession of most holy Mary, the
strength ever to conform ourselves to Thy
most holy will.

Indulgence: 100 days, once a day.

6. Fiat laudetur, atque in æternum superexaltetur justissima, altissima, et amabilissima voluntas Dei in omnibus.

May the most just, most high and most adorable will of God be in all things done, praised, and magnified forever.

Indulgence: 100 days, once a day.

7. Deus meus et omnia!

My God and my all!

Indulgence: 50 days, T. Q.

8. My God, grant that I may love Thee, and as the sole reward of my love, grant that I may ever love Thee more and more.

Indulgence: 100 days, once a day.

9. My God, my only good,
   Thou art all mine; grant that I may
   be all Thine.

Indulgence: 300 days, once a day.

10. Blessed be God!

Indulgence: 50 days, T. Q. (If said devoutly on hearing a blasphemy.)

11. My God, unite all minds in the truth and all hearts in charity.

Indulgence: 300 days, T. Q.

The Holy Ghost

12. O HOLY Spirit, divine spirit of light and love, I consecrate to Thee my understanding, heart, and will, my whole being for time and for eternity. May my understanding be always submissive to Thy heavenly inspirations, and to the teaching of the Catholic Church, of which Thou art the

infallible guide; may my heart be ever inflamed with love of God and of my neighbor; may my will ever be conformed to the divine will, and may my whole life be a faithful imitation of the life and virtues of Our Lord and Saviour Jesus Christ, to Whom with the Father and Thee be honor and glory forever. Amen.

Indulgence: 300 days, once a day.

13. O Holy Spirit, Creator, be propitious to the Catholic Church; and by Thy heavenly power make it strong and secure against the attacks of its enemies; and renew in charity and grace the spirit of Thy servants, whom Thou hast anointed, that they may glorify Thee and the Father and His only-begotten Son, Jesus Christ, our Lord. Amen.

Indulgence: 300 days, once a day.

14. O Holy Spirit, spirit of truth, come into our hearts; shed the brightness of Thy light on all nations, that they may be one in faith and pleasing to Thee.

Indulgence: 100 days, once a day.

15. Come, O Holy Ghost, fill the hearts of Thy faithful, and kindle in them the fire of Thy love.

Indulgence: 300 days, T. Q.

Jesus Christ

16. O MY Jesus, Thou well knowest that I love Thee; but I do not love Thee enough: Oh! make me to love Thee more.

O Love which burnest always and is never extinguished, my God, Thou who art Charity itself, kindle in my heart that divine fire which consumes the saints and transforms them into Thee. Amen.

Indulgence: 50 days, twice a day.

17. Grant us, O Lord Jesus, faithfully to imitate the examples of Thy Holy Family, so that in the hour of our death, in the company of Thy glorious Virgin Mother and St. Joseph, we may deserve to be received by Thee into eternal tabernacles.

Indulgence: 200 days, once a day.

18. Most sweet Jesus, increase my faith, hope, and charity, and give me a humble and contrite heart.

Indulgence: 100 days, once a day.

19. My Jesus, mercy!

Indulgence: 300 days, T. Q.

20. Sweetest Jesus, be to me not a judge, but a Saviour.

Indulgence, 50 days, T. Q.

21. Saviour of the world, have mercy on us.

Indulgence: 50 days, once a day.

22. Jesus, my God, I love Thee above all things.

Indulgence: 50 days, T. Q. (For saying it or inducing others to say it.)

23. Jesu, fili Da-   Jesus, Son of Da-

vid, miserere mei. vid, have mercy on
(Luc. xviii, 38.)   me.

Indulgence: 100 days, once a day.

24. O Jesus Christ, Son of the living God,
Light of the world, I adore Thee; for Thee
I live, for Thee I die. Amen.

Indulgence: 100 days, once a day.

Invocation of the Holy Name

*Indulgences: i. 50 days, every time anyone says to
another:*

25. LAUDETUR Jesus Christus.

PRAISED be Jesus Christ.

or answers: Amen, *or*
In sæcula.

For evermore.

*ii. 25 days, every time anyone invokes the most holy
Name of Jesus.*

*iii. Plenary, at the point of death, to anyone who has
had the devout practice of saluting and answering as
above, or of invoking often the said most holy Name,
provided that he then invokes this holy Name at least
in his heart, if he is unable to do so with his lips.*

*·The same indulgences to preachers and others who
exhort the faithful to salute each other in this way
and to invoke frequently the most holy Names of Jesus
and Mary.*

26. Jesus!

Indulgence: 25 days, T. Q.

27. Jesus! Mary!

*Indulgence: 300 days, T. Q. Invoked with the
heart if not with the lips.*

28. Jesus! Mary! Joseph!

Indulgence: 7 years and 7 quarantines, T. Q.

The Blessed Sacrament

29. **V**ISIT to the Blessed Sacrament, with *Pater, Ave,* and *Gloria* five times, and *Pater, Ave,* and *Gloria* once for the intention of the Pope.

Indulgence: 300 days, T. Q.

30. Jesus, my God, I adore Thee here present in the Sacrament of Thy love.

Indulgences: i. 100 days, before the tabernacle, T. Q. ii. 300 days, at exposition, T. Q. iii. 100 days, for making a reverence passing a church or chapel where the Blessed Sacrament is reserved, T. Q.

31. My Lord and my God!

Indulgence: 7 years and 7 quarantines when said with faith, piety, and love, while looking upon the Blessed Sacrament either during the Elevation in the Mass, or when exposed on the altar.

32. O Sacrament most Holy, O Sacrament Divine,
All praise and all thanksgiving be every moment thine.

Indulgence: 300 days, T. Q.

33. O Jesus in the Blessed Sacrament, have mercy on us.

Indulgence: 300 days, T. Q.

Jesus Crucified

34. **T**HE cross is my sure salvation. The cross I ever adore. The cross of my Lord is with me. The cross is my refuge.

Indulgence: 300 days, once a day.

35. We adore Thee, most holy Lord Jesus

Christ, we bless Thee; because by Thy holy cross Thou hast redeemed the world.

Indulgence: 100 days, once a day.

36. Ecce crucem Domini ✠ fugite partes adversæ, vicit Leo de tribu Juda, radix David. Alleluia.

Behold the cross of the Lord, ✠ flee ye adversaries, the Lion of the tribe of Juda has conquered, the root of David. Alleluia.

Indulgence: 100 days, once a day.

Prayer for a Happy Death

37. O JESUS, while adoring Thy last breath, I pray Thee to receive mine. In the uncertainty whether I shall have the command of my senses, when I shall depart out of this world, I offer Thee from this moment my agony and all the pains of my passing away. Thou art my Father and my Saviour, and I give back my soul into Thy hands. I desire that my last moment may be united to the moment of Thy death, and that the last beat of my heart may be an act of pure love of Thee. Amen.

Indulgence: 100 days, once a day.

The Precious Blood

38. ETERNAL Father! we offer Thee the most precious blood of Jesus, shed for us with such great love and bitter pain from His right hand; and through the merits and the efficacy of that blood, we entreat Thy divine Majesty to grant us Thy

holy benediction, in order that we may be defended thereby from all our enemies, and be set free from every ill; whilst we say, May the blessing of Almighty God, Father, Son, and Holy Spirit descend upon us and remain with us forever. Amen.

Pater, Ave, and Gloria.

Indulgence: 100 days, T. Q.

39. Eternal Father, by the most precious blood of Jesus Christ, glorify His most holy Name, according to the intention and the desires of His adorable Heart.

Indulgence: 300 days, T. Q. To be said in reparation for blasphemies.

40. Eternal Father! I offer Thee the precious blood of Jesus Christ in satisfaction for my sins, and for the wants of Holy Church.

Indulgence: 100 days, T. Q.

The Sacred Heart

41. MAY the Heart of Jesus be loved everywhere.

Indulgence: 100 days, once a day.

42. Jesus, meek and humble of heart, make my heart like unto Thine.

Indulgence: 300 days, T. Q.

43. Sweet Heart of Jesus, be my love.

Indulgence: 300 days, once a day.

44. Sweet Heart of my Jesus,
Make me love Thee ever more and
more *or,*

O sweetest Heart of Jesus, I implore
That I may ever love Thee more and
more.

Indulgence: 300 days, T. Q.

45. Heart of Jesus burning with love of
us, inflame our hearts with love of Thee.

Indulgence: 100 days, once a day.

46. All praise, honor, and glory to the
divine Heart of Jesus.

Indulgence: 50 days, once a day.

47. All for Thee, most Sacred Heart of
Jesus.

Indulgence: 300 days, T. Q.

48. Sacred Heart of Jesus, Thy kingdom
come!

Indulgence: 300 days, T. Q.

49. Sacred Heart of Jesus, I trust in Thee.

Indulgence: 300 days, T. Q.

50. Eucharistic Heart of Jesus, have
mercy on us.

Indulgence: 300 days, T. Q.

51. Divine Heart of Jesus, convert sinners, save the dying, set free the holy souls
in Purgatory.

Indulgence: 300 days, T. Q.

52. O Heart of love, I place all my trust
in Thee; for though I fear all things from
my weakness, I hope all things from Thy
mercies. (Ejaculation of Saint Margaret
Mary.)

Indulgence: 300 days, T. Q.

53. Eucharistic Heart of Jesus, model of the priestly heart, have mercy on us.

Indulgence, 300 days, T. Q.

54. Praised be the most Sacred Heart of Jesus in the Most Holy Sacrament.

Indulgence: 100 days, T. Q.

55. Let us with Mary Immaculate adore, thank, pray to, and console the most sacred and well-beloved Eucharistic Heart of Jesus.

Indulgence: 200 days, T. Q.

56. May the Heart of Jesus in the most Blessed Sacrament be praised, adored, and loved with grateful affection, at every moment, in all the tabernacles of the world, even to the end of time. Amen.

Indulgence: 100 days, once a day.

57. My loving Jesus, out of the grateful love I bear Thee, and to make reparation for my unfaithfulness to grace, I, N., give Thee my heart, and I consecrate myself wholly to Thee; and with Thy help I purpose never to sin again.

(Act of Oblation to be made before a representation of the Sacred Heart.)

Indulgence: 100 days, once a day.

58. O Most Merciful Jesus, lover of souls: I pray Thee, by the agony of Thy most Sacred Heart, and by the sorrows of Thy immaculate Mother, cleanse in Thine own blood the sinners of the whole world who

are now in their agony, and to die this day. Amen.

Heart of Jesus, once in agony, pity the dying.

Indulgence: 100 days, T. Q.

59. O Divine Heart of Jesus, grant, we beseech Thee, eternal rest to the souls in Purgatory, the final grace to those who shall die to-day, true repentance to sinners, the light of the faith to pagans, and Thy blessing to me and mine. To Thee, O most compassionate Heart of Jesus, I commend all these souls, and I offer to Thee on their behalf all Thy merits, together with the merits of Thy most holy Mother and of all the saints and angels, and all the sacrifices of the Holy Mass, communions, prayers, and good works, which shall be accomplished to-day throughout the Christian world.

Indulgence: 100 days, once a day.

60. O Most Sacred Heart of Jesus, pour down Thy blessings abundantly upon Thy Church, upon the Supreme Pontiff, and upon all the clergy; give perseverance to the just, convert sinners, enlighten unbelievers, bless our parents, friends, and benefactors, help the dying, free the souls in Purgatory, and extend over all hearts the sweet empire of Thy love. Amen.

Indulgence: 300 days, once a day.

61. **M**OTHER of love, of sorrow, and of mercy, pray for us.

Indulgence: 300 days, T. Q.

62. Our Lady of the most holy Sacrament, pray for us. (Before the Blessed Sacrament exposed.)

Indulgence: 300 days, T. Q.

63. Our Lady of the Sacred Heart, pray for us.

Indulgence: 100 days, T. Q.

64. Our Lady of Lourdes, pray for us.

Indulgence: 300 days, T. Q.

65. Our Lady of Good Studies, pray for us.

Indulgence: 300 days, once a day.

66. Mary!

Indulgence: 25 days, T. Q.

67. Queen of the Most Holy Rosary, pray for us.

Indulgence: 100 days, T. Q.

68. O Mary, bless this house, where thy name is ever held in benediction. All glory to Mary, ever Immaculate, ever Virgin, blessed among women, the Mother of Our Lord Jesus Christ, Queen of Paradise.

(Reparation for blasphemy against Our Lady.)

Indulgence: 300 days, T. Q.

69. My Lady, and my Mother, remember

I am thine; protect and defend me as thy property and possession.

Indulgence: 40 days, T. Q. (If said in time of temptation.)

70. Mary, Mother of God and Mother of mercy, pray for us, and for the departed.

Indulgence: 100 days, once a day.

71. Mary, Virgin Mother of God, pray to Jesus for me.

Indulgence: 50 days, once a day.

72. Mary, our hope, have pity on us.

Indulgence: 300 days, T. Q.

73. Mary sorrowing, Mother of all Christians, pray for us.

Indulgence: 300 days, T. Q.

74. Sweet Heart of Mary, be my salvation.

Indulgence: 300 days. T. Q.

75. In thy Conception, O Virgin Mary, thou wast immaculate; pray for us to the Father, whose Son Jesus Christ conceived of the Holy Ghost thou didst bring forth.

Indulgence: 100 days, T. Q.

76. To thee, O Virgin Mother, who wast never defiled with the slightest stain of original or actual sin, I commend and entrust the purity of my heart.

Indulgence: 100 days, once a day.

77. O Mary, who didst enter the world

free from stain, do thou obtain for me from God, that I may pass out of it free from sin.

Indulgence: 100 days, once a day.

78. Blessed be the holy and immaculate Conception of the most blessed Virgin Mary, Mother of God.

Indulgence: 300 days, T. Q.

79. O Mary, conceived without sin, pray for us who have recourse to thee.

Indulgence: 100 days, once a day.

80. Most holy immaculate Virgin Mary, Mother of God and our Mother, speak on our behalf to the Heart of Jesus, who is thy Son and our Brother.

Indulgence: 100 days, once a day.

81. Holy Mary our Deliverer, pray for us and for the souls in Purgatory.

Indulgence: 100 days, T. Q.

82. Memorare, O piissima Virgo Maria, non esse auditum a sæculo quemquam ad tua currentem præsidia, tua implorantem auxilia, tua petentem suffragia, esse derelictum. Ego tali animatus confidentia, ad te, Virgo virginum, Mater, curro, ad te venio, coram te gemens peccator assisto; noli, Mater Ver-

Remember, O most gracious Virgin Mary, that never was it known that any one who fled to thy protection, implored thy help, or sought thy intercession, was left unaided. Inspired with this confidence, I fly unto thee, O Virgin of virgins, my mother; to thee I come, before thee I stand, sinful and sor-

bi, verba mea despi- rowful; O Mother
cere, sed audi propi- of the Word Incar-
tia, et exaudi. Amen. nate, despise not my
petitions; but in thy
clemency hear and
answer me. Amen.

Indulgence: 300 days, T. Q.

83. O Holy Mary, my mistress, into thy blessed trust and special custody, and into the bosom of thy mercy I this day, every day, and in the hour of my death, commend my soul and my body: to thee I commit all my anxieties and miseries, my life and the end of my life, that by thy most holy intercession and by thy merits all my actions may be directed and disposed according to thy will and that of thy Son. Amen.

—Prayer of St. Aloysius Gonzaga.

Indulgence: 200 days, once a day.

Prayer for a Good Death

84. O MARY, conceived without stain, pray for us who fly to thee. Refuge of sinners, Mother of those who are in their agony, leave us not in the hour of our death, but obtain for us perfect sorrow, sincere contrition, remission of our sins, a worthy reception of the most holy Viaticum, the strengthening of the Sacrament of Extreme Unction, so that we may be able to stand with safety before the throne of the just but merciful Judge, our God and our Redeemer. Amen.

Indulgence: 100 days, once a day.

The Holy Angels

85. ANGELE Dei, qui custos es mei, me tibi commissum pietate superna, illumina, custodi, rege, et guberna. Amen.

O ANGEL of God, whom God hath appointed to be my guardian, enlighten and protect, direct and govern me. Amen.

or

Angel of God, my guardian dear,
To whom His love commits me here,
Ever this day be at my side,
To light and guard, to rule and guide.
Amen.

Indulgence: 100 days, T. Q.

86. St. Michael Archangel, defend us in the day of battle, that we may not be lost in the dreadful judgment.

Indulgence: 100 days, once a day.

St. Joseph

87. ST. JOSEPH, foster-father of Our Lord Jesus Christ, and true spouse of Mary ever Virgin, pray for us.

Indulgence: 300 days, once a day.

88. St. Joseph, model and patron of those who love the Sacred Heart of Jesus, pray for us.

Indulgence: 100 days, once a day.

89. Grant, O holy Joseph, that ever secure under thy protection, we may pass our lives without guilt.

or

Help us, O Joseph, in our earthly strife
Ever to lead a pure and blameless life.

Indulgence: 300 days, once a day.

90. Remember, most pure spouse of Mary ever Virgin, my loving protector, St. Joseph, that never has it been heard that anyone ever invoked thy protection, or besought aid of thee, without being consoled. In this confidence I come before thee, I fervently recommend myself to thee. Despise not my prayer, foster-father of Our Redeemer, but do thou in thy pity receive it. Amen.

Indulgence: 300 days, once a day.

91. Guardian of virgins, and holy father Joseph, to whose faithful custody Christ Jesus, Innocence itself, and Mary, Virgin of virgins, were committed; I pray and beseech thee, by these dear pledges, Jesus and Mary, that, being preserved from all uncleanness, I may with spotless mind, pure heart and chaste body, ever serve Jesus and Mary most chastely all the days of my life. Amen.

Indulgence: 100 days, once a day.

92. O Joseph, virgin father of Jesus, most pure spouse of the Virgin Mary, pray for us daily to the Son of God, that, armed with the weapons of His grace, we may fight as we ought in life, and be crowned by Him in death.

Indulgence: 100 days, twice a day.

Offering of Masses for the Dying

93. **MY GOD,** I offer Thee all the Masses which are being celebrated to-day throughout the whole world, for sinners who are in their agony and who are to die this day. May the precious blood of Jesus, their Redeemer, obtain mercy for them.

Indulgence: 300 days, T. Q.

94. Plenary Indulgence in Articulo Mortis
(At the Moment of Death)

To all who, with sincere love toward God after Confession and Communion, made on any day they may choose, say the following prayer:

O LORD my God, I now, at this moment, readily and willingly accept at thy hand whatever kind of death it may please Thee to send me, with all its pains, penalties, and sorrows.

The Faithful Departed

95. *V.* Requiem æternam dona eis, Domine.

V. Eternal rest give unto them, O Lord.

R. Et lux perpetua luceat eis.

R. And let perpetual light shine upon them.

Indulgence: 50 days, T. Q. Applicable only to the dead.

96. *V.* Requiem æternam dona eis, Domine.

V. Eternal rest give unto them, O Lord.

R. Et lux perpetua luceat eis.

R. And let perpetual light shine upon them.

V. Requiescant in pace.	*V.* May they rest in peace.
R. Amen.	*R.* Amen.

Indulgence: 300 days, ̄T. Q. Applicable only to the dead.

97. Pie Jesu Domine, dona eis (vel ei) requiem sempiternam.	Dear Lord Jesus, grant them (or him) eternal rest.

Indulgence: 300 days, T. Q. Applicable to the Holy Souls only.

Ejaculations for a Happy Death

98. **J**ESUS, Mary, Joseph, I give you my heart and my soul.

Jesus, Mary, Joseph, assist me in my last agony.

Jesus, Mary, Joseph, may I breathe forth my soul in peace with you.

Indulgences: i. 300 days, T. Q. ii. 100 days, for saying one of the same.

To Our Blessed Lady for the Souls in Purgatory

O TURN to Jesus, Mother! turn,
　　And call Him by His tenderest names;
Pray for the holy souls that burn
　　This hour amid the cleansing flames.

Ah! they have fought a gallant fight,
　　In death's cold arms they persevered;
And after life's uncheery night,
　　The harbor of their rest is neared.

In pains beyond all earthly pains,
　　Favorites of Jesus, there they lie,
Letting the fire wear out their stains,
　　And worshipping God's purity.

Spouses of Christ they are, for He
  Was wedded to them by His blood
And angels o'er their destiny
  In wondering adoration brood.

They are the children of thy tears;
  Then hasten, Mother! to their aid;
In pity think each hour appears
  An age while glory is delayed.

Pray, then, as thou hast ever prayed;
  Angels and souls all look to thee;
God waits thy prayers; for He hath made
  Those prayers His law of charity.
                    —Father Faber.

Short Litany with the Angel of the Agony

JESU! by that shuddering dread which
  fell on Thee;
Jesu! by that cold dismay which sickened
  Thee;
Jesu! by that pang of heart which thrilled
  in Thee;
Jesu! by that mount of sins which crippled
  Thee;
Jesu! by that sense of guilt which stifled
  Thee;
Jesu! by that innocence which girdled
  Thee;
Jesu! by that sanctity which reigned in
  Thee;
Jesu! by that Godhead which was one with
  Thee;
Jesu! spare those souls which are so dear
  to Thee;

Who in prison, calm and patient, wait for
    Thee;
Hasten, Lord, their hour, and bid them
    come to Thee,
To that glorious home, where they shall ever
    gaze on Thee.
                        —Cardinal Newman.

ETERNAL rest give unto them, O Lord.
        R. And let perpetual light shine
upon them.
    V. May they rest in peace.
    R. Amen.

Litany of the Faithful Departed.[1]

LORD, have mercy.
        Christ, have mercy.
Lord, have mercy.

Ancient of days, Thy servants meet
To bow before Thy mercy seat,
Thou Father, Son, and Paraclete.
                    Miserere, Domine.

Have mercy, Lord, on all who wait
In place forlorn and lonely state,
Outside Thy peaceful palace gate.
                    Miserere, Domine.

These were the work of Thine own hands,
Thy promise sure forever stands;
Release them, Lord, from pain and bands.
                    Miserere, Domine.

[1] By the Rev. Frederick George Lee, D.D., in Ave Maria.

Lord Jesus, by Thy sacred name,
By Thy meek suffering and shame,
Preserve these souls from cruel flame.
Miserere, Domine.

By sweat of blood and crown of thorn,
By cross to Calvary meekly borne,
Be Thou to them salvation's horn.
Miserere, Domine.

By Thy five wounds and seven cries,
By pierced Heart and glazing eyes,
By Thy dread, awful sacrifice,
Miserere, Domine.

When here below are lifted up
The sacred Host and blessed cup,
Soon with Thee, Lord, may each one sup.
Miserere, Domine.

By Raphael's powers and Michael's might,
By all the ordered ranks of light,
Battalions of the infinite,
Miserere, Domine.

By martyrs' pangs and triumph-palm,
By saints' strong faith, confessors' psalm,
By Mary's name, like Gilead's balm,
Miserere, Domine.

These souls forlorn, Redeemer blest,
Never denied Thee, but confest,
Grant them at last eternal rest.
Miserere, Domine.

On earth they failed from day to day,
Oft stumbling on the narrow way,
Yet put their trust in Thee for aye.
Miserere, Domine.

Let their chill desolation cease,
Thy mercy shed and give release,
Then grant them everlasting peace.
Miserere, Domine.

Here months and years now come and go,
With summer gleam and winter snow;
Let fall Thy dew and grace below.
Miserere, Domine.

Flowers fade and wither; such their doom,
Men fail and find the gaping tomb:
With Thee Thy gardens ever bloom.
Miserere, Domine.

Vision of peace so calm and bright,
After a long and darksome night,
Clothe them with everlasting light.
Miserere, Domine.

For these poor souls who may not pray—
For gone is their probation day—
We plead Thy cross and humbly say,
Miserere, Domine.

Jesus, for Thee they keenly long,
To company with saintly throng,
And, ransomed, sing the new glad song.
Miserere, Domine.

May they with saints in glory shine,
Joined with angelic orders nine;
Link them with Thee in joys divine.
Miserere, Domine.

Enter may they through heaven's door,
To walk in white on yonder shore,
Forever, Lord, for evermore!
Miserere, Domine.

Made in the USA
Coppell, TX
23 May 2024

32717741R00243